ORDERS AND HIERARCHIES IN LATE MEDIEVAL AND RENAISSANCE EUROPE

PROBLEMS IN FOCUS: MANCHESTER
General Editor: Brian Pullan

Published

Jeffrey Denton (editor)
*Orders and Hierarchies in Late Medieval and
Renaissance Europe*

Peter Lowe (editor)
The Vietnam War

ORDERS AND HIERARCHIES IN LATE MEDIEVAL AND RENAISSANCE EUROPE

Edited by

Jeffrey Denton

Research Professor of Medieval History
University of Manchester

First published 1999 by
MACMILLAN PRESS LTD
Houndmills, Basingstoke, Hampshire RG21 6XS
and London
Companies and representatives throughout the world

ISBN 0-333-67765-X hardcover
ISBN 0-333-67766-8 paperback

A catalogue record for this book is available from the British Library.

This book is printed on paper suitable for recycling and made from fully
managed and sustained forest sources.

10 9 8 7 6 5 4 3 2 1
08 07 06 05 04 03 02 01 00 99

Printed in Hong Kong

CONTENTS

LIST OF ILLUSTRATIONS

Editor's Preface

The chapters of this book originated as papers delivered at a series of one-day conferences of the J. K. Hyde Centre for Late Medieval and Renaissance Studies at the University of Manchester. The Centre was established by the late Professor J. K. Hyde to promote interdisciplinary research. Thanks are due to all who attended the conferences and contributed to the wide-ranging discussion on orders and hierarchies. I am especially grateful to Brian Pullan both for his unstinting work on behalf of the J. K. Hyde Centre and for his unfailingly generous assistance in the preparation of this book. For constant forbearance and support, not least in solving the enigmas created by variously processed contributions, my heartfelt thanks go to David Shepherd.

JEFFREY DENTON

NOTES ON THE CONTRIBUTORS

Peter Ainsworth is Professor of French at the University of Liverpool. Author of *Jean Froissart and the Fabric of History* (1990), he has also published recently on Marie de France. With George Diller, he is preparing a partial edition of Books II and III of Froissart's *Chroniques* for the Lettres Gothiques series, and a new edition of Book III (Besançon MS 865) is also in preparation.

Paul Binski is Lecturer in the History of Art at the University of Cambridge, and has taught at the Universities of Yale and Manchester. He is the author of *The Painted Chamber at Westminster* (1986) and *Westminster Abbey: Kingship and the Representation of Power 1200–1400* (1995), as well as numerous studies of English royal art patronage. His most recent book is *Medieval Death, Ritual and Representation* (1996).

Antony Black is Professor in the History of Political Thought in the Department of Politics at the University of Dundee. He has written on conciliarism (*Council and Commune*, 1979), on guilds and communes (*Guilds and Civil Society in European Political Thought from the Twelfth Century to the Present* (1984), and *Community in Historical Perspective* (1990), an edition of a translation of selections from Gierke, *Das deutsche Genossenschaftsrecht*, vol. 1) and also a general study *Political Thought in Europe 1250–1450* (1992). He is now working on a history of political thought under Islam with a view to producing a comparative study of the development of political ideas in the Middle East and in Europe.

Michael Bush left the History Department of Manchester University in 1994 to pursue a career in historical research. As a comparative historian, he has written a two-volume work entitled *The European Nobility* (1983, 1988), *The English Aristocracy* (1984), and several articles on tenant right and serfdom. As a Tudor historian, he has written *The Government Policy of Protector Somerset* (1975) and a two-volume study of the Pilgrimage of Grace and its aftermath, *The Pilgrimage of Grace: A Study of the Rebel Armies of October 1536* (1996; second volume forthcoming). He has also produced a modern edition of Richard Carlile's *Every Woman's Book* (1826) entitled *Richard Carlile's Philosophy of Sex* (1997); and he has edited *Social Orders and Social Classes in Europe since 1500* (1992) and *Serfdom and Slavery* (1996).

Jeffrey Denton is Research Professor in Medieval History at the University of Manchester. He is the author of *English Royal Free Chapels 1100–1300* (1970), *Robert Winchelsey and the Crown 1294–1313* (1980), and (with J. P. Dooley) *Representatives of the Lower Clergy in Parliament 1295–1340* (1987), and editor (with R. G. Davies) of *The English Parliament in the Middle Ages* (1981). He is working on a monograph, and new editions of texts, concerning royal/ecclesiastical relations, *c.*1300, in France and England.

Maurice Keen was educated at Winchester and at Balliol College Oxford, where he read Modern History, graduating in 1957. Since 1961 he has been a Fellow of Balliol and tutor in medieval history there. His many publications include *The Outlaws of Medieval Legend* (1961), *The Laws of War in the Later Middle Ages* (1965), *A History of Medieval Europe* (1967), *England in the Later Middle Ages* (1973), and *Chivalry* (1984).

Spencer Pearce is Lecturer in Italian Studies at the University of Manchester, where he currently teaches courses on Dante and fifteenth-century Italian art. His principal research interest is in the field of Italian Renaissance thought. He has published articles on Dante, modern Italian poetry, and the Renaissance polymath Girolamo Fracastoro.

Brian Pullan has been Professor of Modern History at the University of Manchester since 1973 and is the author of *Rich and Poor in Renaissance Venice* (1971), *The Jews of Europe and the Inquisition of Venice, 1550–1670* (1983) and *Poverty and Charity: Europe, Italy, Venice, 1400–1700* (1994), and the editor of *Crisis and Change in the Economy of Venice in the Sixteenth and Seventeenth Centuries* (1968) and (with D. Chambers and J. Fletcher) *Venice: A Documentary History, 1450–1630* (1992). He is currently

working on a general history of poverty, charity and poor relief in Italy
from the fifteenth to the eighteenth century.

David Rheubottom is Lecturer in Social Anthropology at the University
of Manchester. He did anthropological fieldwork on the family and
economics in a Macedonian peasant village. More recently he has been
working on an anthropological analysis of politics and kinship in late
medieval Ragusa (Dubrovnik). He is the author of several studies concerning both Macedonia and Ragusa published since 1976.

Stephen Rigby was educated at the Universities of Sheffield and
London and is Reader in Medieval History at the University of Manchester. He is the author of a number of books and articles on social
theory and medieval history including *Marxism and History: A Critical
Introduction* (1987), *Engels and the Formation of Marxism: History, Dialectics
and Revolution* (1992), *Medieval Grimsby: Growth and Decline* (1993), *English Society in the Later Middle Ages: Class, Status and Gender* (1995) and
Chaucer in Context: Society, Allegory and Gender (1996).

INTRODUCTION

Jeffrey Denton

While this is no orthodox textbook, it is nonetheless a coursebook. Its theme is the social structure of Western Europe between c.1300 and c.1600. Its aim is not to provide a comprehensive survey, but to give perspective to the subject and to shed light upon a few different approaches. It is interdisciplinary because an important challenge, still too rarely taken up, of learning about past social development lies in the connected study of various activities and attainments, whether political, literary, artistic or scholastic. It is also essential to achieve understanding of the methodologies of those trained in the separate, perhaps all too separate, disciplines of history, social science, political theory, literary criticism and history of art. The book is introductory in that it opens the door on the work of experts in these fields. In introducing students to the research of leading scholars, in the context of a book concerned with a general theme, the intention is to demonstrate that the world of teaching and learning may not be best served by the preservation of hierarchical notions that set the results of research at the highest end of the educational spectrum and books for courses at the lowest.

This study is largely concerned with the attitudes of a past age towards its own social organisation. These attitudes can only be understood by assessing both beliefs and actions, and by analysing the ever-complex relationship between the two. It is thus a book about theory and practice, or, to express it rather differently, about attitudes and the contexts in which these were expressed and (maybe) lived out. But it takes as its starting point in Chapter 1 an assessment of other kinds of theories: the theories not of the period under study but rather by which our understanding of that period can be ordered – the theories, that is, formulated primarily by social scientists but used, in large measure or in small measure, consciously or unconsciously, by all who study the past.

1

There has been a distinct shift towards an understanding of medieval and early modern social structure as a hierarchy of orders (the functionalist approach) rather than of classes (the Marxist approach). This shift is evident in some of the chapters which follow: see especially Chapters 6 to 9 and in particular the discussion on pp. 147–9. Although a variety of terms were in fact used in the Middle Ages to categorise social distinctions, it has become a commonly expressed belief that the term 'class' is now best avoided because it carries with it modern implications.[1] Chapter 1 analyses the functionalist and the Marxist approaches and suggests that the strengths of each can be brought together in an interpretative framework (a theory of 'social closure') which focuses on interest groups, whether class-based or status-based, and the processes whereby they protected and extended their concerns. Within this framework the evidence concerning the status or role of women, for example, can be reassessed (pp. 17–18, 22–3), as also, maybe, other manifestations of social change discussed in further chapters, for instance the image-making of the English royal court (Chapter 5) or the re-defining of English aristocratic/chivalric society (Chapter 6).

The theories of social scientists are a means whereby social realities can be assessed and described, assisting the processes of historical enquiry, though, of course, never determining the answers to historical enquiry. Study of the past is a kind of dialogue: a double process of studying the evidence for the formulation of principles and theories and of testing principles and theories by analysis of the evidence. The historical examples in Chapter 1 come largely from late medieval England. Three later Chapters, 5, 6 and 7, relate directly to England, spotlighting in turn aspects of kingship, knighthood and commons; then, building upon a brief assessment of Italian nobility *c.*1300 in Chapter 3 (pp. 34–6), the book moves from North-West Europe to South-East Europe with detailed studies of Ragusa, alias Dubrovnik, and Venice (Chapters 8 and 9). The English/Italian poles provide something of a contrast. Yet a primary supposition of this book is that, from the point of view of social stratification, Western Europe can be studied as an entity. Chapter 2 examines this supposition through a comparison between the Christian West and the Islamic Middle East, concluding that despite interesting similarities between the two the Middle East (a) did not accept a hierarchical structure for society as a whole, (b) stressed vertical rather than horizontal groupings and (c) made a greater distinction than the West between the state and the people (see esp. pp. 29–32).

Thus, in our analytical dialogue with the past, there are some firm reasons for treating Western Europe as a single testing ground. One of the most challenging features of recent scholarship, affecting many disciplines, has been to question the very character of social realities and of discourse about those realities. Did historical events and developments and the products of society – its artefacts, its artistic and literary achievements, as well as its own social theories – directly reflect society's organisation and priorities? Or, rather, did these manifestations of activity and endeavour themselves actively constitute the realities? How are we to perceive, and provide a context for, the images of social distinctions created by the past? With these questions in mind, Chapters 3, 4 and 5 scrutinise some of the most notable cultural expressions of the age, the works of Dante, the narratives of Froissart and the images of English kings. Outstanding literary and artistic achievements were, of course, often individual achievements, and, as such, they could be no other than 'unique'; yet they cannot be separated from their cultural and historical settings, nor isolated from political and social influences, acting both upon and through them.

Notions of social order, formulated or assumed, were a natural part of creative image-making. The most striking contemporary model of social structure, the model of trifunctionality, has been widely studied, most notably by Georges Duby in his *The Three Orders: Feudal Society Imagined* (Chicago and London, 1980),[2] a work frequently referred to in the following pages. What was the cultural and historical setting for this (recurring) ideal of society as divided into those who pray (*oratores*), those who fight (*bellatores*) and those who labour (*laboratores*)? The context surrounding, and explaining, the ideal's emergence, or re-emergence, in the West during the early decades of the eleventh century has been examined by Duby, and others.[3] Duby saw the ideal as a hidden, mysterious force, resurfacing time and again over the succeeding millenium. There can be no doubt, however, that whenever it resurfaced it did so not only in different contexts but also in different forms. The threefold division might give emphasis, for example, to wealth and power rather than function (below, p. 11). Indeed, in the West, social distinctions were perceived very commonly as relating not simply to divisions of occupation but also to divisions of political standing and rights (below, p. 32). It is not surprising, therefore, to see the idea of three orders developing as a notion of three political estates: the clergy, the nobility and the 'third estate'. Even so, there are no grounds for interpreting the institutional development of Estates General, and

Parliaments of many sorts, as a reifying, or bringing to fruition, of the ideal. Rather, the ideal was re-invoked and re-expressed in explanation of the developments.[4]

The 'third estate' of late medieval and early modern assemblies certainly did not correspond to the category of 'those who laboured'.[5] Indeed, the third element of the trifunctional ideal was, from the eleventh century onwards, something of a shifting concept. It often came to be closely associated with an urban elite. It emerged in England, as Chapter 7 shows, with a very distinctive 'commons' label. Rarely did it encompass the populace, for there is a sense in which the hierarchical concept of social orders was too important to embrace all. The role of Froissart's lowly 'people' was to talk about the deeds of valiant men (below, p. 64).

The trifunctional notion – always more of a literary model than a scholar's model – was not a fixed idea. It might be revived and re-worded, in particular circumstances, especially it seems in France or in England, to represent and thereby support a perceived enduring reality; but it never, any more than other contemporary models, in itself presented a convincing view of actualities, except of a broadbrush kind. It clearly derived much plausibility from its primary emphasis on the two distinct, though in practice mutually supporting, categories of clergy and nobility.[6] These orders were remarkably secure – indeed, were under constant regeneration. Their position was little shaken by religious trends which saw individual devotion as more important than status[7] or by political ideas which stressed the community or the common good.[8] And they were bolstered as social classifications by the profoundly significant legal and political distinctions between the clergy and the laity. These distinctions, surely more than any other, characterised the age; and, unlike the three orders model, belief in the different spheres of churchmen and laymen was rooted in biblical texts and informed the whole world of learning.

There were other images of social order, notably the much-used organic model, of the body with its head and members,[9] and the metaphor of the ship, which had three levels of twelve orders in Philip de Mézières's late-fourteenth-century *Songe du Vieil Pèlerin*.[10] Whatever the image, the orders of society were set unerringly in a hierarchical framework. Social inequalities were not just facts of life. They were essential to social harmony and a prime element in European Christian thinking. Position in the social hierarchy was, in images as in reality, more significant than function alone (below, p. 107). Society's organisation was an extension of, or a mirroring of, the perceived hierarchical structure of the universe. Two treatises, on the *Celestial Hierarchy* and the *Ecclesiastical Hierarchy*, written in the early Middle Ages under the pseudonym Dionysius the Areopagite, continued to influence reflection on orders and on the correspondences between temporal and spiritual authority, especially among supporters of the Church militant.[11] But belief in cosmic order was certainly not the preserve of staunch papalists and hierocrats, those, that is, who supported priestly authority and priestly government. It was also intrinsic, for example, to Dante's thinking, though strict hierarchical order was mitigated, through divine grace, by human free will and the singular quality of the human soul (below, pp. 46–7). The necessity of ordering was linked to faith in the immanent and the immutable. Order and discipline reflected the intentions of the Creator.

Two major treatises composed *c*.1300 conveniently set the scene for this book. Giles of Rome's *On Ecclesiastical Power*[12] epitomised the hierocratic approach: a fundamentally sacralised ranking of authorities, the celestial linked through intermediaries with the earthly. Giles's stridently clear-cut and deeply traditional ideas were used to defend and explain the pope's supreme authority on earth, spiritual and temporal. On the other hand, John of Paris in his *On Royal and Papal Power*[13] presented consciously moderating opinions, which were more in tune with those of contemporaries, at any rate outside the papal curia. John's work was influenced both by recent heated debates among the friars about the role of the Church and by the realities of royal control and patronage in France. Here is an emphasis on communities, pointing firmly away from rigidly viewed tiers of authority. Here, too, the door is opened on the possibility of a diversity of groupings, and of independent groupings, in the secular world: 'It is not so necessary for all secular rulers to be hierarchically ordered as it is for ecclesiastical ministers.'[14] As we have seen, it is possible – indeed, salutary – to study Europe as a whole, but it was, even so, a Europe of diversities. While there was a flourishing of clerical status and of noble status in late medieval and early modern Europe, many factors, among them the activities of ecclesiastical reformers and of all kinds of traders, produced a greater consciousness and acceptance of diversity than repeated images of social orders and social order would at first suggest.

1

APPROACHES TO PRE-INDUSTRIAL SOCIAL STRUCTURE

Stephen Rigby

'Hostility to theory usually means an opposition to other people's theories and an oblivion of one's own.'

T. Eagleton, *Literary Theory: An Introduction* (Oxford, 1983), p. viii.

It is often the case that practical, empirically-minded historians who believe themselves to be quite exempt from the influence of any abstract social theory are, in reality, the unwitting slave of some defunct sociologist. The two sociological ghosts which haunt all attempts by historians to make sense of late medieval and early modern societies are Marxism and functionalism. This chapter briefly considers these approaches and argues that the strengths of each are synthesised in the neo-Weberian 'closure theory' developed by writers such as Parkin and Murphy. It considers, with the help of evidence drawn mainly from medieval England, the advantages of closure theory for historians and concludes by examining some of the criticisms which can be made of this approach.

Marx's *historical materialism* presents social hierarchies in *dichotomic*, rather than *gradated* or *functional* terms,[1] analysing social relations in terms of one or more binary oppositions: propertied and non-propertied, exploiter and exploited, employer and employee, and so on. For Marx, the key to a society's structure lies in its *relations of production*, that is property or class relations which determine how individuals obtain access to the means of production (or *productive*

6

forces) and to the necessities of life which they produce. Long-term historical development is then presented in terms of a succession of *modes of production* (such as the feudal, capitalist, and socialist modes), each of which is defined by its dominant relations of production.[2] According to Marx, class relations are necessarily *exploitative* since they involve the appropriation by one class, the propertied, of the *surplus labour* created by another class, the producers, as in the payment of rent by peasants to feudal lords in medieval England. As a result, class relations possess an inherent potential for conflict as the producers have an inherent interest in minimising the level of exploitation (for example, the level of rent paid by peasants) while the propertied have an interest in seeking to maximise levels of exploitation.[3] Marx presents these relations of production as the economic *base* of society to which 'corresponds' a *superstructure* of political institutions, law and forms of social consciousness.[4] Thus, in general, the state functions as 'the organised power of one class for oppressing another', as when the feudal state is seen as 'the organ of the nobility for holding down the peasant serfs and bondsmen'. Similarly, particular social ideologies express specific class interests, as when Engels described medieval Catholicism as a 'halo of sanctity' which legitimated feudal relations.[5]

Given the comprehensive scope of Marx and Engels's work, much twentieth-century sociology has been a dialogue, whether implicit or explicit, with historical materialism. Moreover, Marx and Engels's social theory has inspired some of the most original, wide-ranging and theoretically self-conscious analyses of pre-industrial society, as can be seen in the work of historians such as Brenner, Hilton and Razi.[6] Nevertheless, Marxist theory involves a number of problems. In particular, there are the difficulties posed for Marxism by the conceptualisation of society in terms of the metaphor of base and superstructure. Indeed, Marxists have spent much of the twentieth society trying to avoid the implications of this metaphor, either by blaming it on Engels or by qualifying Marx's claims out of existence altogether.[7] The dilemma facing Marxists is that if they overemphasise the determination of society's 'superstructure' by its relations of production, they run the risk of 'reductionism' whereby politics and ideology become simply passive reflections of society's economic base, an approach which Marxists have rejected ever since Engels's famous letters of the 1890s.[8] On the other hand, Marxists have to refrain from ascribing too much importance to the social superstructure, so as to avoid lapsing into a pluralitiy of explanations which dissolve away anything distinctively Marxist about their analysis.[9] The usual solution to this dilemma has been to adopt, in their actual historical analyses, an explanatory pluralism little different from that of non-Marxist historiography, while maintaining an explicit commitment to the primacy of the economic at the level of theory.[10]

Very similar problems arise for Marxism when it attempts to account for those *non-class* forms of social inequality based on status, which often cut across social divisions based on property, such as gender, race, language or religion. Again, one response to this problem is for Marxists to lapse into 'reductionism' by explaining such relations through the 'needs' of class relations, as when the social inequality of women is explained in terms of its benefits for the reproduction of the dominant mode of production of the time.[11] Alternatively, once more, Marxists can simply opt for pluralism and add non-class social relations *ad hoc* to their analysis. It was these problems with the model of base and superstructure and with non-class forms of social inequality, as well as pure political animosity, which led to the alternative account of social stratification which became dominant among the *functionalist* sociologists of the mid-century.

In contrast with the dichotomic conception of social inequality characteristic of Marxism, the functionalist perspective presents society as a *gradated* hierarchy of *functionally defined* groups which together form an organic whole. Liberal, functionalist stratification-theory took from Weberian sociology a rejection of Marx's claims for the primacy of economics or class relations, emphasising instead the *multi-dimensional* nature of social inequality conceptualised not just in terms of property and wealth but also in terms of power and status.[12] In the place of the sharply distinguished classes of Marxist social theory, functional sociology presented social structure in gradated terms, inequality being distributed more or less continuously along society's major dimensions of inequality.[13] While Marxists tended to deny the importance of differences of social esteem on the grounds that they 'tell one nothing about the concrete structure of inequality' from which such esteem is ultimately derived,[14] functionalist stratification theorists came to see *status*, defined in terms of lifestyle and the estimation of one's esteem in the eyes of others, as the key to social stratification.[15] In this perspective, subjective conceptions of the social structure are not merely a second-order, superstructural reflection of some underlying social reality but are themselves actively constitutive of the social hierarchy. However, for specific groups to be ranked in terms of their status or prestige in the eyes of their contemporaries necessarily requires, as was made explicit in the work of Talcott Parsons, the existence of some degree of consensus, that is a *common value-system* which provides shared grounds of evaluation of social functions, rather than the opposed class interests emphasised by Marxism.[16]

The perspective of American stratification theory thus differed from that of Marxism in three main ways. First, it stressed the importance of non-class forms of social differentiation. Second, it analysed society in terms of the subjective evaluation of social roles by contemporaries rather than just of objective property rights and relations of production. Third, it emphasised consensus and social harmony rather than the inevitable conflict assumed by the dichotomic approach.

Although the functionalist conception of social structure was initially worked out in relation to modern society, it was to have an influence on the work of a number of historians, such as Blum, Mousnier and Fourquin. These writers argued that social inequality in medieval and early modern society was based not on a hierarchy of objectively defined economic *classes* but rather on an 'evaluative differentiation' of the functions of different social *orders* or *estates*. In this society, 'opinion', in the form of shared judgements about the value of different social roles, lay at the heart of pre-industrial social stratification, and the position of each order 'rested upon the esteem accorded by the society to the functions performed by each estate'. Such estate-functions had '*no necessary connection* with the production of goods or with any other economic activity', although the ownership of wealth was of 'much importance' for the internal hierarchy of each order. In short, in pre-industrial society, social status was not based on income: income was based on social status.[17] This distinction between the societies of orders characteristic of pre-industrial society and the class-societies of capitalism is now so commonplace that it constitutes the orthodoxy of sociology primers.[18]

With an emphasis on the existence of consensus about the evaluation of specific social functions, functionalist historians have inevitably tended to minimise the extent of conflict within society and instead stressed social collaboration and harmony.[19] Thus, Keen characterises late medieval England as a 'deference society' since, 'in the minds of men of that age, the relations of deference and service that existed between the grades [of society] were the basis of social order, of its essence: they had not yet come to regard social distinctions as divisive, as forces with the potential to tear society apart'.[20] Mousnier even adopted the functionalist claim that inequalities of status act as a socially useful means for meting out rewards which ensure the provision of particular functions, as when a society faces a sustained military danger so that a military elite is particularly highly valued and then rewarded accordingly.[21] Where pre-industrial social revolts *did* occur, they are seen by these historians not as the result of inherent class conflicts but rather as cross-class alliances occasioned by some specific crisis, such as a poor harvest or military defeat, and as political in their focus, targeting the state rather than the propertied.[22]

This interpretation of pre-industrial social structure as a hierarchy of orders rather than of classes is, as Peter Burke pointed out, in danger of becoming an outdated 'Aunt Sally' which its opponents ritually knock down. Yet Burke himself concludes that, for the study of early modern society at least, the orders model is perhaps the 'least misleading' of the theoretical frameworks available to us.[23] Certainly, historians have been happy to apply this approach to a wide variety of societies, from those of the Ancient world to those of early-modern Europe.[24] What then are the weaknesses of the functional perspective and its application by historians to pre-industrial society?

First, there is the problem that functionalist theory vacillates between, on the one hand, seeing society in terms of a number of dimensions of stratification (wealth, status and power) and, on the other, presenting *one* of these dimensions (status) as the most important, thus downplaying other forms of inequality, particularly property divisions. Second, the functionalist approach faces problems in its account of social inequality as a 'rational' mechanism by which society allocates rewards to groups which perform particular functions. After all, Mousnier and Fourquin themselves accept that social evaluation can sometimes, or even 'usually', be based upon criteria which are 'quite irrational and largely erroneous' and that even principles of stratification which were 'rational' in their origin can continue to prevail even after the initial reasons for their emergence have disappeared.[25] But in this case we are left with the puzzle of why such irrational and erroneous opinions emerge or why they persist, even though they are no longer beneficial for society. In practice, even if we accept that pre-industrial society *was* stratified (at least in certain respects) on the basis of status-evaluation, this does not mean that we necessarily have to offer a 'rational' explanation of the criteria used to arrive at such opinions, a point vividly illustrated by the dominant social evaluation of the Jews in medieval English society prior to their eventual expulsion in 1290.[26]

A third problem with the functional perspective is that it tends to take societies at their own word about their social stratification and so ignores the potential for disparity between theory and social reality. Yet, why should we accept what medieval people said about their own society as the basis of *our* historical description of that society? After all, in everyday life we constantly distinguish 'between what somebody professes to be and what he really is'.[27] In other words, it is quite possible that a disparity can emerge between 'opinion' – or ideology – and reality. As Crone puts it, in pre-industrial society, wealth was based on rank and not vice versa, '*or at least that was the principle*'.[28] Mousnier likewise admits that, while the clergy were the 'first order' of seventeenth-century France in terms of social theory and law, it was, in fact, the nobility who enjoyed actual social primacy.[29] Similarly while Fourquin emphasises that medieval social theorists portrayed their own society in religious terms, he himself presents medieval society as a 'military society of orders' in which a military elite had pride of place. Furthermore, Fourquin argues that medieval social stratification should be seen in terms of the evaluative differentiation of social roles by contemporaries, but he also offers his *own* view of medieval society as one divided into 'elite, commons and marginals'.[30]

Indeed, the inhabitants of pre-industrial Europe themselves could adopt a variety of different social perspectives according to their immediate purposes. In particular, the similarities between individuals who were, in theory, members of different orders tended towards a division of society into horizontal strata defined in terms of their wealth or power rather than into the three functionally defined estates (those who pray, those who fight, and those who work) familiar from traditional medieval social theory.[31] As Aristotle had put it, 'In every state there are three parts, viz the very rich, the very poor, and thirdly the intermediate class.'[32] Thus, in a sermon before the parliament of 1433, Bishop Stafford divided English society into, first, the commons (the cultivators, artificers and *vulgares*), second, the knights, esquires and merchants (or the knights and *mediocres*), who were the 'hills' of society, and, third, the bishops and magnates, who were the 'mountains' of society.[33] The horizontal equation of the members of different orders is not simply the work of class-obsessed modern historians but could also be adopted by contemporaries when the need arose.

The final weakness of the functional perspective is that it tends to overemphasise social consensus and to underestimate the extent and significance of social conflict.[34] This weakness is closely linked with a tendency to 'reify' society, to make it into an agent which does things and has opinions, as when Blum argues that the hierarchical arrangement of orders in pre-modern society 'rested upon the esteem *accorded by the society* to the functions performed by each estate'.[35] Yet 'society' is not an independent reality or an historical actor which can make evaluations of the worth of 'its' members separate from the actions of the individuals who make it up. As a result, there is no reason why all of the individuals who actually comprise any particular society should necessarily share a single opinion about the value of the functions performed by other members of society. Rather, the individual members of particular social groups may see their own group as the most important and thus most deserving of primacy in the social order or, as is more frequently the case, may come to question particular privileges claimed by other groups. The latter was certainly the case in late medieval England where the endemic friction between lord and peasant over the terms of the social contract played a crucial part in bringing about the end of villeinage and the achievement of peasant freedom.[36] We need not assume, as Marshall did, that the only alternatives facing the medieval peasant were either outright rebellion or total social acquiescence.[37] In fact, in late medieval England, local friction and piecemeal conflict were rather more typical than either the class harmony favoured by the preachers or the social anarchy which threatened briefly for a few weeks in 1381. Such conflict, while hardly revolutionary, was crucial in determining which paths of social and economic development were opened up to England and which were closed off.[38]

Thus, many social theorists, even those who mounted their own critiques of Marxism, such as Dahrendorf, Giddens, and Parkin, have rejected the functionalist emphasis on social harmony, preferring to see social relations as potentially antagonistic, even though they do not see such social conflicts as limited to, or reducible to, those of economic class.[39] This approach was based on an alternative reading of Weber, one in which status groups were portrayed as combative and monopolistic appropriators of power and material privileges and whose closure of opportunities to outsiders could provoke resistance from those who were excluded. It was *this* reading of Weber which was to form the basis for the account of social structure offered by 'closure theorists' such as Parkin and Murphy.[40]

In his discussion in *Economy and Society* of the competition for economic resources and opportunities, Weber discusses the process by which a group of competitors seizes upon the characteristics of some other social group, such as race, language, religion, or descent, as a pretext or ground for the latter's exclusion from access to resources and so comes to 'form an "interest group" against outsiders'. By this 'monopolisation' of resources, the members of the group attempt to guarantee themselves advantages and achieve 'the closure of social and economic opportunities to outsiders', although such closure 'may provoke a corresponding reaction on the part of those against whom it is directed'. Status groups and economic classes based on property ownership are specific forms of such interest groups, which seek the monopolistic appropriation of rewards and opportunities.[41] In the work of writers such as Neuwirth, Collins and Murphy, Weber's undeveloped remarks about social closure have been turned into a broader framework within which to analyse social structure,[42] but the essentials of such closure theory have been set out with particular clarity in the work of Frank Parkin.[43] In Parkin's view, Weber's theory of *social closure* offers a set of common concepts and a vocabulary with which to analyse all structured social inequalities, including those between classes, those within particular classes, and those between communal- and status-groups based on race, religion, or gender. For Parkin, all of these particular forms of social closure are 'different means of mobilising power for the purpose of engaging in distributive struggle'. Closure is thus the process by which social groups attempt to maximise their rewards and opportunities. It exists in two main forms: exclusionary and usurpationary.

In the case of *exclusionary closure*, one group attempts 'to secure for itself a privileged position at the expense of some other group through a process of subordination', this downward exercise of power leading to the creation of 'a group, class or stratum of legally defined inferiors'. Such exclusionary closure is not limited to that achieved by the property-based classes of Marxist analysis but can be affected by a variety of criteria, including race, religion, gender, language, or lineage. Closure theory thus insists that 'social conflict' is not simply mounted from below (as popular revolts, strikes, and so on) but can also be inspired from above through the attempt to extend the exclusionary closure enjoyed by 'insiders'. For example, when, after 1298, the abbots of Battle set about undermining the unusually free tenure of the customary tenants of the abbey's *leuga* (the land within a league of the abbey's altar), their offensive was just as much an example of class conflict as the ultimately successful resistance to it organised by the tenants of the *leuga*.[44]

Parkin distinguishes two main modes of exclusion: the *collectivist* and the *individualist*.[45] In the former, one possesses privileges as a member of a group (for instance, a racial group) into which one is born. As a result social mobility is reduced and group 'reproduction' between the generations is encouraged. In the latter case, exclusion is effected by criteria which are purely individual, as in the possession of private property or academic qualifications under modern capitalism or membership of the Communist Party in the Soviet Union, and which thus tend to encourage individual social mobility. In practice, these two modes of exclusion are likely to be combined, although Parkin claims that there has been a long-term historical shift away from the collectivist and towards the individualist end of the spectrum. Traditional, pre-capitalist, agrarian societies, are thus said to have been characterised by the dominance of hereditary or 'collectivist' forms of exclusion, such as 'aristocratic lineage'. As a result, upwards social mobility 'was an unusual exception to the explicit mode of exclusion in operation', so that, as Murphy puts it, society consisted of 'a system of bounded collectivities which were separate, unequal, closed and with each in its place'.[46]

Although strategies of exclusion are the predominant form of closure in any society, Parkin emphasises that such exclusion can provoke attempts at *usurpationary closure*, that is 'the use of power in an upward direction', as the excluded attempt to win a greater share of resources and 'to bite into the privileges of legally defined superiors'. Exclusionary closure normally works by obtaining the sanction of the state: property relies upon the policeman. Usurpationary closure, by contrast, often involves mass mobilisation and direct action, tactics which can bring it into conflict with the state's claim to have a monopoly of legitimate violence. However, in particular circumstances, both exclusion and usurpation can be effected by means of the strategies of legalism and collective mobilisation. In order to mobilise support, attempts at usurpationary closure normally have to appeal to some alternative standard of distributive justice from that which justifies the status quo. For instance, in the Peasants' Revolt of 1381, John Ball argued that, in the beginning, 'all men were created equal by nature', thus allowing him to reject feudal servitude as a human invention which was contrary to the will of God.[47]

Parkin argues that particular social groups can also adopt the strategy of *dual closure*. In these cases, a social group which is subordinated by one form of social exclusion is, in turn, itself responsible for, or benefits by, the exclusion of some other social group. An example might be that of white workers, whose class position is defined by their exclusion from access to the means of production but who themselves attempt to exclude non-white workers from competing for employment. Weber argued that in the monopolisation of resources and the exclusion of outsiders 'it does not matter which characteristic is chosen' as the pretext for exclusion: 'whatever suggests itself most easily is seized upon'.[48] But, if this were the case, it would not be possible to explain why female workers have not achieved exclusionary closure against men or why blacks in the Deep South were unable to enforce white skin as the 'pretext' for exclusion. Parkin argues that in such cases one subordinated social group is able to exclude some other subordinated group because the latter has already been defined as legally or socially inferior by the state or the dominant class and is therefore vulnerable to exclusion. This certainly seems to have been the case with the popular hostility experienced by the Jews in twelfth- and thirteenth-century England. This animosity was not merely the result of economic griev-ances of debtors to moneylenders. After all, Christians were soon to take the place of the Jews as the major source of credit within the economy but they were not to be accused of ritually murdering young boys or expelled from society as traitors and blasphemers. It was not simply that people disliked being in debt to the Jews or that they envied their wealth. Rather, what was particularly resented was the sense of injustice generated at being placed in an inferior position to those who, accord-ing to society's dominant ideology, were themselves supposed to be in perpetual servitude.[49]

Thus, for closure theory, any one individual is the member of a multiplicity of overlapping social sets, each of which, according to closure theory, is defined in terms of its relative access to, or exclusion from, social resources such as economic wealth, social status and politi-cal power.[50] Indeed, as Marx and Engels long ago pointed out, the members of any particular social group are, as individuals, 'on hostile terms with each other as competitors': workers are in competition with each other for employment, peasants for land, nobles for royal patron-age, and clerics for promotion. One of the main ways in which the competing members of such groups come to feel a subjective sense of shared identity is through carrying on 'a common battle' against another social group.[51] Murphy usefully distinguishes between the dif-ferent forms of organisation or identity of excluded social groups.[52] At the one extreme are those who, despite a situation of social exclusion on some common grounds, are 'isolated from one another and disorganised, forming little more than an amorphous plurality'. At the other extreme are 'firmly-rooted sentient communities' with strong subjective senses of identity such as minority groups herded into racial ghettoes, although, as the 'circumspect' attitude of the Jews in medieval England emphasises, such self-conscious communities are not always able to mobilise successfully to achieve usurpationary closure.[53] A third alternative is the creation of 'associational groupings based on the shared qualities of the plurality', whether permanent, as in the case of trades unions and political parties, or more short-lived, as with the 'crowd' typical of so much pre-industrial social protest.[54] For Parkin, which of these responses emerges is related to which mode of exclusion is at work, in particular whether it is based on individualist or collectivist criteria. He argues that collectivist types of exclusion should 'in ideal-typical terms . . . produce a subordinate group of communal character' rather than one marked by intense social fragmentation.[55]

The advantage of closure theory for the historian is that it synthesises the strongest elements of both the Marxist and the liberal perspectives. First, from historical materialism, closure theory inherits an emphasis on the antagonisms and tensions arising from the struggle over the distribution of social rewards and opportunities between dominant insiders and subordinated outsiders. Yet, unlike the Marxist tradition, closure theory does not see such conflict as necessarily fatal for society or as leading society towards some particular goal, such as the maximum development of the productive forces or socialism. Second, from the functionalist perspective, closure theory retains an emphasis on the variety of non-class criteria which can be used as the basis for exclusion. It refuses to reduce these various sources of social power to a mere superstructure of class relations and insists on the existence of multiple dimensions of social inequality and sources of social power. Similarly, the concept of dual closure allows closure theory to recognise the existence of intermediate groups in the social hierarchy whose importance was traditionally stressed by American stratification theory. Closure theory therefore provides us with a series of concepts and a vocabulary which enable us to make a unified analysis of both inter-class and intra-class divisions as well as the inter-communal conflicts which pose so many problems for Marxist social theory.

Finally, given the level of generality at which much of closure theory is pitched, historians studying the structure of any particular society may wish to combine Parkin's approach with the comprehensive account of social structure offered by Runciman. For both Parkin and

Runciman, the structure of any particular society can be seen as a hierarchy of groups defined in terms of their allocation of power (or, in Parkin's terms, their ability to effect closure). Runciman distinguishes three different *modes of power*: the *economic*, the *coercive* and the *ideological*, based respectively upon access to the means of production, to the means of political and military coercion, and to the means of persuasion. These three 'dimensions' of social structure are 'always mutually interdependent', and even inter-convertible (so that power in one dimension is translated into power in another), but are 'never fully reducible to one another'. Although in any particular society, it may be the case that 'the way that power is allocated in one dimension determines the way that it is allocated in the others', there is no universal rule that one mode of power should have primacy, as was claimed by Marx's metaphor of economic base and political and ideological superstructure.[56]

In order to refer to the entire spectrum of social groups defined by their allocation of power, Runciman coins the ugly but extremely useful term *systacts*, that is 'groups or categories of persons sharing a common endowment (or lack) of power by virtue of their roles' and who thus have a common interest in maintaining or augmenting the power (economic, coercive or ideological) attached to such roles. Familiar types of systact include *status-groups*, defined by Runciman as groups distinguished by 'a common value system and life-style accorded differential esteem'; *castes* whose membership is hereditary, linked to a place in the division of labour, and positioned in a ritual hierarchy of purity and pollution; *orders*, whose social location 'is juridically defined'; and *estates*, which are systacts 'constitutionally entitled to separate representation in government'.[57] We can then reserve the term *class* for, as Runciman puts it, a systact 'whose members stand in a common relation to the processes of production, distribution and exchange of goods and services' rather than using the term more generally to refer to *any* social group defined in terms of domination or subordination.[58]

To Runciman's list of systacts, it is crucial to add *gender*, that is the way in which the biological differences between the sexes are socially interpreted so as to become the bases for specific forms of access to, or exclusion from, wealth, status and power.[59] Sociologists and historians often present the family – which is assumed to have a male head – as the key mechanism which gives individuals access to wealth, power and status and transmits privilege over the generations and as the basic unit of social stratification. As Andreas Capellanus put it in the twelfth century, 'A married woman changes her status to match that of her husband.'[60] The weakness of this perspective is that it fails to take account of social inequalities *within* the family, in particular those between men and women.[61] As Judith Bennett argues, despite the material inequalities experienced by the women of different classes in medieval England, it was still the case that women of all classes 'encountered political, legal, economic and social disadvantages that distinguished them sharply from their father, brothers, husbands, and sons'. As a result, women of the peasantry, as women, 'faced limitations fundamentally similar to those restricting women of the more privileged members of society'.[62]

It is easy to imagine that, since society can be conceptualised in terms of three dimensions of inequality (wealth, status and power), social groups and institutions have to be inserted into one of these dimensions (for instance, class into wealth, or race into status, or party into power). Certainly, feminist social theorists have debated whether the systematic social exclusion of women, such as that which characterised the patriarchal societies of late medieval and early modern Europe, had its grounding in society's ideological practices or forms of material production.[63] In practice, however, any one criterion or ground of social exclusion may be intersected by any or all of the three dimensions of social power (economic, coercive and ideological) so that a particular systact may come to experience social inferiority 'in all three dimensions of social power and inequality'.[64] Moreover, a reduction of the exclusion in one dimension of social inequality by no means has to result in a corresponding advance in the other dimensions. For instance, the growth of economic opportunities enjoyed by London women during the labour shortage of the later Middle Ages was not accompanied by any corresponding growth in their political power or legal rights, a fact which was to make such economic gains difficult to defend in the long term.[65] It thus becomes extremely difficult to speak of '*the* status of women' in pre-industrial society or to assess long-term changes in the net balance of their social exclusion when their status was characterised by a unevenness and inconsistency between the different areas of social life.[66]

Closure theory thus emphasises that individuals are not just ranked in one dimension of social inequality (of property ownership, esteem or whatever) but are instead positioned at the meeting point of a number of 'axes'[67] of social inequality. Any particular society can then be seen as an aggregate of multiple forms of social closure. Murphy has argued that the weakness of this approach is that it tends to ignore the interconnections between specific forms of social closure and that historians or sociologists must also provide an account of society's *deep structure* of closure.[68] Murphy attempts to do this by distinguishing between *rules* and *forms* of closure. A *rule* of closure is the criterion upon which exclusion is based, it is the line (such as race, gender or property-rights) along which insiders are distinguished from outsiders. A specific rule of exclusion is said to exist in a principal, derivative or contingent *form*. A *principal* form of exclusion is 'the main determinant of access to, or exclusion from, power, resources and opportunity' in a particular society, such as the legal title to private property in capitalist societies or Communist Party membership under state socialism. *Derivative* forms of exclusion exist where a principal form of exclusion provides the excluders with some supplementary means for developing associated forms of exclusionary closure as when the possession of wealth gives access to educational privilege. Finally, Murphy defines *contingent* forms of exclusion (rather generally) as those which are 'not directly derived from the principal form of exclusion' but whose very nature and existence is contingent upon the principal form of exclusion in society. Thus, he claims that the gender exclusion of modern society can be seen as 'contingent on' capitalist forms of exclusion.[69]

Armed with these concepts, Murphy argues that we can then characterise a society's overall *structure* of exclusion, the most common form of which is the *tandem* structure in which there is one principal form of exclusion along with its derivative and contingent forms. Second, there is the *dual* structure where there are two complementary principal forms of exclusion (such as race and class in apartheid South Africa), each of which can have its own derivative and contingent forms. Third, there is the possibility of a *polar* structure characterised by two competing or opposed principal rules of exclusion, each of which, once more, would have its own derivative and contingent forms of exclusion.

Yet, Murphy's attempt to construct a deep structure of closure is not entirely convincing. It is certainly true that specific forms of exclusion can be the basis for other forms of exclusion. For instance, within the medieval church, noble birth, while by no means a *sine qua non* of promotion, undoubtedly provided a number of advantages in the struggle for clerical advance.[70] What is more problematic is why, in this kind of analysis, one *rule* of exclusion (for example, gender) is said to be a contingent *form* of another rule of exclusion (for example, capitalist property relations) rather than simply a form of exclusion *sui generis*.

More specifically, even if we accepted this possibility in the abstract, it is not clear why exclusion on the grounds of gender is presented by Murphy as 'contingent on' capitalism when he himself rightly acknowledges that exclusion on the grounds of gender 'in many ways' antedates capitalist private property.[71] But, if this is the case, why not see gender exclusion as compatible with a wide variety of forms of property relations and thus as a social reality in its own right?[72] Once we do this, it follows that patriarchal societies would not simply have a 'tandem' structure, with one principal form of exclusion (property) and its derivative and contingent forms (such as gender). Rather, they have a 'dual structure' with two principal rules of exclusion: property and gender. In practice, of course, we may also have to add order, race, religion etc. as rules of exclusion in their own right. We then end up with a view of any particular society as an aggregate of primary rules of exclusionary closure, each of which may be the precondition for other forms of exclusion but none of which can be reduced to, or explained by, one fundamental form of exclusion.[73]

Once we see society as an aggregate of multiple forms of closure, there is no reason why social ranking in terms of economic classes and of functional estates or legal orders should be mutually exclusive. In this perspective, the long-running debate about whether medieval England was a class society or a society of orders can be seen to be about as productive as arguing whether an elephant is 'really' a quadruped or a mammal. Both approaches are equally valid but, in practice, which we adopt will tend to reflect our own academic interests. If we are interested in the manorial policies of the ecclesiastical landlords, such as their abandonment of direct management of their demesnes in the period after c.1375, we will then tend to stress the *similarities* between them and their lay counterparts.[74] Thus, while the theorists of the Middle Ages presented their own society in terms of mutually dependent orders, each defined by its functions,[75] it is certainly possible for twentieth-century historians to see medieval society as divided into economic classes, such as landlords and peasants, employers and labourers, merchants and artisans, each defined in terms of its property rights.

Yet, adopting the class approach where profitable does not mean that we have to ignore or deny the differences between lay and ecclesiastical landlords or to deny the existence of the status-privileges of specific orders. Certainly, if the power and status enjoyed by the lay aristocracy of late medieval England can largely be seen as a result of its class position and property rights, the position of the clerical order presents us with a very different picture. The social status enjoyed by the clergy was not simply the *consequence* of the ownership of wealth. On the contrary, access to the immense institutional wealth of the Church was itself the consequence of one's rank and functions within the ecclesiastical hierarchy even though such functions had 'no necessary connection with the production of goods or with any other economic activity'.[76] While it may be the case that, as Doyle argues, 'power differentials unrelated to wealth are quite inconceivable',[77] this does *not* mean that inequalities in the social distribution of power and status in medieval England were simply the *result* of economic inequalities. Access to wealth, the mode of its possession, and the ability to transmit property to successors fundamentally differed between the lay and ecclesiastical magnates: class and status co-existed as forms of social inequality. Thus, even if we reject the doctrine of the three orders as an accurate description of medieval society,[78] this does not mean that we have to see *all* status distinctions as merely imaginary, ideological misrepresentations of social reality. Although the importance of its class relations means that medieval England was not simply a 'society *of* orders', it was, most certainly, a 'society *with* orders' since the 'vertical' division between clergy and laity was one of the main features which gave medieval society its specificity. The co-existence of classes and orders was not, therefore, just a feature of pre-industrial society during some early modern period of transition from a medieval society of estates to a modern society based on classes. Rather, both class and order were fundamental to English social structure within the medieval period itself.[79]

If closure theory has a number of advantages for the historian, what are the *historical* criticisms which can be made of this approach?[80] Firstly, historians are likely to insist on the need for a more nuanced picture of historical development than that provided by closure theory with its claims for a long-term shift from traditional societies based on hereditary, collectivist forms of exclusion, such as aristocratic lineage, to modern societies, characterised by individualist forms of exclusion, such as private property, academic qualifications or Communist Party membership, and by high social mobility.[81] Certainly, when we look at the example of medieval England, the extent of the privileges flowing from aristocratic lineage or noble status *per se* seem remarkably limited. Where they did exist, as in the privileges enjoyed by the upper nobility, the parliamentary peerage, they were a relatively late development and were never extended to include tax exemption or reservation of office. While the nobility enjoyed immense power and prestige, its position was, essentially, the result of its property ownership as an economic class of landed magnates, not of its descent as a hereditary order of aristocrats. In England, unlike some other parts of Europe with their poor or even landless 'nobles' who could be traders, artisans or agricultural workers, class and status were fused and the aristocracy was given a unity by a lifestyle based on its position as the class of substantial landowners.[82]

Furthermore, we need to qualify the claim that the importance of landed wealth in late medieval England minimised social mobility and 'enabled the same families to monopolise power over long periods of time'.[83] The difficulties of ensuring male heirs, the dispersal of property in the absence of such heirs, the effects of royal favour, the consequences of political involvement, and the variety of routes into the ranks of the nobility all meant that social mobility was by no means as limited as is often thought.[84] Nor was it the case that there was a simple unilinear trend towards greater social mobility. On the contrary, entry to the upper ranks of the English nobility may have been easier in the thirteenth century than it was to the narrower and more clearly defined 'peerage' of the late fourteenth century.[85]

Finally, the picture of medieval English society as based on collectivist forms of exclusion has to be further qualified by the importance of the power, wealth and status enjoyed by the clergy.[86] In late medieval western Europe, the insistence on clerical celibacy meant that the clergy were not a 'closed hereditary estate' like the secular clergy of the Orthodox Church in eighteenth- and nineteenth-century Russia.[87] Instead, the privileges of the clergy were based on individualist, non-hereditary forms of exclusion rather than on the collectivist forms of exclusion supposedly typical of traditional societies. Again, the claims for a transition from collectivist to individualist forms of exclusion has to be qualified by the historical evidence.

A second area of empirical criticism of closure theory arises from Parkin's and Murphy's claim that the specific forms taken by usurpationary closure are related to whether social exclusion exists in a collectivist or an individualist form. In particular, they argue that collectivist types of exclusion should 'in ideal-typical terms . . . produce a subordinate group of communal character' as in the 'firmly-rooted sentient communities' of racial ghettoes.[88] The example of women in medieval English society would seem to provide an important exception to this generalisation. Although experiencing a social exclusion on the collectivist criterion of gender, women's subordination within the household meant that they did not form a separate community and that their social organisation tended to the amorphous, rather than the communal, end of the spectrum. Although they objectively constituted a systact within late medieval society, women do not seem to have advanced from constituting a systact 'in itself' to become a systact possessed of a common consciousness or able to take collective action 'for itself'.[89] Rarely do we see women acting in concert, as did the women of Leicester in the 1380s when they threatened to stone William Swinderby for his over-enthusiastic preaching against feminine pride and weakness.[90] Nor is there any evidence that women were more likely than men to be attracted to heresies, such as Lollardy, as a form of social protest.[91] Unlike women in modern society, medieval women could not exploit the sense of injustice between a social ideology premised on ideals of equality of legal status and individual opportunity and the reality of their social inferiority to offer an associational response to their social exclusion. On the contrary, the official ideology of medieval England portrayed the inferiority of women as natural, inevitable and divinely sanctioned.[92] Thus, despite their social inferiority to the men of their own class, women did not attempt to achieve usurpationary closure on the grounds of gender in alliance with the women of other classes, from whom they were divided by their lifestyle and class-interests, or even with women of their own class. Women's resistance to their social exclusion was thus more likely to be individual, rather than collective, in character, as is perhaps indicated by the prosecution of townswomen as 'gossips' and 'scolds'.[93] Women certainly did participate in collective social unrest, as in pre-plague Thornbury where they seem to have been firmest in their support for the campaign to establish the villagers' freedom.[94] But such actions tended to be motivated on class grounds, arising from women's status as peasants or as artisans, rather than from their position as women *per se*.

Personal experience suggests that, before concluding, I should address directly the objection which is most likely to be raised against closure theory by empirically-minded historians, that is the charge that, like any sociological theory, closure theory constitutes a 'Procrustean bed', an *a priori* schema to which the historical evidence is illegitimately adjusted and twisted.[95] That this is far from being the case is suggested by the fact that the opponents of closure theory amongst the ranks of sociologists have attacked it for precisely the *opposite* reason, namely that it offers only 'a conceptually weak empiricism'. Closure theory's concepts are criticised by these opponents for being essentially descriptive rather than explanatory so that closure theory does not help us to understand the inequalities of class, gender or race but 'only defines things differently'.[96]

In a sense, the criticisms made by the sociological opponents of closure theory are valid, but whether we see this as a reason to reject closure theory depends upon what we as historians expect of theory in the social sciences. If we expect social theories to be explanatory and predictive, like the general laws of the natural sciences, we will inevitably be dissatisfied by the descriptive nature of closure theory. However, in history and historical sociology, the events we deal with are not like the predictable orbits of the planets but are more like car accidents, that is events which are totally in accordance with the laws of physics but which cannot be predicted by or deduced from such laws. Just as a car accident requires some particular *post factum* explanation (the driver was drunk, the brakes failed, or whatever), so the existence of any specific form of exclusion in any particular societies is, as Parkin puts it, 'only explicable in historical terms'.[97] Thus, however useful it may prove to be, closure theory can never anticipate the results of historical research nor provide universally valid explanations of why particular social relations exist or why they change. Closure 'theory' is 'theoretical', then, only in the sense that it provides definitions of some key concepts in social analysis and that it offers general 'orienting statements' for research rather than in the strict sense of supplying precise, predictive propositions like those familiar from the natural sciences.[98]

If I have emphasised here the advantages of closure theory for historians and social scientists, this is not to claim that closure theory is some revolutionary new way of seeing society which makes all previous historical work redundant. On the contrary, the strength of closure theory is its synthesis of previous sociological approaches and its provision of a comprehensive analytical framework within which existing historical studies of particular social groups, such as the peasantry, clergy, and women, can be incorporated. Closure theory offers us a set of intellectual tools, a unified vocabulary, and a package of concepts which help to make specific social hierarchies intelligible to us. It helps us to clarify existing questions, assists us in expressing our answers to them more clearly, and suggests new questions to us. However, the answers to these questions can only be obtained by the traditional methods of empirical historical investigation. The modesty of closure theory's claims may disappoint those with a loyalty to more ambitious sociological theories or who seek a means of providing *a priori* answers to their historical questions, but it is likely to make such theory more, not less, attractive to historians.

2

EUROPEAN AND MIDDLE EASTERN VIEWS OF HIERARCHY AND ORDER IN THE MIDDLE AGES: A COMPARISON

Antony Black

A comparison between the different views about hierarchy and order of Europe and the Middle East may throw into clearer relief the character-istics of each set of ideas. Religiously inspired ideas of equality were present in both Islam and Christianity but with different meanings and outcomes. In Islamic law, ethics and theology – that is the *Shari'a* (religious code) and its exposition in *fiqh* (jurisprudence)[1] – all Muslims are supposed to be equal regarding the rules they must follow and the rights they have in the sight of God. There is one Islamic community (*'umma*) and differentiations within it are not important. In certain legal contexts, however, women have a position inferior to men.[2]

Similarly, all baptised Christians were alleged to have the same fun-damental moral duties and rights. One significant difference, however, was that the *Shari'a* attempted, in theory, to cover all aspects of social and legal life and action, whereas the Christian ethic explicitly rejected the rule of law (or legalism) in morals and left much to be determined by the individual – or the community of the church. The doctrine of the Holy Spirit and belief in its guidance was of critical importance here. Hence shared duties and rights were less clear and less extensive. Many more duties and rights could be determined, for example, by local, secular law. On the other hand, the distinction between male and female was less pronounced in Christianity.

The most significant differentiation between persons in Islamic eyes was between Muslims and others. Of the non-Muslims, those who were 'people of the book' (that is, monotheists) were protected (*dhimmi*), and should be left in peace, provided they accepted conquest with military–political subordination and paid the designated special taxes.[3] Polytheists and others (unbelievers), however, had no place in Muslim society.

Only non-Muslims could be slaves.[4] On the other hand slaves, ex-slaves and descendants of slaves could play a prominent part in Islamic society in the army, the civil service, commerce and culture. In the medieval West, on the other hand, non-Christians and, indeed, non-Catholics had no defined or secure social status. In the West serfdom for Christians was widely accepted as legitimate, except by radical thinkers.[5] The foregoing ideas about religiously determined status were widely diffused in both societies. Yet again, there was present in medieval European literary culture a concept of *humanitas* (common humanity) which was not found in Islam; this derived from ancient Greek and Roman thought.

The next most often articulated social distinction in Islamic countries was between the elite and the masses (*khassa wa'umma*: the special and the general). If we divide expressions of socio-political ideas into the three major genres of *fiqh*, advice to kings (considerably influenced by Iranian tradition) and philosophy (works in the neo-Platonic and neo-Aristotelian mode), this distinction was most often articulated in advice to kings and philosophy, and only occasionally in *fiqh*. So far as one can judge, this distinction was also widely disseminated; it is probably of Iranian origin. This implied a socio-economic division between, on the one hand, the ruler and his retinue, the religious scholars ('*ulamā*), military commanders, wealthy merchants – that is, the religio-political, cultural and economic elite – and, on the other hand, everybody else. It is especially striking that this was sometimes related to a philosophical distinction, perhaps derived from Plato or from the Platonic tradition, between those with greater and lesser mental capacities. It is still more striking that such a distinction was found in works of *fiqh*, not only after these had become influenced by philosophy of Greek origin, but as early as al-Shafi'i (767–820: one of the foremost and most influential of the early formulators of *fiqh* and eponymous founder of one of the four Sunni schools of law). He stated that there are two kinds of religious knowledge (*ilm*): 'one is for the general public and no sober and mature person should be ignorant of it'. The second 'consists of detailed duties and rules obligatory on men' (concerning which 'there is no text and perhaps no tradition'); 'the public is incapable of knowing this kind of knowledge nor can all specialists obtain it'.[6] The point was that one's obligations were dependent upon one's ability to know.

This elite/masses distinction was to be strongly reinforced in the Ottoman socio-political culture by a fundamental distinction between *askeri* (literally warriors but including religious and secretarial functionaries) and *re'ayya* (the common people, literally the sheep). The *askeri* were the state, in the sense of the political class ruled directly by the Sultan-caliph; the *re'ayya* were never addressed directly by the Sultan, only through his officials. This distinction was important not least because the *askeri* were defined as the recipients of taxation, which the *re'ayya* provided.[7] From around 1600 the Ottoman reform literature argued persistently that the decline of the state (that is of 'the destined rule of the House of Osman') was due, among other things, to the confusion of these two classes, in particular to the seepage of *re'ayya* upwards into the *askeri* through commoners' ownership of military landholdings (*timar*) and their inclusion in the army.[8]

This distinction also appears to have been widely diffused in Islamic, and certainly in Ottoman, culture. It was of great practical importance. On the other hand, there was significant social mobility in Islamic societies earlier than in the West, due (as in Europe after *c*.1050) to the prospects offered by the religious profession and by commerce. This may have declined as time went on; the status of *'ālim* (religious scholar: plural *'ulamā*) often became hereditary. Yet again, the pleas of Ottoman reformers for the maintenance of status boundaries were consistently unsuccessful. In both European and Middle Eastern social thought, we find in aristocratic and learned circles frequent expressions of contempt for the common people.[9] In both cases, this was contrary to strict religious teaching, but appears to have been a fairly widespread attitude. In the Middle East, as in India, certain occupations, e.g. tanning and refuse collection, were widely regarded as inherently dishonourable.[10]

There were two other ways in which social groups (*ta'ifa*) were formulated in the Islamic Middle-East. A fivefold classification is found in some philosophical thinkers, such as al Farabi (c.870–950) and Nasīr ad dīn Tūsī (1201–74). This divided society into (1) the wise, (2) religious and other intellectual experts, (3) mental practitioners (such as accountants and doctors), (4) warriors, and (5) economic producers. Again, philosophers and royal advisers sometimes divided society into four groupings: (a) men of the pen, (b) men of the sword, (c) men of business, and (d) agriculturalists.[11] These fivefold and fourfold classifications were perhaps adaptations of the Platonic (Indo-European) division into three orders: the fivefold classification divided the philosophers (or *oratores*) into three, (1), (2) and (3); the fourfold classification divided the producers (or *laboratores*) into two, (c) and (d). The reason for the fourfold categorisation may have been a pre-Islamic Iranian (in fact, Sassanian) model: this divided society into (i) knights and princes, (ii) religious officials, (iii) physicians, scribes and astrologers, (iv) farmers and others of low standing.[12] It is clear, however, that the later classification of Islamic times is closer in substance to the Platonic or Indo-European than to the earlier Iranian one.

These divisions were articulated in literary traditions. The fourfold one became a commonplace of Ottoman reform writers, who used here the Arabic term *rukn* ('pillar') for social group.[13] It was introduced into Ottoman discourse from Tūsī via Dawwani (1427–1501/2) and Kinalizad (1510–72).[14] It was most elaborately expounded by Katib Çelebi (writing 1653). He compared the four groups to the four bodily fluids (blood, mucus, yellow gall, black gall). The point made by Çelebi and others was that the four groups must be kept in their correct balance or proportion with each other, if society was to remain stable and healthy.[15]

Although these were concepts articulated by a literary elite, the distinction between religious scholars, the soldiery, merchants and agriculturalists was clear and of great practical importance. The division of Plato's 'producers' into merchants and agriculturalists may suggest a greater public esteem for merchants, deriving from the relatively elevated view of their calling in Islamic societies.[16] These statements were, however, reflections rather than constituents of social phenomena.

Prima facie, the most important contrast with Europe was that the terms used in Islamic society for social groups – *ta'ifa* and *rukn* – did not imply inequality. There never was in Islamic societies any official, *de jure* acceptance of hierarchy or class structure as such. Rather, what were articulated here were groups based upon a division of labour. Such an attitude is also found in the theory of the 'circle of power'; according to this, the ruler depends on the army, which depends upon prosperity, which depends upon justice, which depends upon religion, which depends upon the ruler . . .[17] In this image there is no inequality but a circular relationship of mutually interdependent factors. In Europe, by contrast, hierarchy and socio-political inequality were widely accepted and explicitly sanctioned, among other things, by a philosophico-theological tradition deriving from Christian Neoplatonism: for example, Gregory I's statement, much quoted, of Christian society as patterned upon the divinely ordained hierarchical cosmos.[18] The hierarchical concept indicates not only diversity but also a subordination of *horizontal* ranks. Such a view was also implied by means of the ('organic') analogy between society and the body, widespread in literature, sermons and popular imagination, but seldom found in Islam. The reason for the extraordinary popularity of the organic image was surely that it had a firm scriptural basis in St Paul. This had, from the early Church, been articulated in theology; the Church is the body of Christ. This refers *explicitly* to a legitimate diversity of functions and it usually also *implies* inequality of status.[19] Again, Thomas Aquinas argued that human society without sin would have had not only a division of labour but actual inequality.[20] The language of *diversi gradus*, *dignitates*, and so on meant not only a division of labour but also that some are legitimately subordinate to others, at least in moral status, and usually also in legal status: lords and vassals, kings and subjects, clergy and laity. Part of the essence of church–state controversy in Europe was of course precisely whether the subordination of clergy to laity should be legal as well as moral. Such hierarchy can include intermediaries (for example, God, pope, bishops, priests, laity) which might be seen to reflect a kind of 'feudal' order.

The *regnum/sacerdotium* distinction in theory does not exist in Islam, though it is sometimes roughly paralleled by a distinction between the concepts of *dīn* (religion) and *dawla* (rule) and again between men of the pen and men of the sword. (There is no real analogy between the occasional division of Christendom into *ecclesia*, *regnum* and *studium* and the way in which the Ottoman elite was divided into men of the sword, men of (religious) knowledge and men of the (bureaucratic) pen.)[21] In all theoretical writings the contrast between secular and religious is much slighter in Islamic society due to a fundamental difference in the character of religion. Not only was there no priesthood, but the *Shari'a* was intended to embrace this world as well as the next. Yet, the *de facto* relationship between the Sultan with his retinue and the *'ulamā* could, on occasion, be much closer to that between king and clergy than theory would have us suppose.

By focusing upon horizontal distinctions we may be missing a more fundamental contrast between European and Middle Eastern society and social awareness. Islamic societies were characterised to a much larger degree than in Europe by vertical divisions based upon kinship groups and groups of a religious character. In religious groups, most notably *Sūfī tariqas*, there was a strongly subordinate master/pupil relationship; but each group formed its own unit in society separate from other groups. Masters and disciples in no way made up classes; rather what we have is a society made up of segments or cells. Kinship, that is the extended family, clan, or tribal group, sometimes embracing a common place of origin or religious affiliation, counted for far more than in the West. Indeed, Islamic society was, one might say, essentially constituted of households, and at the upper level of dynastic clans. While these did exist in the West, the horizontal groupings were of much greater importance there.

Let us conclude by relating these social divisions to political life. In Islamic societies, concepts of social division played hardly any part in discourse about power and authority, about the nature, origin or structure of the polity. This reflected – and no doubt reinforced – a tendency towards a *de facto* division between coercive and military power, on the one hand, and society, religion, economy and the administration of *Shari'a* justice, on the other. One might express this by saying that 'civil society' was more distinct from the state than it was in Europe. This gulf between the social and the political held for the radical distinction between Muslims and non-Muslims, for, while the Sultan must be a Muslim, his senior servants might on occasion be Christians or Jews.

Furthermore, in Islamic thought there was never any suggestion that these groups or parts of society should have any political functions. Rather, all groups were equally subject to the *Shari'a* on the one hand, to the Sultan on the other. It is true that men of the sword and men of the pen were alike associated with the Sultan as the instruments of his rule over the *re'ayya*. But they themselves, as men of the sword or men of the pen, had no authority. The one exception – and an important one – was that the *'ulamā* could make independent statements on what was religiously lawful or unlawful.

Thus, in both societies, we have a rather similar conception of parts of society based upon the division of labour, deriving in the Islamic case from Plato and Zoroastrian culture, and in the West from St Paul, Plato and Aristotle.[22] In both societies such ideas helped to reinforce the legitimacy of a division of labour; they also reflected – and perhaps encouraged – a somewhat similar organisation of urban crafts into guild-like institutions with religious social and economic functions.[23] Only in Europe, however, did such social groups become the instruments of political participation or representation: as in the three estates of parliamentary assemblies, or in the merchant oligarchies and popular crafts of cities. In the West, moreover, the organic analogy commonly referred not just to social differentiation but to the distribution of political powers and rights.

This partly reflected – and certainly consolidated – a fairly fundamental difference in the way in which the military–agricultural complex was organised in the two societies. Discussion of this topic has been bedevilled by attempts to export the concept of feudalism to non-European cultures. In both societies there was – almost invariably – a correlation between military service duly performed, or the expectation that it would be performed, and tenure of landed wealth: how else could you raise cavalry? But in the Middle East the *iqta* or *timar* was, in theory at least, always at the disposition of the ruler and never heritable.[24]

It is striking that European political writers and philosophers recognised the justice of subordination to a ruler for the sake of a common good even if (especially from the fourteenth century onwards) they saw servitude as unjust. In other words, political ranking may have been acquiring a stronger rationale than socio-economic ranking.[25] Islamic societies, on the other hand, seem rather to have enshrined and clung to what Crone has identified as a *tribal* concept of equality, which worked against the formation of any kind of legitimate state.[26]

While religio-juridical equality was more firmly based in the East than in the West, a new notion of equality emerged in the West from around the twelfth century. This was socio-civic equality, inspired by the Greco-Roman republican tradition and, in particular, by Cicero. In this view, inequalities of political power had to be justified by contribution to the common good; access to public office should be determined by ability not birth.[27] This also justified election. This development does not seem to have taken place in classical Islamic societies, which is perhaps one reason why patrimonial authority remained in place until yesterday.

3

DANTE: ORDER, JUSTICE AND THE SOCIETY OF ORDERS

Spencer Pearce

Dante Alighieri, as any reader of the *Divina Commedia* can attest, was a consummate artist; and like any great artist he offers us in his work a vision, at once personal and universal, of the life of his times. The purpose of this chapter is to look behind this truism with a view to discerning how Dante perceived the society with which he was familiar and also what he made of – both what he thought about and, in his poetry and prose, created out of – the facts of social and political life in the period (1265–1321) through which he lived. Dante was no neutral observer of these social and political realities, but a poet who wrote in full consciousness of the intellectual, social, political, and religious affiliations and commitments which gave form and meaning to his life as he lived it and (even more important) relived it, in memory and imagination, in his verse. It might be as well to begin, therefore, by setting Dante in his social and cultural context and declaring his interests; for these naturally shaped the vision *of* contemporary society which he presents in his work and also the vision *for* that society which he develops, publicises, and promotes: the ideal against which he measures and finds wanting the civil and ecclesiastical polity of his day.

Dante appears to have thought of himself as belonging to the lesser nobility of his native city of Florence, although it is by no means certain that he was actually accounted a member of the social and military order of Florentine horsemen or *milites*, whose upper ranks were filled by those formally invested with the dignity of knighthood. What is the case is that the conferment of this dignity upon his great-great-grandfather, Cacciaguida, whom he introduces to his readers in Canto 15 of *Paradiso*, was a source of pride and satisfaction to him. Knighted by the Emperor Conrad III, Cacciaguida had died during the course of the Second Crusade in about the year 1147, and thus earned his place in Paradise among the ranks of the blessed associated with the heaven of Mars. One of his brothers was called Eliseo, and they may have belonged to the ancient Florentine family of the Elisei; but this too is far from certain, and of Cacciaguida little more is known than what we are told in Dante's poem. The Alighieri held lands in the vicinity of Prato, where they also appear as small-time moneylenders and speculators in grain; the family home, however, was in Florence, and there is evidence that the Alighieri household of Dante's own day was established in the city on the site occupied three generations earlier by Cacciaguida's son Alighiero. This was in the parish of San Martino del Vescovo in the *sesto* or urban district of Porta San Pietro, the district which Dante represented during his two-month tenure of office as one of the city's six Priors in 1300.[1]

The Florentine constitution of 1293, known as the Ordinances of Justice, had barred nobles from election to the Priorate; but this ban had been relaxed in 1295 (except in the case of regularly ordained knights and their families) to grant eligibility to those nobles who signalled their commitment to the constitution by joining one of the merchant or artisan guilds from among whose membership the city's executive officers were drawn. Noble or not, Dante was registered with the guild of physicians and apothecaries, appearing on the rolls for 1297 as 'Dante d'Aldighieri degli Aldighieri, poeta Fiorentino', and so qualified for office.[2] As is well known, his brief period as Prior led subsequently to his permanent exclusion from the city he so passionately loved. For Dante fell victim to the strife which divided Florence into perpetually warring factions, a situation which the Ordinances of Justice had sought to remedy by instituting the office of *Gonfaloniere della giustizia* or 'banner-bearer of justice' and by imposing indemnities and restrictions on the nobles or (to employ the language of the Ordinances) magnates. This factionalism had its origins in the rivalries and feuds which divided the great noble families and which prevented the nobility from presenting a united front against the political disabilities imposed on them by the merchant oligarchy which in effect controlled the city.

Dante was identified with the White Guelf faction, which was in the ascendant during his term of office as Prior. What divided the Whites from their opponents the Blacks was in part their attitude to commerce, on the one hand, and to the Ordinances of Justice, on the other. Vieri de' Cerchi, the leader of the Whites, as a banker and a merchant and one of the richest men in Europe, exercised considerable covert influence over all the merchant guilds in Florence and considered the interests of the magnates to be best served by accommodation with the constitution of 1293. Both his policy with regard to the Ordinances of Justice and the commercial interests this policy was designed to protect, however, served only to provoke the scorn of the flamboyant and impetuous leader of the Blacks, Corso Donati, who, less wealthy but proud, represented the feudal nobility of ancient blood, who were ill-disposed to accept the 'democratic' control foisted on them by wealth and commerce. In 1301, Pope Boniface VIII, hoping to secure a measure of influence in the fiercely independent republic of Florence, employed Charles of Valois to engineer the return to power of the exiled Corso and his faction, in consequence of which Dante was himself to face exile.[3]

The condition of Florence's politically divided nobility was mirrored in most of the other urban communes of central and northern Italy. Increasingly, as a result of marrying wealth or of engaging in trade on their own account, the nobility was becoming indistinguishable from the merchant class whose energy and initiative were responsible for a new prosperity, and who demanded the political independence they saw as indispensable to its maintenance. The violent dispute at Florence between Blacks and Whites supplemented the antagonism between Ghibellines and Guelfs, which had become institutionalised on a national scale in the early decades of the thirteenth century and persisted well into the fourteenth, despite the fact that the Ghibellines had lost any effective power in Tuscany with the decline in imperial fortunes in Sicily and peninsular Italy marked by the death in 1250 of the Emperor Frederick II and the subsequent defeat at the hands of Charles of Anjou of Frederick's illegitimate son Manfred, in 1266, and grandson Conradin, two years later. Essentially, the Ghibellines were long-standing feudatories who looked to the Romano-Germanic Emperor as the source and guarantor of their rights to land and jurisdiction, while the Guelfs repudiated imperial suzerainty and sought for their expanding and increasingly prosperous communes the largest possible measure of political independence.

What, at Florence and elsewhere, was a struggle for local supremacy in the government of the commune was projected on to the European stage in terms of the wider conflict between Empire and Papacy. For if the Ghibellines looked to the Emperor for the legitimation of their right to govern, the mere fact of the Guelfs' anti-imperial stance served to identify their interests with those of the Papacy, which was, of course, the only other European institution of comparable standing to which the Guelfs, in their turn, could look for support. Dante blamed his personal ruin on the forthright opposition of Corso Donati, the duplicity of Boniface VIII and the dishonourable conduct of Charles of Valois, and he consigns all three of them to Hell.[4] But what he condemned most heartily were the root causes of the disorder in society of which his personal misfortunes were but a minor symptom: the mutual encroachments of Empire and Papacy, the failure of these two greatest of European institutions to fulfil their proper responsibilities, and, in the moral vacuum created by this lack of leadership, the unbridled greed which appeared to lie behind so much of the inter- and intra-communal violence in an era which saw the rapid commercialisation of the urban centres of central and northern Italy, Florence foremost among them.[5]

It is perhaps clear from what has been said that the nobility of the Italian communes in the years around 1300 did not constitute a homogeneous social group. The situation in the south was different, but the nobility of central and northern Italy embraced a wide membership which included enfeoffed commoners and impoverished notables of ancient lineage, as well as powerful dynastic landowners, townspeople prominent in administration or grown rich by trade, and individuals who had achieved a position of dominance (often by violent means) in the *castelli* or fortified villages of the remoter areas.[6] Among the ranks of the nobility there were significant differences in economic and political power and social prestige – differences, that is, of economic and social class. In the case of the Florentine nobility, few any longer drew their revenues exclusively from their lands in the *contado* or countryside beyond the city walls: typically, they combined ownership of land in the *contado* with commercial or banking interests in Florence itself, and many of them passed without apparent difficulty between a variety of economically complementary activities. Nevertheless, one of the effects of commercial expansion was to produce a certain amount of friction between what might be called 'old' and 'new' money. A factor which contributed to the personal antipathy between Corso Donati and Vieri

de' Cerchi, apart from Corso's wholly anachronistic contempt for commerce, was the circumstance that the Cerchi were relative newcomers of
obscure origin, who had settled in Florence from Acone in the Val di
Sieve in 1154 or shortly thereafter. Dante, through words he gives to
Cacciaguida, expresses the regret that they ever made the move: 'the
intermingling of people was ever the beginning of harm to the city'.[7]

Although Dante elsewhere alludes to the mixed population of
Florence – legend had it that the Florentines were descended from
'noble and virtuous Romans' on the one hand, and from 'crude, war-
roughened Fiesolans' on the other[8] – it would be a mistake to conclude
that he thought that mixed descent as such was responsible for the city's
social and political problems. Certainly, he thought that a city has an
optimum size, and that the fivefold increase in the population of Florence since Cacciaguida's time had to be reckoned a factor in the city's
decline. But that decline was primarily, for Dante, a question of moral
degradation: along with the 'new people' it was the 'sudden gains' that
had 'engendered pride and excess' in a people blinded by avarice and
envy.[9] 'Roman' and 'Fiesolan', in Dante's usage, are moral categories.
The Florentines whom Cacciaguida celebrates in *Paradiso* 15 and 16
were 'Romans', in that they were upright, sober, thrifty, and chaste;
those whom Dante addresses from his place of exile in 1311 as 'most
wretched offshoot of Fiesole' are perverse and arrogant miscreants
whom 'the insatiable greed of avarice has urged all too willing into
every crime' – notably, at the date of the letter, defiance of the Emperor
Henry VII and of the political order for which he stood.[10] What Dante
lamented was the steady transformation of the old military order into
an economic class or classes: the fusion of the nobility with the merchants and the assertion of a false and anarchic independence had led
to the exacerbation of economic and social divisions and to the political
factionalism which had eroded the unity and coherence of the juridically constituted *societas militum*, which during Cacciaguida's lifetime
had remained firm and effective. What united this association of noblemen was the assumption of leadership, a claim to hereditary jurisdiction
over others, and the assertion of a right to bear arms. These privileges
were still claimed, with due allowance for the circumstances of a more
complex urban society, by the nobles of Dante's generation. What
Dante felt was under threat, or had indeed already suffered demise
(though he saw it momentarily reborn in the person of Henry VII), was
the grandeur and simplicity of a way of life informed by the chivalric
code of honour, courtesy, and valour; a way of life which Cacciaguida

and many other nobles whose names Dante records with approbation in the *Commedia* once represented so well.[11]

It is this way of life – the ideological and cultural dimension of nobility – which figures most prominently in Dante's conception and representation of the knightly order. This comes as no surprise, given his cultural interests and the moral tenor of his thinking. In his exile Dante eschewed party allegiance, and although, in his strong intellectual support for the imperial ideal, he came to appear Ghibelline rather than Guelf (and was condemned as a Ghibelline when an amnesty was offered by the Florentine government to certain of the exiled Whites in 1311), he became, as Cacciaguida says, a party unto himself, standing outside and above the factions he so abhorred.[12] Nonetheless, culturally speaking, Dante belonged to what may be considered a Guelf tradition, nourished as it was by French and, in particular, Provençal manifestations of the chivalrous and courtly life, and by the literary culture associated with it. For the Counts of Anjou, rulers in Provence, the Kingdom of Naples and, between 1266 and 1282, Sicily (itself, under Frederick II, a centre for the diffusion of Provençal culture), were the backbone of the Guelf alliance in Italy. In his allusions to Charles I of Anjou in *Purgatorio* 7, Dante appears to be swayed by the admiration, traditional among Florentine Guelfs, of a decisive, magnanimous, and imposing knight.[13] This in spite of the criticisms of his government and his methods which appear elsewhere in the *Commedia*, even in the mouth of his young grandson, Charles Martel, whom the protagonist of the poem greets with obvious affection in the heaven of Venus in *Paradiso* 8.[14] The elder Charles may be admired, if not without reservation, for his aristocratic valour; the words of the younger breathe that courtesy which, in Dante's conception, is a defining characteristic of the civilised life.

The notion of 'courtesy' (*cortesia*) had been the subject of significant refinement in the Italian poetry of the thirteenth century and in the youthful Dante's own verse, which had raised lyric poetry in the Italian vernacular to new philosophical heights. Central to this development was the conception of 'courtly love' first elaborated in the courts of Provence and codified in the late twelfth century by Andreas Capellanus in his *De Amore*.[15] In the courtly love tradition the ennobling love of a beautiful, virtuous and high-born lady replaces fidelity to the liege-lord or to the Christian faith – the predominant motives to action in the earlier literature of knightly heroism, the *chansons de geste* – as the principal inspiration of the lover's noble deeds. In the tradition which

Dante takes up and extends, *cortesia* had become detached from its association with the noble military order and was assuming the status of an ideal to be cultivated by all those who aspired to a civil and civilised life. When Manfred died, the brilliant Hohenstaufen court in southern Italy came to an end and Italian chivalry lost its chief point of reference.[16] This loss of an ultimate and unified court (*curia*) did not mean, however, that 'courtesy' or 'courtliness' (*curialitas*) was no longer to be found in the peninsula, 'because courtliness is nothing other than the well weighed norm for those things which are to be done' and 'whatever in our actions is well weighed is called courtly'. All that it meant was that this courtliness, deprived of its institutional focus, found an ideal one instead: 'for though in Italy there is no court in the sense of a united one like the court of the King of Germany, nevertheless its members are not lacking. And just as the members of that one are united by one prince, so the members of this are united by the grace-giving light of reason.'[17] In the increasingly secular, mercantile, and anti-feudal climate of the Guelf cities, courtesy came to be seen as an interior, spiritual quality that has nothing to do with the accident of wealth or of aristocratic birth.[18]

This is an interpretation of courtesy or nobility – the two are one and the same thing – for which Dante argues most vigorously in the fourth treatise of his prose *Convivio* (*The Banquet*). Nobility, says Dante, cannot be based on inherited wealth, because riches, being intrinsically ignoble, have no necessary connexion with nobility and can neither confer it nor take it away. Bestowed without regard for distributive justice by the blind goddess Fortune, wealth, however much is accumulated, can never satisfy the deepest human longings, promotes the vice of avarice, induces fear of loss and attack, and provokes the envy and hatred of others.[19] If the inheritance of wealth is no guarantee of nobility, then neither, affirms Dante, is the inheritance of blood. 'Let no member of the Uberti family of Florence, or of the Visconti family of Milan, claim: "Since I come of a noble family-line, I, too, am noble", for the divine seed does not descend into a stock or family-line; it descends, rather, into individual people, and . . . it is not a family-line that makes individuals noble, but individuals who ennoble a family-line.'[20] God is directly responsible for the creation of what is distinctively human in every human being, namely, the intellectual soul; and nobility is a divine quality, a grace, with which God endows the soul whose body is perfectly disposed to receive it.[21] Given that 'nobility', in its generic sense, 'signifies in any being the perfection of its own particular

nature',[22] in human beings it implies beauty, health and strength of
body but, above all, possession of those marks of specifically human
excellence which are the moral and intellectual virtues.[23] Dante's identification of nobility with virtue, in strict accordance with which an
expression such as 'evil nobleman' becomes a contradiction in terms,[24]
clearly elevates the concept of nobility into the realm of normative
values. It does not, however, lose contact with sociological realities; for
the social nobility was, he thought, in so far as the general corruption
allowed, best placed to aspire to this ideal of nobility.

It is to just such people that Dante addresses himself in the *Convivio*,
the *Commedia*, and his other vernacular works: people who possess
'excellence of mind' but who, 'through the unfortunate neglect entailed
by activities in the world, have left education to men who have turned
this lady into a prostitute. These noble people are princes, barons,
knights and many others of like nobility, women no less than men, a
vast number of both sexes, whose language is not that acquired through
education, but the vernacular.'[25] Education in Latin is largely the preserve of those – lawyers, physicians, and most of the clergy – whose
pursuit of wisdom is partial, and adulterated by the desire for personal
gain, be it money or status.[26] Thus the public for whom Dante writes
consists of layfolk without Latin in whom 'true nobility is sown' and who
are capable of understanding, but who are deprived of the 'most noble
perfection' of knowledge by lack of access to centres of learning or by
'family and civic responsibilities, which quite properly absorb the ener-
gies of the majority of men'.[27] Although Dante's definition of nobility
entails its extension beyond the ranks of the social nobility, it may be
observed that in listing his addressees, he observes the customary hierarchical order of 'princes, barons, knights', and only then adds 'many
others of like nobility', not only men but also women. He may be
addressing the noble of heart, irrespective of social rank or gender; but
the primary targets of his instruction and admonition, in the *Commedia*
as in the *Convivio*, are those whose social function it is to guide and
govern others, those who have the political and moral leadership of lay
society.

If, in the unfinished *Convivio*, Dante's aim is to share with the truly
noble some crumbs he has gathered from the table of philosophical
knowledge, in the *Commedia* he sets himself the even more exalted and
urgent task of moral and spiritual guidance. In the famous letter to Can
Grande della Scala, lord of Verona, the patron to whom the third part
of the poem is dedicated, Dante declares that 'the aim of the whole and

of the part is to remove those living in this life from a state of misery, and to bring them to a state of happiness'.[28] This aim is to be achieved by the effective treatment of the subject-matter of what the poet, in a reference to the *Commedia* in the same letter, calls his 'treatise' (*tractatus*). This subject is 'the state of souls after death'; or, if one passes from the literal sense of the work to its all-important allegorical meaning, 'man according as by his merits or demerits in the exercise of his free will he is deserving of reward or punishment by justice'.[29] The poet's journey through the three realms of the afterlife, then, is designed to illustrate the consequences, as determined by God's justice, of the use to which individuals put free will (*libertas arbitrii*), their freedom to choose between good and evil. The order which governs the disposition of the groups of souls which the protagonist encounters on his journey is not social, but moral and metaphysical: the worse the sin, the heavier the burden of guilt, the deeper the sinner finds himself in Hell, at the centre of the dull, heavy, and imperfect Earth; the deeper and more radiant a soul's love of God, the more exalted it is among the luminous ranks of the blessed in the Heaven above the heavens, in the purely spiritual realm beyond all space, time, and materiality. While the structure of Hell and the hierarchy of the saints in Heaven are determined by a scale of absolute moral values, the choice of individuals to represent the various points on that scale is contingent upon the experience and purposes of the author. If we pass from the nobility to the other end of the social spectrum, we realise that for this purpose the peasantry is completely ignored by Dante. The *Commedia* contains, it is true, a number of what may be called vignettes of country life, passages in which moments in the life of the villein are evoked with some sympathy. It has been noted, however, that, in all such cases, these evocations are included only as vehicles of extended similes: in the *Commedia* 'no labourer appears in his own right. Dante places no representative of the Italian people as a whole in Heaven, Purgatory, or even Hell. For Dante these men and women existed at the periphery of his mind; they dwelt in another world.'[30] Certainly, the glimpses of the peasant's existence afforded by such passages are insufficient to counterbalance the weight of this judgement. It must be said, however, that the choice of 'personnel' in the *Commedia* is also affected by considerations of Dante's audience and of his mission. The poet's words will act upon that audience, Cacciaguida tells his great-great-grandson in *Paradiso* 17, 'as does the wind, which smites most upon the loftiest summits'; and it is for this reason that 'only the souls known of fame' have been shown to him during the course of his journey; 'for the mind of him who hears rests not nor confirms its faith by an example that has its roots unknown or hidden, nor for other proof that is not manifest'.[31]

Among the exemplary figures who populate the *Commedia* there are a number who do not meet Cacciaguida's criterion of 'souls known of fame'. Of course, as Dante insists in *Purgatorio* 11, fame is a relative, transient phenomenon; and the fact that history knows next to nothing, for example, of the gluttonous Ciacco (*Inferno* 6.34–93) or the indolent Belacqua (*Purgatorio* 4.96–139) tells us little about their passing notoriety in the Florence of Dante's day. Ciacco may have been a courtier: Dante entrusts to him words about the political strife between Black and White Guelf factions in his native city (*Inferno* 6.64–75), just as later he puts into the mouth of another courtier, Marco Lombardo, an expression of his regret for the decline of 'valour and courtesy' (*Purgatorio* 16.116). Belacqua, on the other hand, was a lutemaker, an artisan. He is obliged to wait in Ante-Purgatory for a period equivalent to his own lifetime before beginning the purgation of his sinful inclinations because, as he informs his questioner, he 'delayed good sighs until the end', repenting only on his deathbed.[32] This was doubtless a result of his indolence. But Belacqua also belongs to a category of persons – those who have to work for a living – who are almost inevitably bereft of right judgement when it comes to higher concerns. These, Dante tells us in the *Convivio*, are 'ordinary people' (*populari persone*) who, 'having been engaged from an early age in some gainful occupation, by dint of necessity . . . concentrate their mind on this to such a degree that they take no interest in anything else. And since attaining possession of the virtues, both moral and intellectual, is not the work of a moment but must be acquired through constant practice, whereas they devote themselves to practising some professional skill and make no effort to be discriminating in matters outside that, it is impossible for them to possess discrimination.'[33] Such members of the populace are neither noble nor candidates for nobility in Dante's sense of the word: in the circumstances in which they live their lives and fulfil their function in society the highest human excellence is, in all but the most exceptional of cases, beyond their reach.

The same stricture applies of course to the social nobility who engage in banking or commerce. Even preoccupation with that most noble of tasks, the government of earthly kingdoms, frequently constitutes an obstacle on the path to human perfection. There is in Ante-Purgatory a place – the so-called Valley of the Princes (*Purgatorio* 7 and 8) – which is reserved for those whose involvement in earthly affairs proved a distraction from that single-minded cultivation of knowledge and virtue in which the supreme earthly happiness consists and which alone constitutes an adequate preparation for the joys of Heaven. Behind this view of things lies the familiar distinction between the active and the contemplative life and the pre-eminence accorded to the latter. 'It must be clearly explained here that in this life we may enjoy two forms of happiness, distinguished according to two paths that lead to them, one good, the other best: they are the active life and the contemplative respectively. For although the happiness to which we attain through the active life is certainly good (as has been said), the contemplative life brings us to supreme happiness or blessedness, as the Philosopher demonstrates in the *Ethics*.'[34] This ultimate form of earthly happiness is reserved for the very few: the fact is that the majority of human beings, as Dante frankly acknowledges at the beginning of the *Convivio*, 'cannot find the leisure required for cultivating the mind'.[35] Human existence, then, appears to be directed towards a goal and a perfection which at best can only ever be imperfectly realised on earth.

However, it is important to stress that, for Dante, the realisation of human perfection in this life is a corporate activity: it is, as he explains in his treatise on world government, the *Monarchia*, a goal for which 'the whole human race in all its vast number of individual human beings is designed; and no single person, or household, or small community, or city, or individual kingdom can fully achieve it'.[36] This goal, 'the activity proper to mankind considered as a whole', is 'constantly to actualise the full intellectual potential of humanity, primarily through thought and secondarily through action (as a function and extension of thought)'.[37] Not all can devote themselves to the primary activity of thought, but all can contribute to the realisation of the common goal in the measure which their nature and circumstances allow. That human beings are born with different characters, temperaments, and capabilities is a result of the stellar and planetary influences which preside over the conception and development of each and every individual. Nature, activated for this purpose by divine providence, ensures by the eternal circling of the heavens that, as human beings, we all have something different to contribute to the human community. This is made clear in the *Commedia* by Charles Martel, by way of explaining how his miserly brother Robert could be so different from their grandfather Charles, who had enjoyed a reputation for great liberality. Charles asks the pilgrim Dante:

'Now say, would it be worse for man on earth if he were not a citizen?'
'Yes,' I replied, 'and here I ask for no proof.' [For Dante accepts as
axiomatic the saying of the 'master', Aristotle, that 'man is by nature
a social animal'.[38]] 'And can that be, unless men below live in diverse
ways for diverse duties? Not if your master writes well of this for you.'
Thus he came deducing far as here, then he concluded, 'Therefore
the roots of your works must needs be diverse, so that one is born
Solon and another Xerxes, one Melchizedek and another he who
flew through the air and lost his son.'[39]

It is in this way that God's providence, working through the system of
secondary causes we call nature, ensures that the human community
is not without lawgivers like Solon, generals like Xerxes, priests like
Melchizedek, and inventors like Daedalus. 'If the world there below
would give heed to the foundation which Nature lays, and followed it,
it would have its people good', continues Charles; however, the fact is
that, for motives of waywardness, wilfulness or expediency, the disposition with which individuals are naturally endowed is frequently ignored; and this is one reason for the disorderly state in which society
finds itself: 'you wrest to religion one born to gird on the sword, and
you make a king of one who is fit for sermons; so that your track is off
the road'.[40]

One implication of these words is that each individual has a function
in society which he or she is providentially suited to fulfil. Daedalus,
artificer supreme, represents those gifted with the technical expertise
which provides for the practicalities of civilised living; Solon, Xerxes,
and Melchizedek represent the leaders, civilian and military, of lay
society and those responsible for leadership in the religious sphere. It is
tempting to see behind this allusion to social functions the tripartite
division of medieval society commonplace in Dante's time and much
discussed by recent historians.[41] On this analysis medieval society
presents us with three estates or social orders distinguished in terms of
the different social functions they fulfil: the *laboratores* are those who
work, the peasantry; the *bellatores* are those who fight: the princes,
barons, knights and others to whom Dante addresses himself, whose
task it is to defend and govern society; and the *oratores* are the preachers, priests, and pastors, whose apostolic mission it is to look after the
spiritual needs of the Christian souls entrusted to their care.

Now, Dante would obviously have recognised the trifunctional
scheme, but he nowhere invokes it as a basis for social analysis or

evaluation. That his view of society was a functional one is clear from what has been said: given that human potential can only be fully realised by the human race as a whole, society exists in order to enable individuals to contribute to the achievement of this goal to the extent to which they are able, and depends in turn on the ability and willingness of individuals to perform the variety of social functions which nature has providentially suited them to perform. However, in the social world of late-thirteenth-century and early-fourteenth-century Italy – in circumstances in which the upper echelons of the ecclesiastical hierarchy were heavily involved in secular politics, noble knights could be merchants, and ignoble merchants could acquire notable esteem and wield considerable political power – the functions traditionally assigned to the three orders had become confused: they no longer mapped neatly on to the membership of the social groups identified in the trifunctional scheme, which must have appeared an abstraction of increasingly limited applicability, if indeed, given the growing specialisation and differentiation of activities, it was applicable at all to the complex social world of the populous Italian cities.[42]

Dante clearly recognises the existence of manifold functions in society, and of a definite hierarchy among them, according as they serve the needs of the human community, from the most basic necessities of life to the realisation of the human potential for intellectual and spiritual growth. The labourer, however, is someone whom Dante appears to take for granted: the satisfaction of the human need for food, clothing, and shelter is of interest to him only in its ethical dimension, as something to be enjoyed in moderation, austerity and restraint in the consumption of material goods being preferable to self-indulgence and display. It is not the labourers (nor, indeed, the simple clerks) but the leaders of the human community that engage Dante's attention. He is interested in the governors rather than the governed: in those who 'gird on the sword', but also in those 'fit for sermons' and, most important, in the correct division of responsibilities and the right ordering of the relationship between these two significant social groups, the nobility and the clergy.

Dante was not a social analyst and does not discuss the relationship between churchmen and princes in terms of estates or orders. He was, however, a political theorist, and as such he had a keen interest in how things might best be disposed if social order – the sway of lawful authority and the operation of justice – were to be established and maintained. That the way in which things are 'ordered', 'disposed', 'ordained', or 'directed' is a fundamental preoccupation with Dante is indicated by the repeated use in the *Monarchia* of the Latin verb *ordino*. While the cognate noun, *ordo*, is occasionally employed with the meaning 'arrangement', 'disposition', the predominant sense which attaches to the term in the *Monarchia* is that of 'relationship': logical relationship or, significantly, the determinate relationship of one thing to another, the fixed arrangement of things, in the natural world – the order of nature or of the universe. He once uses *ordo* of the relationship of members to one another within a collegiate body (*Monarchia* 2.6.2), but nowhere of a social group, class, or order.[43] The poet's use of Italian *ordine* in his vernacular works follows a similar pattern. In *Paradiso* 9.116 *ordine* denotes a group or rank of individuals, but with reference not to the earthly social order but to an order of beatitude: the rank among the blessed enjoyed by those souls whom the protagonist meets in the heaven of Venus. The most concentrated use of *ordine*, and the only instances of the use in Dante's works of the word 'hierarchy' (*gerarchia, gerarcia*), occur in *Convivio* 2.5 and *Paradiso* 28, in discussions concerning the nine 'orders' of angels and their organisation, three by three, into three 'hierarchies'. However, *ordine* in the *Commedia* refers with greatest frequency to the order manifest in God's creation. 'All things have order among themselves, and this is the form that makes the universe like God', declares the lady Beatrice, Dante's guide in the third part of the poem, at the beginning of *Paradiso*.[44]

The harmonious relationship between all that exists is the liveliest imprint left on the creation as a whole by the hand of its Creator. This relationship is essentially hierarchical; for all things in the created universe have a determinate place in the 'chain of being'; that is to say, in the hierarchy whereby they are all linked, from the elements at the one extreme to the angels at the other, by a continuous and minutely graded scale of increasing perfection. Human beings, by virtue of the fact that they are bodily creatures who are nevertheless endowed with an immortal soul, occupy a crucially significant position between the higher animals and the angels, between the material universe and the spiritual. It is inevitable, therefore, that individuals of the species will occupy a place on the scale of being which, if not precisely equidistant from beast and angel, will fall closer to one or the other.

> Although I have spoken so far only of there being various grades at the generic level, the same can also be said with regard to individuals, in that each human soul receives the divine goodness in a way which

differs from that of others. And so in the intellectual order of the universe there is a scale of ascent and descent along almost continuous grades from the lowest to the highest and from the highest to the lowest, just as there is in the sensible world, as we observe. Further, between the angelic nature, which is purely intellectual, and the human soul there is no intervening grade; rather, one is more or less continuous with the other in the scale of grades. Again, between the human soul and the most perfect soul among brute animals there is no gap: we see many men who are so base and have sunk so low that they seem scarcely distinguishable from beasts. Likewise, it must be stated and firmly held that some men are so noble and of such high calibre that they are to be considered more or less angels; otherwise the human species would not be continuous in both directions, which is inconceivable.[45]

It might be thought that this consideration, with its clear distinction between 'superior' and 'inferior', offers ontological grounds for distinctions of a social kind; but it does not. For while cosmic forces shape the human frame and temperament, the soul itself is characterised by an infusion of 'divine goodness' which is unique. To the extent that the human individual is a product of processes occurring in the natural world, that individual is subject, like the rest of the material creation, to the operation of natural laws; but, as a being endowed with a unique and immortal intellectual soul, this same individual is a child of God's grace, and consequently, in respect of both origin and destiny, is free from determination by the laws of nature. Nobility or human perfection is, as we have seen, a grace bestowed without regard to natural parentage or social distinctions of birth; and to the extent that it is not an original endowment, but is also the fruit of the cultivation of the moral and intellectual virtues, all human beings, in so far as their circumstances allow, may strive to become 'noble'. Unlike stones or trees or asses, human beings are perfectible, in virtue of the possession of free will. They may choose to cultivate virtue or, alternatively, as many unfortunately do, they may choose to abandon their freedom and enslave themselves to natural appetite.[46] In consequence of this moral freedom the human community finds itself in a unique position with respect to the rest of creation: whereas in the non-human world, the cosmic order is already perfectly fulfilled, in the world of human affairs it remains an ideal as yet unrealised – a model of harmonious unity-in-diversity which human agency has still to recreate.

The realisation of this order in the social and political sphere depends, for Dante, upon a recognition of the ends of human existence and the establishment of conditions in which these ends may best be pursued. First and foremost, it requires peace: 'universal peace is the best of those things which are ordained for our human happiness'.[47] Now, the greatest obstacle to peace among nations, and to social harmony within them, is *cupiditas*, 'the stubborn greed' which has assumed such proportions that it 'has extinguished the light of reason'.[48] If justice, as Thomas Aquinas puts it, is 'the habit whereby a person with a lasting and constant will renders to each his due',[49] then greed leads men to act unjustly, appropriating what rightfully belongs to others. The most conspicuous instance of such injustice, in Dante's view, is the usurpation by pope and emperor of the authority and jurisdiction which properly belongs to the other. It is so very scandalous precisely because it involves the two supreme arbiters of western Christendom, whose duty it is to set an example of justice and moral rectitude to those they govern. In the historical circumstances of his own lifetime, it is rather the abdication of authority on the part of successive emperors that Dante criticises. Addressing Albert I of Austria, son of Rudolf I of Habsburg and uncrowned Emperor at the fictional date of the *Commedia* (1300), the narrator of *Purgatorio* attacks him for the greed which has led him to concentrate on increasing his German possessions and the consequent neglect and disorder to which he has consigned his kingdom in Italy, the garden of the Empire. 'O German Albert, who do abandon her that is become wanton and wild and who should bestride her saddle-bows, may just judgment fall from the stars upon your blood, and be it so strange and manifest that your successor may have fear thereof! For you and your father, held back yonder by greed, have suffered the garden of the Empire to be laid waste.'[50]

Given, then, the collapse of imperial power in Italy – until Albert's successor, Henry VII, appeared on the scene, Dante continued to regard Frederick II as 'the last emperor of the Romans'[51] – the chief cause of scandal in Europe were the pretensions to world dominion cherished by the Papacy. The old view – often referred to as the Gelasian doctrine, after Gelasius, the fifth-century pope who enunciated it – was that the rule of Christendom was divided equally between two powers invested with supreme authority, in spiritual and in temporal affairs respectively; but this view had been steadily eroded as a result of the religious revival of the eleventh century and a succession of popes, notably Gregory VII (1073–1085), Innocent III (1198–1216),

and Boniface VIII (1294–1303), who had asserted in increasingly un-
compromising terms the absolute supremacy of the authority of the
Church. In brief, the pope, as Christ's vicar on earth, was held to derive
his power directly from God, whereas emperors, kings, and heads of
state generally were considered to derive theirs from the pope. The
most tangible expression of this claim was the territorial expansion of
the Papacy in central Italy. Nicholas III (1277–1280) had taken advantage of the weakness of Rudolf of Hapsburg to secure the cession to the
Papacy of the Romagna in 1278; and Boniface VIII entertained similar
designs with respect to another of the emperor's Italian provinces,
Tuscany. This project ended in personal humiliation for Boniface and
a severe check to papal ambitions, administered by the equally ambitious French monarch, Philip the Fair; but not before Boniface's intrigues had affected the situation in Florence and Dante's personal
fortunes in the way we have already described. It is possible that
Boniface, a shameless nepotist, intended to enfeoff with Tuscany one of
his Roman kindred.[52]

It is specifically for the sin of simony, the misuse of his sacred office
for his personal aggrandisement and that of his clan, that Dante con-
demns Boniface to Hell.[53] Greed and the misuse of power go hand in
hand, and these are the failings with which Dante taxes the clergy as a
whole, secular and regular alike: they have betrayed the Gospel and the
ideals of their order. Indicating Jacob's ladder, the ladder of contemplation which Dante sees in the heaven of Saturn and which leads from
things of earth to those of Heaven, Benedict of Nursia complains that
'no one now lifts his foot from earth to ascend it, and my Rule remains
for waste of paper. The walls, which used to be an abbey, have become
dens, and the cowls are sacks full of foul meal. But heavy usury is not
exacted so counter to God's pleasure as that fruit which makes the heart
of every monk so mad; for whatsoever the Church has in keeping is all
for the folk that ask it in God's name, not for kindred, or for other
filthier things.'[54] By the time Dante wrote *Paradiso* and the *Monarchia*,
he had arrived at a religious radicalism which considered the Church to
be a purely spiritual institution, to which the ownership of property was
utterly alien. Any resources of a material kind – including the infamous
Donation of Constantine, whereby the first Christian emperor was held
to have transferred the government of the western Roman Empire to
the pope – could only be held by the Church in trust for the poor of
Christendom, to whom the Church's wealth belongs as their inheritance. 'The emperor could however consign a patrimony and other

resources to the guardianship of the Church, provided it was without prejudice to the superior imperial authority, whose unity admits no division. And God's vicar could receive it, not as owner but as administrator of its fruits for the church and for Christ's poor, as the apostles are known to have done.'[55] Paradoxically, whereas an evangelical poverty – full and literal acceptance of the injunction laid by Jesus upon his disciples to 'provide neither gold, nor silver, nor brass in your purses, nor scrip for your journey'[56] – is the poet's remedy for the avarice of the clergy, he suggests that the emperor is put beyond 'the thing most contrary to justice', namely greed, by placing all ownership, all jurisdiction, in his hands. For 'where there is nothing which can be coveted, it is impossible for greed to exist, for emotions cannot exist where their objects have been destroyed. But there is nothing the monarch *could* covet, for his jurisdiction is bounded only by the ocean. . . . From this it follows that of all men the monarch can be the purest embodiment of justice.'[57]

Jurisdiction is not the same as material enjoyment, and Dante's argument clearly presupposes an emperor high-minded enough to be content with the privilege of sitting in supreme judgement over kings and princes whose territories and possessions are, in reality, only nominally his. For Dante envisages the emperor not as supplanting the rulers of kingdoms and city-states, but as the focus of that unity-in-diversity which is the Christian commonwealth. 'Mankind is to be ruled by him in those matters which are common to all men and of relevance to all, and is to be guided towards peace by a common law'; nevertheless, 'nations, kingdoms and cities have characteristics of their own, which need to be governed by different laws', and, in general, it is in accordance with local laws that decisions affecting a particular locality will be taken.[58] Dante's conception of the emperor – source of humankind's unity and peace, secured through universal law – is indeed an exalted one. Just as God, the unmoved mover, is the single source of motion in the cosmos, and the movements of the heavens and of all things below are regulated by the single movement of the Primum Mobile (the 'first movable thing', the outermost and swiftest moving of the heavenly spheres), so too, if the political universe is to reproduce the ideal order demonstrated in the universe at large, the emperor will be the one source of all political action and imperial law its most general regulatory mechanism.[59] Dante insists that this God-like imperial authority is conferred directly on his chosen instrument by God himself, and can in no sense be said to derive from the authority of the Church. The Church's

responsibilities complement those of the emperor, but are quite different in kind.

The separation of spiritual and temporal authority, of which the
Monarchia is designed to offer a rigorously logical demonstration, rests
ultimately on Dante's conception of human nature. Although humans
are unitary beings, they have a dual nature, material and corruptible in
respect of their mortal body, spiritual and incorruptible in respect of
their immortal soul. The unique distinction among God's creatures
which belongs to human beings in virtue of this duality of nature is that
they have also a dual finality; that is to say, human existence has one
goal in so far as human beings are mortal, and another in so far as they
are immortal.

> Ineffable providence has thus set before us two goals to aim at: that
> is, happiness in this life, which consists in the exercise of our own
> powers and is figured in the earthly paradise; and happiness in the
> eternal life, which consists in the enjoyment of the vision of God (to
> which our own powers cannot raise us except with the help of God's
> light) and which is signified by the heavenly paradise. Now these two
> kinds of happiness must be reached by different means, as represent-
> ing different ends. For we attain the first through the teachings of
> philosophy, provided that we follow them putting into practice the
> moral and intellectual virtues; whereas we attain the second through
> spiritual teachings which transcend human reason, provided that we
> follow them putting into practice the theological virtues, that is, faith,
> hope and charity.[60]

The two goals of human existence, therefore, and the means of
reaching them have been revealed to us by the philosophers on the one
hand, and by the scriptures and God's personal revelation in the incar-
nate Christ on the other. However, we come into the world 'simple
souls',[61] ignorant *tabulae rasae* on which experience writes what we need
to know concerning our human nature and supernatural destiny. In
particular, if human greed is not to lead us astray, we require the
instruction and admonition of reliable guides. 'It is for this reason that
man had need of two guides corresponding to his twofold goal: that is
to say the supreme Pontiff, to lead mankind to eternal life in conformity
with revealed truth, and the emperor, to guide mankind to temporal
happiness in conformity with the teachings of philosophy.'[62] Although
Dante acknowledges that the pope is the emperor's guide in matters of

revealed religion,[63] he insists on the parity that exists between them and the independence they enjoy, each in his rightful sphere. This parity is brought out nowhere more strikingly than in words spoken by Marco Lombardo in *Purgatorio* 16. 'Rome, which made the world good, was wont to have two Suns, which made visible both the one road and the other, that of the world and that of God. The one has quenched the other, and the sword is joined to the crook: and the one together with the other must perforce go ill – since joined, the one does not fear the other. If you do not believe me, look well at the ear, for every plant is known by the seed.'[64] The discord sown by the seizure of the imperial sword by the bearer of the papal crook is an effect of the failure to recognise that Christian Rome has two great luminaries, and that these *duo magna luminaria* are not to be identified in the traditional way, as sun (pope) and moon (emperor), but as two suns of equal magnitude.[65]

Dante thus operates a clear distinction between the sacred and the secular, between the one group that can unequivocally be said, in virtue of its distinctive mission and manner of life, to constitute an order, and the rest of society, to whose spiritual needs it is ordained to minister. This vertical division between clergy and laity complements the horizontal division remarked upon earlier between governors and governed and suggests that the poet's thinking in this area is dominated by dichotomies rather than by patterns of any other kind. It is of interest to note, however, that the horizontal and vertical divisions within the human community that appear most significant to his philosophical cast of mind (for which the identification of logical distinctions and root causes is a fundamental preoccupation) are precisely those which Geoges Duby acknowledges to lie behind the traditional trifunctional scheme. 'Triplicity arose,' he writes, 'out of the conjunction of two kinds of dissimilarity, that instituted by the *ordo* – there were the priests and the others – conjoined with that instituted by *natura* – there were nobles and serfs.'[66] It is clear that what Dante offers readers of the *Commedia* is no sociological analysis of the society of his times, but a moral portrait of humankind. This portrait is informed by beliefs about how, at the most general level, society is best organised and by the tension which exists between the ideal form this organisation ought to take and the realities of human conduct in a changing world. He appeals in particular to society's rulers, all of whom, even those who are citizens of independent communes like Florence, he regards as subjects of the one imperial authority. His purpose as a poet, in the best rhetorical tradition, is not simply to entertain or enlighten, but to persuade to virtue.

He wishes to affect the way his chosen public behaves, to lead those charged with the guidance of humanity, and in particular with the governance of lay society, to act in a manner more nearly conformable to the ideal which he suggests human reason can discover to be the goal of earthly existence. This ideal is the abstract but objective standard by which particular policies and actions are to be judged. It is, as we have seen, an ideal of earthly order – of the just ordering of relationships in political society – and it is objective in the sense that it is already embodied and visible in the structures of the universe as a whole. The perfection of each kind of being resides in the full realisation of its specific nature. Specific to human nature is the radical dualism of mortal body and immortal soul, in virtue of which the human being belongs to both the temporal and the spiritual order, to the realms of both nature and grace – neither of which is reducible to the other.

The supernatural goal of human nature is that in which religious faith instructs us; the temporal goal of earthly existence has been revealed by philosophy. Hence the importance for Dante of the philosopher. *The* philosopher, without further qualification, is Aristotle, whose *Nicomachean Ethics* provides the foundations for the ethical and political views Dante expresses in the *Monarchia*.[67] With the introduction of the philosopher alongside the emperor, there emerges from this work the conception of three orders – not social ranks, but the three orders of experience over which, each in his respective sphere, the philosopher, the pope, and the emperor independently preside. The pope's task is to lead the human race to eternal life through revelation; that of the emperor is to lead the human race to temporal happiness through philosophy; that of the philosopher is to arrive at those truths which are accessible to human reason. The philosopher's authority 'does not in any way detract from that of the emperor; rather, the latter authority without the former is dangerous, and the former without the latter is rendered weak, not because of anything intrinsic to it, but because people tend to act irrationally. So when these two operate in unison each is at its most beneficial and carries its fullest weight.'[68] The emperor's task is not philosophical but political: he is to ensure the peace and stability in which alone philosophy can flourish and the goal of philosophy – the realisation of the human community's full intellectual potential – can be reached. These same conditions also encourage the pursuit of humanity's supernatural goal; but it is no part of the political power's task to define what that is, any more than to settle properly philosophical issues. Dante does not claim that these three offices, those of emperor, philosopher, and pope, do not differ in dignity; for 'this earthly happiness is in some sense ordered towards immortal happiness',[69] just as, of the two forms of happiness available to us in this world, that attained through contemplation is superior to that enjoyed in virtue of the active life.[70] What he does insist upon, however, is that all three exercise supreme and exclusive authority in their own sphere: the pope in matters of faith, the philosopher in the conduct of rational inquiry, the emperor in the world of practical politics. Provided that in the exercise of their authority they remain true to its nature, they will recognise the limits of that authority and show respect for the other kinds of authority by which their own is restricted. The result will be the spontaneous harmonisation of their independent activities, a concord deriving precisely from their separation and independence under God, the exclusive and direct source of the authority each enjoys.

Dante's ideological standpoint is unique, as is his philosophical blueprint for society. The reflections of contemporary social and political realities in his work emphasise the ways in which they manifest disorder and deny the order which ought to govern relationships within the human community. For Dante, order, or right relationship, signifies justice, 'since in its intrinsic meaning justice implies a rightness of order';[71] the observance of justice is the only guarantee of peace; and peace is the indispensable condition for the complete fulfilment of human potential, and so for complete human happiness, in this life. Dante's blueprint for society involves only the general principles which must be observed if political unity and social harmony are to be secured; it offers no direct account of social stratification or of contemporary status groups. It does, however, rest on a hierarchical view of society, in which social distinctions are important, not in themselves, but in so far as they reflect a hierarchy of moral worth and dignity of function. These values – moral worth and social function – are, on the other hand, fundamental expressions of human freedom. For, ideally, social function should be determined by a person's endowment of natural propensities and talents, which, if properly nurtured and freely embraced by the person concerned, will lead to the fulfilment of his or her nature as a uniquely endowed individual. As a human being, the same individual has moral responsibilities determined by the human nature shared with all other human beings: this, for its fulfilment, requires that the individual's freedom be employed for the cultivation of wisdom and virtue in accordance with rational ethical principles, as given expression by Aristotle, and the revealed truths of the Christian faith.[72] Dante's is a

fundamentally religious view of human destiny: as all things return to
their origin, so the human soul, which issues directly from the hand of
God, can find repose only in returning to its Creator. All the more
remarkable, then, is the poet's insistence on the importance and validity
of activity in this life directed towards the fulfilment of a purely earthly
goal of human existence: the practice of rational contemplation and the
work of political harmonisation on which the contemplative life depends. The idea that the ecclesiastical order somehow included or
subsumed the temporal order was bound to provoke reactions such as
Dante's. The uniqueness of his solution to the problem lies in what he
considers to flow, as a matter of demonstrable logic, from the dualism
inherent in human nature: distinct temporal and spiritual goals
demand, of their nature, distinct authorities to preside over their
fufilment. The temporal happiness of humanity is defined by the supreme philosopher and made possible by the emperor's political power;
the means whereby eternal happiness is to be secured are the province
of the spiritual authority invested in the pope. It is only by observing
their strict separation and by fidelity each to their own guiding principles, that politics, philosophy, and religion can successfully perform
their respective tasks in the universal human community and ensure
that peace and concord which Dante so earnestly desired.

4

FROISSARDIAN PERSPECTIVES ON LATE-FOURTEENTH-CENTURY SOCIETY

Peter Ainsworth

'Li vaillant honme, li peuples . . . et auquns clers.'

Jean Froissart (*c*.1337–*c*.1404) was the author of one of the great historical enterprises of the later Middle Ages.[1] His Chronicles[2] span almost
the whole of the fourteenth century, concluding with the accession of
Henry IV. Selective in viewpoint and emphasis as they undoubtedly
are, they embrace many of the major political and military events of that
period, and address at least some of its more serious social disturbances.
This chapter[3] focuses on the principal ways in which the discourse of the
chronicle – as Froissart practised it – presents to the reader a lively but
selective vision of social order, structure and hierarchy. A second aim
is to show how Froissart's text sometimes takes us one stage further
forwards by *subverting* – momentarily, but no less unforgettably for that
– the very image of social order that it purports to uphold. This
important feature is explored through close analysis of an episode from
Book II depicting a key moment in the struggle between Louis, count
of Flanders, and the people of Ghent, under their leader Philip van
Artevelde.

Froissart was enormously popular in the nineteenth century because
of his undoubted appeal to the Romantic imagination, and justifiably
celebrated as a great narrative artist by Sir Walter Scott,[4] who loved his

vivid recitals of battles, sieges, embassies and military campaigns. But it is sometimes argued nowadays, though not a little unfairly, that Froissart is not Philippe de Commynes: he displays none of the latter's overt awareness of the truly interesting questions posed by the emerging modern European state and its government. There can be no doubt that, of the two, Commynes is by far the more sophisticated and perspicacious historical commentator, though Commynes's Memoirs *as discourse* need to be interrogated just as critically as Froissart's Chronicles if one is not to be led astray by their particular use of rhetoric and of a carefully focused viewpoint,[5] and study of Froissart's style and discourse can be an excellent introduction to study of Commynes, as indeed of other chroniclers and memorialists. Froissart is currently commanding the serious attention of historians of the later Middle Ages. An important collection of essays appeared in 1981 under the title *Froissart: Historian*;[6] this was followed in November 1995 by the first international colloquium devoted exclusively to him as poet, historian and writer.[7]

That Froissart sometimes fell prey to his own taste for the frankly sensational cannot easily be denied, as is confirmed by the following extract from Geoffrey Brereton's translation for Penguin Classics (currently the only widely available translation into English):[8]

At that time there departed this life in rather strange circumstances, in the castle of La Hérelle which he held, ten miles from Amiens, Sir Jean de Picquigny, strangled, it was said, by his chamberlain. One of his most trusted knights, called Sir Lus de Bethisi, also died in the same way. May God have mercy on their souls and forgive them their misdeeds.

A very strange thing happened at about the same time to an English squire belonging to the troop of Sir Peter Audley and Albrecht. They had gone raiding one day to a village called Ronay and began plundering it just as the priest was chanting high mass. This squire entered the church and went up to the altar and, seizing the chalice in which the priest was about to consecrate the blood of Our Lord, he spilt the wine on the ground. When the priest protested, he gave him a back-hand blow with his gauntlet, so hard that the blood spurted on to the altar. After this, they all left the village and, while they were riding across the country, with the robber who had committed the outrage carrying the chalice, the plate and the communion cloth against his breast, this thing suddenly happened

which I will relate; it was a true example of God's anger and venge-
ance and a warning to all other pillagers.

His horse and he on it began whirling madly about in the fields and
raising such an outcry that none dared to go near them; until at last
they fell in a heap with their necks broken and were immediately
turned to dust and ashes. All this was witnessed by the comrades who
were present and who were so terrified that they swore before God
and Our Lady that they would never again violate a church, or rob
one. I do not know whether they kept their promise.

There are quite a few episodes like this to be found in the Chronicles.[9]
However, they should not be allowed to detract from other passages in
which Froissart displays much greater critical judgement and distance.
I do not propose, here, to rehearse or replicate the studies of Froissart
as historian so usefully collected by John Palmer. My line of argument
will be, rather, that the Chronicles offer us an object lesson concerning
the need for the serious historian to consider not merely what is
selected, deleted and set down by any writer of 'history', but also to
investigate how the material that is left is ordered and assembled. For
writing as process and result also confers order, not just upon the raw
materials gathered and collated by the inquirer, but on society itself – in
so far as the writer's final vision or revision of social and political
phenomena impinges on the social order. It may reinforce, encapsulate
(with relative degrees of adequacy, 'success', accuracy or faithfulness),
but may also query or even begin to challenge that order or the ideologies which support it. At the very least, the *chronicle* may lay bare
emerging symptoms or patterns of social change, whether the *chronicler*
is fully aware of this or not. Whether or not this was perceived by
his contemporary or subsequent readers is another matter, to be addressed, briefly, towards the end of the chapter.

An essay on the present scale cannot hope to do justice to every issue
raised by the foregoing paragraph. Attention will therefore be focused
in turn on those aspects of Froissart's writing which, it will be argued,
pose the most interesting problems within the perspective chosen for
the volume as a whole. In a word, the emphasis will be on discourse: its
structuring properties, and the relationship between these and social
structure (as perceived by the writer) as well as ideology. As to subject-
matter, I propose to deal first with Froissart's most conservative 'discur-
sive orchestration' of society, before turning in contrast to selected
episodes in which he writes about various threats to its stability.

In one of the earliest manuscript versions of Book I of the Chronicles, Froissart refers to his work as 'our history of the kings'.[10] A clerk in minor orders, the chronicler became priest at Les Estinnes in Hainault in 1373, and ended his ecclesiastical career as canon of Chimay (now in modern Belgium, province of Hainault) where he was buried some time after 1400. The Chronicles themselves evince scant interest in church history – except, *post* 1378, when Froissart writes about the Great Schism. He sees it as a scandal, as a totally reprehensible failure of Christian charity on all sides, and as a poor example to the flock.[11] It also appears that he was not a little worried about the impact it was having on benefices, perhaps including his own. The anecdote quoted above betrays his strong aversion, moreover, to those who desecrated or pillaged church property.

For all that he was a cleric, however, Froissart's vision was pre-eminently aristocratic, chivalric and even *royal* in emphasis and pre-occupation.[12] Familiar with the French and English royal households, the chronicler spent the period 1362–9 on the personal household staff of his compatriot Queen Philippa of Hainault, wife to King Edward III of England. As depicted in the Chronicles, the relationship between secretarial clerk and royal lady appears to have been one of fervent admiration and devotion, not unlike the attitude of lover to lady as found in the lyric poetry of the period.[13] Froissart, we should recall here, saw himself primarily as a poet devoted to the service of Venus. Inspired and imbued by the spirit of the erotic and allegorical *Romance of the Rose*, the lyric and narrative poetry of Guillaume de Machaut and the entire literary heritage of Arthurian romance in both verse and prose, Froissart was the author of numerous *chansons*, *rondeaux*, *pastourelles* and narrative poems.[14] He was also the author of an unusually long (some would argue, unusually fastidious) Arthurian romance, *Meliador*, written in rhyming couplets and using the narrative technique of interlace – whereby several parallel or nearly coterminous intrigues are skilfully marshalled, each thread of the plot being successively picked up and put aside once again, as another comes back to the forefront.[15] As we shall see, these techniques and habits were carried over, to a limited but significant extent, into the approach adopted by Froissart for his prose chronicle.

Probably at the behest of an earlier patron, and in his earliest adult years, Froissart had already undertaken a *verse* history of the wars between the French and English kings and their respective allies.[16] The Chronicles as we now have them constitute a vast compilation in *prose*, in which the interlace techniques just referred to are still manifestly present. They are informed by a similar chivalric and courtly ideology as is to be found in the verse works: that of *armes et amours*, love and war. Like his fellow clerks, the heralds and secretaries to the monarchical orders of chivalry (with whom he shared certain professional interests and functions),[17] Froissart saw fit to record for posterity the great deeds performed by the knights who served their kings in their wars, and to offer thereby a repository of exemplary conduct and precept to young aspirants to knighthood. This is a further reason for the Chronicles displaying such a consistent predilection for all matters relating to *armes et amours* – and consequently excluding much else besides that would not have appealed to his patrons or to a wider, but still wholly aristocratic, readership.

The deeds he records for this compendium of edifying chivalric doxa and precept must be authenticated if they are to pass muster: it would be indefensible to attribute erroneously to a given knight any deeds, good or evil, which the latter had not in fact performed. To that end, the chronicler seeks out wherever possible, like the true journalist-reporter he depicts himself as, reliable eyewitness accounts of representative and exemplary events.[18] He readily uses the testimony of heralds, especially if they had been involved in a particular engagement. Thus the narrative of particular events constantly veers towards an ideal, largely black-and-white, standard of behaviour.

This is most apparent in Froissart's numerous accounts of remarkable feats of arms performed during sieges, skirmishes or battles. Translations tend to edit these out; it is therefore instructive to read an unabridged sequence of some 50 or more pages from one of the critical editions now only to be found in research libraries. One discovers that there is a distinctive rhythm and order to the presentation of this kind of event.[19]

Froissart is especially fond of the dramatic depiction of incident or spectacle, on the battlefield, during a siege or in the throne-room. The reader is fed a complex pattern of textual 'signals' which encourage the creative, visual, and even auditory powers of the imagination to somehow re-run the scene or confrontation in the mind's ear and eye.[20] The process would have been still more acute for contemporary readers who had the additional visual stimulus of the illuminated miniatures which adorned many of the manuscript pages. These were usually based on the episode that one was about to read, and derived from either the rubric or text of the entire episode. What the artist chose or was required to depict would have pre-structured to some extent the reader's reception of the unfolding narrative.[21] On the other hand, Froissart himself was good at providing (implicit) suggestions as to how a scene might be depicted by the miniaturist:

> These lords made their way to the country manor house of the lord Bertrand which showed clearly enough how rich a personage he was. Bertrand came to greet them in his hall, receiving them with great cheerfulness, and speaking to them with gentle courtesy; then he led them into a chamber decked out and adorned as though for the king, where a number of his friends had assembled that very hour. When all had duly come together and were ready to commence formal discussions, the door of the chamber was closed behind them.[22]

Whether or not episodes such as this were prefaced by a miniature, the chronicler was in any case an unrivalled master at recreating a sense of dramatic space and of what it must have been like to *be there*.[23] Well known for his concise evocations of the heraldic panoply and display of a feudal army going into battle ('There you might have beheld great nobility of banners, pennons and blazonry. And I tell you, it was won-drously beautiful to behold'),[24] Froissart can also bring to life the trials and frustrations experienced by 'other ranks' such as sappers and engineers:

> By day three of the attack on Mortagne, the ship had been duly prepared and fitted with its pile-raising machine, and was ready to start clearing the wooden stakes from the river. Then those who were put to this task set about it with a will, as they had been ordered. And so they began to seize and to attempt to raise the twelve hundred or so wooden piles that had been driven into the bed of the Escaut, but had so much difficulty that they were only able to raise one of them, and only after prodigious physical effort. And so the leaders and master engineers overseeing the operation had to admit that the best they were likely to achieve in a day's work was the removal of no more than a twelfth of the whole. So the count, wearied by the enterprise, gave orders that it be abandoned forthwith.[25]

It is, however, the 'great and the good' who occupy the vast majority of Froissart's pages. He provides us with many idealised portraits of men and women who, in his eyes, provide examples of probity, integrity and fitting courtly or moral behaviour, associating at the same time his personal destiny with theirs, by virtue of his clerkly function:

> Duke Wenceslas [of Brabant] was liberal in his giving, gentle, courteous and affable; the legacy he would have left the world would have been impressive indeed, had he lived long; but he perished in the flower of his youth, for he armed himself for battle most willingly; for which reason I who have written and chronicled this history lament the fact that he should not have enjoyed a good four score years or more, for he would have achieved many noble things in his lifetime. He was greatly displeased by the Schism, and told me so readily enough, for I enjoyed his confidence and was well acquainted with him, even though I may say that I have known a good two hundred princes during my time of travail here on the earth, but never saw a more humble, personable or approachable lord than he, save for my lord and good master my lord Guy, count of Blois, who recommended that I write this history. These were the two princes from my own generation whom I found to be the most endowed with humility, liberality and goodness, strangers to any kind of malice, and who were most to be commended to others, for they lived generously but honourably on their revenues, without oppressing or exploiting their people, and without establishing within their domains any novel customs or evil ordinances. Now, let us return to what I was supposed to be writing about from the outset.[26]

It must be admitted that Froissart was, in many respects, the largely complacent *choreographer* of chivalry and royalty, servile in his almost liturgical portrayal of the rituals of chivalrous society and of the achievements of the eminent. Jousts, battles, skirmishes, royal entries, parliamentary assemblies and staged confrontations between rival magnates abound in his pages. However, this kind of stately, circumstantial writing does not solely fix, articulate or orchestrate the brightly illuminated evolutions of a glorified caste. It can also serve, on occasion, to point up the inherent tensions or contradictions lying just beneath the surface of an otherwise ordered society. For the chronicler was just as fascinated by the dramatic potential afforded by stories concerning the sudden, headlong fall of those who suddenly found themselves cast down from high places by the unpredictable revolutions of Dame Fortune's wheel. One, notorious illustration must suffice:

Then the duke of Lancaster, accompanied by these lords, prelates, dukes, earls, barons and knights and the most prominent citizens of London, went to the Tower, all of them on horseback, and, reaching the open space in front of it, they dismounted and went inside. King Richard was brought down and came into the hall vested and arrayed as a king, wearing an open mantle and with the sceptre in his hand and the crown with which he had been crowned upon his head. No one stood at his side or supported him when he began to speak, uttering these words in the hearing of all:

'I have been sovereign of England, duke of Aquitaine and lord of Ireland for some twenty-two years, and this sovereignty, lordship, sceptre, crown and heritage I resign fully and unreservedly to my cousin Henry of Lancaster, asking him in the presence of you all to take this sceptre in token of possession.'

He held out the sceptre to the duke of Lancaster, who took it and handed it to the archbishop of Canterbury. Next King Richard lifted the golden crown from his head, placed it in front of him and said: 'Henry, fair cousin and duke of Lancaster, I give and deliver to you this crown with which I was crowned king of England, and with it all the rights belonging to it.'

The duke of Lancaster took it, and again the archbishop was at hand to receive it from him. These two things done and the king's resignation thereby given and accepted, the duke of Lancaster called for a public notary and required a record to be made in writing, with the signatures of the prelates and lords who were present. Soon after Richard returned to his room, while the duke of Lancaster and all the lords who had attended mounted their horses. The two royal jewels mentioned above were put in strong-boxes and taken to the treasury of Westminster Abbey. The lords all went back to their houses to await the day when the parliament was to be held in the Palace of Westminster.[27]

Here in a few paragraphs penned towards the end of the chronicler's long life is the human drama, shot through with pathos, of deposition, forced abdication and imminent personal destruction, mitigated to some extent by the relatively reassuring transfer of legitimate power from one great magnate to another by means of a regulated, ceremonial process. We are thus made to feel the 'naturalness' of the sequence of events whereby King Richard becomes mere 'Richard' by following the logical thread of Froissart's circumstantial sentences.[28]

Much earlier in his career Froissart had written about a much more disquieting kind of reversal: the violation of the normal structures or orders of society in France during the *Jacquerie* of 1358. Tyranny wrought from below, and attempts to overthrow the divinely sanctioned authority of princes and knights are depicted in Book I as *bestournement* (topsy-turvydom), distorting the true order of things so that they appear to be presented through a refracting prism. Whereas the knights are portrayed with their proper accoutrements – sword, lance, war-horse and emblazoned surcoats – the rebels are presented as an undifferentiated mass of dark (dirty), stunted peasants.[29] The social causes of popular revolt and the contributing factor of dereliction of duty on the part of the *noblesse* do not entirely escape Froissart's intelligence. But social disorder is seen by him essentially as a breakdown in good government,[30] encouraging in its turn insurrection or outright rebellion. Such rebellion, whether in France in 1358 or in England in 1381, is seen not solely as dangerous and reprehensible; it is presented as an unacceptable challenge to divinely appointed authority.[31]

In the Prologue to the later manuscript versions of Book I (*c*.1390 and *c*.1399), Froissart reworked the old commonplace of the three orders. His is an unfamiliar but nevertheless reactionary reformulation, enrolling the writer in the service of an unimpeachable chivalry, and therefore of an immutable social order:

> And so the world may be divided up and categorised in various ways. First come the men of valour who exercise their limbs in battle so as to secure the glory and renown afforded by this world; the people speak of, rehearse and talk about their deeds; whilst certain clerks write down and record their deeds and acts of valour, so that they may be retained and fixed in memory perpetual.[32]

From here is derived the quotation at the beginning of this chapter. Froissart as the 'secretary' of chivalry appears to reaffirm his commitment to and confidence in the dominant social order.

Even so, in the remainder of this chapter I wish to argue that there is another, more discordant voice to be heard in the Chronicles. It is an intermittent voice, but it coincides with some of Froissart's most compelling writing. As I hope to demonstrate, the episodes examined below show how the chronicler's text sometimes 'behaves' more subversively than its author. We shall discover that the sheer *writerliness* of these episodes has the effect of provoking certain insistent questions in the reader's mind. We begin to suspect, that is to say, that Froissart is trying somehow to write uncomfortable realities out of his system, and out of the political system he still wished to preserve. By a curious paradox, the more truly literary the chronicler's writing becomes, the more it seems to invite us to mistrust the smooth, self-evident surface of its ostensibly effortless discourse. And the more metaphorical the prose becomes, the more it lays bare the ground of its own ideological allegiance. Froissart the writer hoped to preserve for posterity the unruffled image of his gilded protagonists. What remains, however, is the power of the writing, provoking us to ask searching questions of what may initially have struck us as little more than a bland, seamless and vainglorious (narrative) spectacle.

When Froissart and 'popular revolt' are mentioned in the same breath, the usual well-known pages tend to be cited once again: Wat Tyler and King Richard, the rebels at Smithfield, and so on.[33] If the editor of a monograph on the Great Revolt of 1381 is looking for illustrations, illuminated manuscripts of Froissart's Chronicles are almost invariably the first port of call. The material considered below attempts to avoid the pitfalls of using over-familiar passages by looking instead at the relatively less well-known struggle between the guildsmen and townspeople of Ghent and their overlord, Louis de Male, count of Flanders (between 1378 and his death in 1384).

According to the Dutch historian J. van Herwaarden,[34] Book II's coverage of these events[35] is not only enthralling but is also of considerable historical value. He describes this part of the Chronicles as a mature work, offering its readers insights that are at once shrewd and intelligent concerning the causes and consequences of the differences between Louis and his Flemish subjects. Froissart clearly understood the perils arising from private feuds between prominent families in towns such as Ghent or Bruges, witness his account of the bloody rivalry between Jan Yoens, dean of the shippers, and Gijsbrecht Mayhuus (another, wealthier shipper) and their respective clans. He also clearly understood the extent to which urban society in the Flemish Low Countries was dominated by the guilds or *métiers*, especially the shippers and weavers. Nor did it escape his notice that this same urban society, especially at Ghent, was made up of a hierarchy of interrelated layers of influence. The most important of these was the *poorterij*, composed of the aristocracy of those persons owning land within the original *portus*.[36] However influential they may have been, however, Froissart (who was based not all that far away, at Les Estinnes-au-Mont or Valenciennes) was not afraid to upbraid these men for giving in too easily to the pressure and power exercised by a handful of presumptuous demagogues, thus allowing tyranny to flourish. The *poorters* ought, in his opinion, to have aligned themselves unambiguously with the count of Flanders, their natural ally and feudal lord.[37] If Froissart exaggerates their role to some extent (the revolt was in reality led by a coalition of *poorters*, shippers, weavers and minor guilds, possibly with the reluctant involvement of some of the fullers),[38] he correctly identifies the important role played by the *Franc de Bruges*, whose agrarian membership, states Van Herwaarden,[39] tended to support the count's interests at the expense of those of the towns.

Recent events in Flanders (Froissart was writing about them *c*.1386–8) seem to have touched the chronicler on the raw. Born to a middle-class family in Valenciennes *c*.1337, he must have watched the events of 1379–82 with a mixture of horror and fascination. Before reaching the point in his narrative where he will be able to write of the (reassuring) defeat of the rebels on 27 November 1382 at West-Roosebeke, he reminds his readers that the Maillotins of Paris and the entire peasant population of the Ile de France and Normandy were just waiting for an excuse to overrun the towns and territories of their overlords. The success of 'popular rebellion'[40] in Flanders would have fuelled a much wider conflagration. Book II will also, of course, record the Great Revolt of 1381 in England, and *misbehaviour* in the Low Countries (it will be hinted) was the bad example which encouraged the men of Kent and Essex to march on London.

What Froissart feared most, it would appear, was the destruction of a divinely sanctioned social order. As Van Herwaarden remarks, a good society for the chronicler is one in which the realm is governed wisely and justly by a prince intent upon maintaining peace at home, and who can therefore enjoy the full support of his barons, senior churchmen and townsmen.[41] Peace and internal good order depend, then, on a social contract and order ordained by God. The prince does not bear the sword in vain: an old but resilient doctrine. This is a view of society in which the lord is respected and feared, but where he is in turn required to respect his subjects and their needs. On either side, pride and presumption are unthinkable, which is why Froissart is not slow to record his strong disapproval of the pride of the men of Ghent and of the overweening presumption of their leader and captain, Philip van Artevelde – descendant, of course, of that temporarily successful agitator of the previous generation, Jakob. However, it is just as important to note that the chronicler is not inured to the courage of the rebels. Just before the battle of the Beverhoutsveld (3 May 1382), he puts the following words into the mouth of no less a personage than their principal adversary, Count Louis:

> 'Let us go and fight these wretched folk; one must allow that they have courage,' the count would remark: 'they would much rather die by the sword than by famine'.[42]

As for Louis, the chronicler seems – on first reading, at least – to level no reproach at him at all. Froissart holds the inhabitants of Ghent, their captains and allies entirely responsible for the insurrection. Or so it would appear. In fact, at least one section of the Book II narrative – namely the prelude to and aftermath of the battle of the Beverhoutsveld – betrays a more nuanced attitude to the moral, if not the political, responsibilities of the various parties to the conflict, including Louis of Flanders. The narrative undoubtedly conveys much more than it purports to. To the extent that we have here what literary critics would recognise as a 'surplus of meaning' or 'second, configured message', the episodes in question can be described as proto-literary. We may not recognise them, consequently, as *history* in the modern sense of that term; but they betray even so a distinctive historical perspective on events that deserves close analysis. The constituent elements of this perspective or vision include conventional narrative, carefully reconstructed or, more probably, *imagined* scraps of conversation rendered largely in direct speech, a friar's sermon and an *exemplum*. These varieties of discourse are seamlessly combined; but a second reading allows them to echo each other ironically, to cancel each other out or to suggest a new configuration for the 'truth'. The first feature that we encounter consists of two biblical glosses on events as they are set to unfold: one occurs as part of a rousing speech by Philip van Artevelde himself; the other is given in indirect speech, and consists of a pre-battle sermon delivered by a team of friars to the rebels assembled at Ghent. Both glosses provide us with an initial commentary on the political situation as it begins to evolve into conflict. The author seems, so far, to stand aloof, though he is of course responsible for putting words into the mouths of his protagonists. However, little by little elements of the gloss start to infiltrate the ostensibly factual, and morally neutral narrative. Exegesis begins to invest the story-telling, a feature betrayed by the discreet presence of echoes from episodes deriving from the Old or

New Testaments. The resulting text tends towards irony, since the exegetical elements seem more and more to put into question the 'self-evident' progress of events. In short, it makes us question what precisely is going on, who is really responsible, and who is the bigger villain, Louis of Flanders or Philip van Artevelde. In this way, the Chronicles cease to speak univocally about their ostensible topic, and start to speak instead – or simultaneously – of something else altogether.

Sermons and Parables: From Exodus to the Gospels

Late in 1379, Louis of Flanders attempts to appease his Ghentish subjects by haranguing them from a window high up in the Town Hall overlooking the crowd assembled below in the square:

> There he reminded them of how a lord was to be loved, trusted, feared, served and held in honour by his subjects; there he showed them how they had done the very opposite; there he recalled to them how he had protected, kept and defended them against all foes; there he showed them how he had kept them in peace and profit and in all prosperity.[43]

Within two years the situation has deteriorated beyond remedy. All attempts at reconciliation have come to naught, and Louis (now at Bruges) is preparing to crush the pride of Ghent at the end of a long blockade which has reduced men, women and children to famine and destitution. Peace negotiations at Tournai have only hardened Ghentish resistance to an overlord who has declared that he 'will have mercy on not a single citizen of Ghent who falls into his hands'.

Meanwhile, a secret council of war is arranged at Ghent at which Philip van Artevelde and Pieter van den Bossche, a former 'disciple' of Jan Yoens, decide to stake their all on an armed conflict. They are prepared to perish in the attempt; if they do so, at least they won't die alone:

> In just a few days from now, our town of Ghent will be the most honoured town in Christendom, or the most cast down. At least, if we perish in this struggle, we shall not die alone. We shall live or die honourably.[44]

Van Artevelde now finds a convenient window from which to address the crowd, his rhetoric betraying its Froissardian source at a mile's distance. He begins by reducing all present to tears. The people of Ghent, he argues, can do no other than throw themselves upon the mercy of their count:

> 'For when he sees us in this condition, on our knees before him and with our hands joined in supplication for mercy, he will surely have compassion on us, if it so pleases him; but I cannot but conclude from what I have been told by some of those on his council that the greater part of those present here today and who approach him thus will suffer no other fate than that of a shameful death after due judicial process and imprisonment. Now consider well if you wish to sue for peace on such a basis.'[45]

After calming the wails prompted by this revelation, Philip sets out the procedure to be followed for an act of collective submission and penance, craftily offering himself as a sacrificial lamb.

> 'And I myself shall, as the very first amongst our company and to assuage his fury against us, offer my head to him on a plate; for I am more than ready to die for the love of Ghent.'[46]

Philip now passes swiftly on, however, to an alternative strategy: combat to the death, with every last Ghentish soul called to the colours. Their courage, he argues, will surely awaken the compassion of God Himself: the militia of Ghent will go forth like Judith, against the heathen forces of this new Nebuchadnezzar.[47]

A third alternative – collective surrender promptly followed by what Philip warns them will be their collective burning alive in the church buildings of Ghent after the arrival of Louis' forces – commends itself to the crowd no more warmly than the first, and the people therefore prepare themselves to face the armed might of Flanders on the battlefield. After all, their provisions are almost exhausted; all they have left, says Froissart, is 'a mere seven cartloads of victuals, made up that is to say of five cartloads of bread and two of wine'. If their venture fails, concludes Philip, they will have nothing to look forward to but a massacre.

Before setting out, the 5,000 men selected to fight receive the benedictions and prayers of their friends and relatives. They spend the first night in the fields about a league outside Bruges, their destination. The next morning, a Saturday (the Jewish sabbath – a detail which links Old and New Testaments, as we are about to see), they all go to mass, 'as those awaiting the grace and mercy of God', and are regaled with a sermon duly comparing Louis of Flanders to Nebuchadnezzar and to Pharaoh:

> There it was explained to them by their clerks, friars preacher and others, how they were to be compared with the people of Israel whom Pharaoh had kept a long time in servitude; and how thereafter, by the grace of God alone, they were delivered out of Pharaoh's hand and led by Moses and Aaron to the land promised to them, whilst Pharaoh and the Egyptians perished and were slain. 'In this wise, good people, declared the preachers in their sermons, have you been held in slavery by your lord the count and by your neighbours in the city of Bruges.'[48]

The drift of this sermon is clear enough, though we should remember that for believers in the Middle Ages the Exodus had a typological meaning. The deliverance of the Israelites through the passover and the crossing of the Red Sea symbolised and anticipated the redemption of sinful mankind through the shedding of the blood of the perfect sacrificial lamb, Jesus Christ. In the same way, the miraculous food provided for the Israelites in the wilderness – heaven-sent manna – was a sign of the coming, many years later, of the *true* bread of heaven, Jesus Christ once again. Taken together, the two episodes from the Old Testament Exodus story thus announce the eucharistic meal: blood/wine and manna/bread, the earliest anticipation of which was the passover meal. Not until the New Testament, however, did the real significance of the manna given in the desert become clear to the Jews. It was when Jesus performed the miracle of the feeding of the 5,000 that He chose to reveal Himself as the true bread of God:

> Most assuredly, I say to you, Moses did not give you the bread from heaven, but My Father gives you the true bread from heaven. For the bread of God is He who comes down from heaven and gives life to the world.[49]

Jesus' exposition of the Exodus story is not to be found literally reproduced in the friars' sermon. But we do find it in Froissart's narrative, and in an unexpected context: the speech made by Philip van Artevelde as part of the preparations for battle. As the friars' sermon ends, Philip scrambles up onto a baggage wagon, and proceeds to address the 5,000 men of Ghent. This time the words used recall those of Jesus in Luke ix, 62: 'No one, having put his hand to the plough, and looking back, is fit for the kingdom of God', which in this gospel closes a chapter which includes the feeding of the 5,000 with five loaves and two fish. It is not so much the kingdom of God that is at stake here, however, as the honour of Ghent. The conclusion to Philip's harangue seems entirely down-to-earth and pragmatic:

> My lords, you see spread before you all your provision of food; I entreat you therefore to share it now graciously amongst yourselves, as brothers ought to do, with no unseemly behaviour, for, when all has been consumed you will have to buy more, if you wish to survive.[50]

What follows, however, is a dignified and richly symbolic alfresco meal. It is worth noting that Van Artevelde's words are reminiscent of St Paul's advice to the Corinthians on the appropriate manner in which to approach the Lord's supper.[51] We should also recall that the provisions consumed by the 5,000 men of Ghent are 'five wagons full of freshly baked bread, and two wagonloads of wine'. The narrative and its solemn style thus fuse together (i) the manna in the wilderness, (ii) the miracle of the feeding of the 5,000, and (iii) the Lord's supper:

> At these words they came together in humility; the carts were un-loaded and portions of bread distributed to each unit and division, and the wine barrels were up-ended. There they partook together reasonably and peaceably of both bread and wine; and each had as much as he needed. What is more, when the meal was concluded each man found himself strong and fit, and in better condition and more ready for the fight than if he had had much more to eat.[52]

The narrative presentation of this second 'mass' (the mass proper has already been celebrated, before the sermon) seems to court blasphemy. It is in any case extraordinary, but arguably lends dignity and pathos to the last moments shared together by the Ghentish rebels before they set out to fight. How, then, are we to explain its presence? It may have been included because Froissart wanted to account somehow for the impending defeat of the count of Flanders and his mounted chivalry at the hands of what he saw as mere urban militia. The quasi-eucharistic meal perhaps conferred supernatural powers upon these *poorters*, weavers and fullers; on this occasion, God was with them to bring down the might and hubris of Flanders.

The implied theological gloss or commentary betrays, perhaps, a measure of sympathy on the part of the chronicler for the citizens of Ghent; it may also testify to his growing awareness of the increasing political significance and social dignity (and power) of the *poorters*. It surely prepares and to some extent justifies the imminent nemesis of Louis de Male, who has shown himself unfit to govern his county and incapable of maintaining its peace and prosperity. From this perspective, the rebels of Ghent are presented as the scourge of God, used to punish His enemy and exercise His justice. Yet even this 'explanation' along traditional, conservative lines fails to satisfy altogether, perhaps because the episode does not seek to *explain*. What the sequence does do, by dint of its poetry and discreet pathos, is to raise at least a modicum of doubt regarding the moral position of each of the parties to the conflict. It betrays, in short, a certain malaise on Froissart's part with regard to the balance to be struck between the hubris of what remains a rebellious community in arms against its rightful overlord, and that of a feudal suzerain whose governance verges on the tyrannical and therefore merits punishment. The narrative will conclude, in fact, with Louis de Male alone and unaided, hiding in an old woman's smoke-filled cottage somewhere in the backstreets of Bruges, tucked under the coverlet[53] of a child's bed. This detail picks up a reference in an earlier episode to the destruction by the mob of the cradle emblazoned with his arms in which Count Louis had lain as an infant.[54]

While the victorious men of Ghent comb the streets outside in search of Louis, Froissart invites us to ponder what thoughts might have passed through the count's mind in those perilous moments, as he considered to what a lowly pass God and Dame Fortune had brought him that day.[55] The *chronicler* will affirm, none the less, that God was with Louis on this occasion, since He clearly chose to deliver him from mortal danger. The *text*, on the other hand, has done *its* work, leaving us with a pleasingly open ending to a narrative dealing with trials that may befall all kinds and conditions of men, be they princes, clerks or Flemish guildsmen.

In the last analysis, Froissart the chronicler must be seen as resolutely conservative in his social outlook. He remains the chronicler of chivalry and of aristocratic ideology. What I hope has emerged from this necessarily brief analysis, however, is the need to avoid premature conclusions when considering the perspectives opened up by the *chronicle*'s (as opposed to the *chronicler*'s) representation of 'popular' revolt. Froissart's aristocratic readers may not have responded to the exegetical gloss quite in the same way as that proposed above. They may not even have noticed its presence. Whatever its ultimate significance may be, it opens a window on to disturbing new social realities and changes in the last quarter of the fourteenth century. To this extent, it constitutes a seismic wave, however attenuated the trace.

5

HIERARCHIES AND ORDERS IN ENGLISH ROYAL IMAGES OF POWER

Paul Binski

The relationship of the academic disciplines of history and art history has long been one of polite antagonism, founded (and I write as one who trained initially as an historian before turning to art history, and who is thus culpable on both fronts) on the eminently unreasonable assumption that history is in some way concerned with the real, and art history with the merely epiphenomenal, that is the marginal or subsidiary. I think few historians would seriously subscribe to this view now, though it should be said that the positivistic (essentially untheoretical) leanings of most art historians until the last decade or so, coupled with their inclination to practise connoisseurship, has undoubtedly opened them to the charge of lacking a genuinely historical method. On the face of it the rise of interdisciplinarity might be said to have subverted this hierarchy of subjects within the academy (and this is where an essay on hierarchies should perhaps begin). But here art historians cannot overplay their hand. In the field of medieval imagery it can fairly be said that our work has scarcely begun. The ideological structuring of medieval art has only become an object of serious enquiry very recently, though such studies as have appeared have very rightly gone to the heart of the matter in challenging glib assumptions about the nexus of social 'reality' and representation, and the notion that art – and medieval art especially – is transparently illustrative of prior or given social conditions.[1] The product of this challenge has in effect been a radical re-empowerment of art as discourse in the widest sense: art does not illustrate but constitutes, or *re*-presents, social conditions, and is one agent in the formation of those conditions in the first place.

In stressing the active agency of medieval art in representing or constituting medieval orders and hierarchies, we enter a field beset with problems. Though it might frequently be clear which high-ranking patrons paid for, and therefore legitimated, certain images, the processes whereby those images came to be formed in the way that they were, and the ways in which those images were read and understood by their audiences, are seldom recoverable. We can construct accounts of the production of medieval art, but not of its reception. This point is vital to assessing the motivation and impact of art production. No less important is the relationship between the public and the private. For an image to work in a way that is other than magical or apotropaic (intended to turn away evil), it must be seen; and logic would suggest that an account of hierarchical art should examine images in the public domain subject to the hierarchies of power which produced and controlled it. But what were the boundaries of the public domain in the Middle Ages, and how did they evolve? This issue is exposed clearly and rather cruelly in the sphere of the most well-documented field of English royal display, the palace, of which it might be said that we know a great deal at the positivistic level, but scarcely anything (yet) at the social and ideological level. Boundaries between the public and private were not constants. In the case of major palaces like that at Westminster it is still unclear how major spaces adorned with significant royal images actually functioned, whether those functions were determinate – very often they were not – and whether changing descriptions of notions of the public and private, as for example in the emergence from *c*.1300 of the 'privy' palace, also had radical implications for the ways older images were reinscribed in unexpected and unintended social contexts.[2]

Exactly the same caveats apply to the extremes of the case, the most private and the most public images. The medieval English court is not noted for its patronage of books, and suffers from comparison with contemporary France; but in neither case can the issues of readership, function and importance raised by book ownership really be established, except by deduction from the nature of the objects themselves. This has to be borne in mind in assessing recent accounts of the ideological formation of French royal imagery in illuminated chronicles.[3] Nor, in England, was there ever an important royal policy of commissioning exterior images of the type which characterised medieval Italy – one thinks of the sculpted self-representations of Frederick II, Charles of Anjou or Boniface VIII. There are perhaps three exceptions: the Eleanor Crosses, commissioned by the queen's executors in the 1290s and clearly placed strategically vis-à-vis their various urban contexts, notably in London at Cheapside and Charing; the image of a king sculpted over the cityward gatehouse of Caernarvon Castle probably under Edward II; and the series of sculptures of monarchs executed on the cathedral-like façade of Westminster Hall facing London, under Richard II in the 1390s.[4]

The thirteenth-century neo-Aristotelian writer Giles of Rome said that in the field of public address subtleties were wasted on the populace as a whole.[5] English court art appears for the most part to have agreed. Many of its images cannot (yet) be described as being merely or essentially propagandistic; but many of them do appear to have had the character of self-address, being those images of the court designed by the court for itself. So in assessing orders and hierarchies in English royal imagery, we may do well to consider other issues which touch on this issue of self-reflexiveness: those which relate to allegorical self-presentation, those relating to the field of display of court art, and those which relate to its myths. How might these be connected?

Images of Hierarchy: The Monarch Enthroned

From one perspective the royal Great Seal offers an obvious instance of an image in the public domain whose functions required it to be both recognisable and stable as the central icon of state. But seals, whether private or official, actually offer a complex field of signification. Precisely because the stablity of an image like a seal relates to the question of its authenticity, moments of fairly drastic change to the semiotic character (the way it is composed of signs) of a seal may be revealing at the levels both of production and consumption, that is reception.

One such moment occurred in 1259 when the appearance of Henry III's Great Seal had to be modified to accord with the terms of the Treaty of Paris negotiated with the French in that year.[6] Henry's first Great Seal of 1219 displays a conventional formula: on the obverse the king sits frontally on a bench holding a sword in his right hand and an orb with a foliated stem in his left, the counterseal showing the monarch on horseback wielding a sword and shield. All this was in line with the corresponding seal of King John. In 1259 Henry was required to give up his claim to Normandy, Anjou, Touraine, Maine and Poitou, and since his first Great Seal styled him *Dux Normannie et Aquitanie comes Andegavie* its legend now had to be changed. But Henry also undertook something technically uncalled for, namely to redesign the images on the seal, a fact known to us because the recorded mandates for the seal's redesign state that its form was prescribed to the king's goldsmith, William of Gloucester, in the form enjoined on him by Henry and his keeper of the works. The new design thus probably reflects the king's direct intentions, an important issue given that the precise agencies responsible for forming the king's image are not always known in the Middle Ages. Henry's new specification is revealing. First, the obverse was changed by placing the monarch not on a low cushioned bench but upon a much more showy high-backed openwork throne. This throne design had already been used in one other significant context, namely on the seal of Henry's brother Richard Earl of Cornwall as King of the Romans, adopted in 1257.[7] Henry's seal also shows leopards or lions at the throne's base and sides, alluding either to the charges of the English royal arms or, as Wormald suggested, to the imagery of the throne of Solomon described in the Bible.[8] Finally, in place of the sword in the right hand of the king, we find instead a long rod with a bird, probably a dove, on its tip.

At this point the strategy of meaning of the new seal starts to emerge: in addition to the quasi-imperial throne type and Solomonic lions, we find in the rod a direct allusion to the seal of St Edward the Confessor, which shows the king seated holding a sword and, in his right hand, the same dove-headed rod. The rod, here as elsewhere, in fact now formed a standard element in the iconography of the Confessor. On Henry's seal the sword has, as it were, migrated to the counterseal where it continues to be shown in the equestrian monarch's right hand. In effect the new seal amounts to a link in the chain of ideas promoted precisely by the various ways in which the cult of Henry III's patron saint, St Edward, was itself formulated in hagiography and other images in the period. Thus here, as elsewhere at Henry's court, St Edward appears as the wise Solomonic ruler, as the bearer of the dove-headed rod of virtue, and as the peaceable (that is not merely sword-bearing) monarch; and it is to him, in virtue of these linked ideas or signfying practices, that Henry has annexed himself.

1. Second Great Seal of King Henry III, 1259, obverse (a) and reverse (b), Dean and Chapter Library Durham 1.2.Reg.6a. Reproduced by permission of the Dean and Chapter of Durham.

The principal point that emerges from this is that the construction of such images relied on thinking that was essentially *allegorical*: through its signs, ostensibly innovative but actually conservative, the seal discloses that Henry is the successor of the virtuous Anglo-Saxon ruler to whom he was distantly related. The allegorical associations are connected to contemporary mythological thinking, in other words to those ways in which St Edward's own rule and life – his work as a saint and a king – were represcribed during the reign of Henry III, most especially in the Anglo-Norman cult literature about Edward composed for Henry's court. And we are justified in locating the seal's meaning within an allegorical mode of thought precisely because this is one of the very few occasions when the reception as well as planning of a royal image is recorded, precisely in allegorical terms. In 1259 the *Liber de Antiquis Legibus* made special note of the change of style of Henry's seal and its exchange of attributes, adding in a margin 'thus was fulfilled the prophecy which says: "By reason of wondrous change, the sword shall be severed from the sceptre"', an allusion to the allegorical prophecies of Merlin which were cited more than once in opposition to Henry's rule.[9] A set of allegorical strategies understandable to us as compensatory in character – one set of claims to French soil renounced and replaced by a strengthening of the sense of lineage to English soil and history at a time of tension between the king and his barons – is matched in opposition by another which hinted at the emasculated character of the new image, the sword of course famously standing for prowess in medieval symbolism.

Henry's second Great Seal thus 'failed' at least in the short term at one obvious level – namely that, whatever its broad public impact, it could be greeted with scepticism by those adroitly using exactly the same strategies by which it was formed – and this serves to remind us that the common view of royal images of power as essentially propagandistic is one founded on frequently intelligent assumptions about the meaning and intentionality of such images, but seldom (because there is no evidence) on the actual historical conditions of their reception. Images can fail as well as succeed, and their extremely delicate position within the medieval field of critiques of images is as well exposed by this instance as by others – for example, the public statues of Boniface VIII which the pope had erected to himself later in the century, which brought about accusations of idolatory in the course of his downfall.[10]

The second instance I wish to discuss involves a similar type of image also produced, it would seem – and here we have no documentary evidence to go on – at a time of relative political instability: the portrait of Richard II in Westminster Abbey dating to the later 1390s. This image belongs to a different and new genre, the painted portrait, which had appeared earlier in the fourteenth century in Italy.[11] Portrait likenesses had already evolved within the field of royal representation on the tombs of Edward III (1380s) and Richard II, complete by 1395, in the first case probably, and in the second case certainly, by contractual requirement. Richard's gilt-bronze effigy stands as an official public likeness of the king, and it is reasonable to assume that the large picture now displayed in the nave, and measuring 2.14 metres in height, corresponded to it. From recent conservation work on the most celebrated image containing a likeness of Richard, the Wilton Diptych of c.1395, we know that issues of likeness were of mounting importance, because close examination of the Diptych, assuredly produced for Richard and doubtless as much under his control and will as Henry III's second Great Seal, shows clear signs of the way the king's profile was modified and adjusted by the painters in their anxiety to 'get things right'.[12]

But the Westminster portrait is also self-evidently of a different kind from that on the Diptych in scale, presumed context and internal pictorial structure. The form of the Diptych with Richard kneeling before the Virgin and Child, and being presented by his sponsors St Edmund, St Edward and St John the Baptist, is that of a profoundly personal devotional image-type which was already widespread by this date in panel paintings and manuscript illuminations produced throughout Western Europe, and which was to form an important component of 'bourgeois' religious art patronage after 1400.[13] The Diptych, and the way it registers a sense of luxurious personal display, is simply a peculiarly magnificent (and enigmatic) instance of the genre of private panel or altarpiece. Nothing is known, though much might be surmised, about the circumstances of its manufacture, display and reception. In contrast there appears to be a reasonably strong tradition that the large portrait was always on show in Westminster Abbey, probably in the choir; it might in any event stand for a type of large-scale official substitute likeness for the king suited to any public or quasi-public venue such as the Great Hall of a palace like that at Westminster. If so, it would accord with the relatively new practices of commissioning large-scale sculpted or painted portraits of heads of

2. Westminster Abbey, portrait of Richard II, *c*.1395–9. Reproduced by permission of the Dean and Chapter of Westminster.

state either singly or in combination, which had appeared at the courts of the Emperor Charles IV at Prague (to whom Richard was related), or of King Charles V of France.[14]

But, context and scale aside, the images also function differently. Of the two, the Diptych is actually the more conventional because it shows the king in profile, the normal form of painted portraits of the fourteenth century and much of the fifteenth century.[15] The great portrait is in contrast absolutely frontal, like the image on a seal – and in this it is strikingly modern, being perhaps the first frontal portrait image of its type from the period. We relate differently to profile and frontal representations: in the former the profile image, because it 'edits' out the full face, is the more passive representational type. Thus Richard is differentiated from the active agency of the Virgin Mary and Child, each in a dynamic three-quarter profile. He is the subject both of their religious power and of our scrutiny. In the large portrait the image stares and faces us down, and though in one sense Richard is its subject, at the level of engagement it is the viewers who are subject to the image. Richard is shown in the finery of his presence bearing an orb and sceptre – audience and not coronation regalia – while actually honoured in his absence. This is an image of the king's estate, whose structure and disposition are fundamentally public. Arguably, its purpose, as in effect an icon of presence – and icons, religious representations, were the only contemporary image-types to be structured in anything like this way – relates to what we know of Richard's own court in the later years of his reign. Thus in 1398 during his 'tyranny', Richard was described as sitting in the midst of his court between dinner (that is lunch) and vespers, and when 'he looked at any one, that man had to bow the knee'.[16] Catching the subject's eye and thereby reducing that person to subjecthood amounted to a decorous and doubtless less-than-amusing game of ocular control. In this sense the Westminster portrait, far from being a representation of the ideal unassailable monarch, stands as a monument to royal paranoia; and it is up to the historian to choose whether or not the prior 'context' for such a stance lies in the political or personal insecurities of Richard at the end of his reign.

Though it has been argued that 'naturalistic' royal images, and especially statues, were one part of medieval strategies of political legitimation, Richard's images precisely expose the hazy boundaries between what is naturalistic and what is conventional, emblematic, socially-grounded and artificial. Richard's great portrait might be understood

to resemble a seal both substantively and in its capacity to be reproduced as an official likeness, as indeed it was – but as a portrait its index
of signification plainly differs from artefacts like seals. Yet the fact of its
being a portrait does not simply align it with an uncomplicated natural-
ism. The possibility that it can be understood in the light of etiquette at
court might emphasise its naturalistic or referential value, but connects
that reference with practices themselves highly regulated and artificial
in nature. Richard's portrait cannot be said to illustrate or document
what are taken to be 'prior' realities of social life; we might just as fairly
suggest that it had a constitutive role, exemplifying the court's practices
even in the king's absence by making the subject genuflect before it, as
before a religious icon. In a sense the image *is* the court's practice. This
is not an idol in the sense that Boniface VIII's self-images were construed by some to be, as sculptures: but the sense of an insecure
monarch contesting and setting aside medieval taboos on frontal representation as the sole preserve of the religious image, and hence making
claims through that image, is powerful, our lack of knowledge of the
'success' or 'failure' of the image notwithstanding.

Court Display and Material Culture

So far I have examined emblematic or naturalistic representations in
order to explore the interpretative possibilities to which they give rise,
and to expose the blurred boundaries between these representations
and other forms of discourse, such as hagiography or court etiquette. I
have suggested that these specialised artefacts are neither illustrative,
nor socially autonomous. But we should now go on to state that how
such images are made, and of what, is as important as what they show.
Both images of Richard, the Wilton Diptych especially, register a
marked sense of luxury conveyed not only by their subject-matter –
their depiction of fabulous textiles and regalia – but also by the oil and
tempera media and gilding used in their production. Arguably even the
use of portraiture exemplifies the capacity of the socially privileged to
command highly specialised, and still relatively rare, modes of representation. The Diptych is also a famous example of the International
Gothic Style, which the art historian Erwin Panofsky located persua-
sively within currents of change in aristocratic European art around
1400 provoked by massive and rapid social mobility. Panofsky, follow-

ing the sociologist Veblen, suggested that the ostentation of the Inter-national Gothic Style in its courtly guise was a form of conspicuous consumption by a newly threatened aristocratic class increasingly con-scious of the need to stress class difference.[17] In this connection we might postulate an analogy between the refined and exclusive habits of the International Gothic Style and fourteenth-century sumptuary laws, which separated accumulation and display by taking luxury commodities or fashions out of circulation and hedging them about with socially-specific signifying practices: in other words, a coun-terpart to commodity 'enclaving' in the sphere of representation and taste-formation.[18]

Enclaving of this type points to the character of the 'regimes of value' which existed throughout the Middle Ages, which did not need to take as their objects representations or true commodities at all. This brings me to what I take to be a central, but still rather neglected, point in understanding the practical and ideological formation of much medi-eval art produced under elite patronage: its emphasis on the objective material constituents of an artefact that was accorded any importance. I stress this point partly to counter the central role given to discussions of style or design, as opposed to material culture, in the discussion of medieval patronage (for example, Robert Branner's conception of the 'Court Style' under Louis IX of France) – not because I think discussion of style is unimportant, but because it, together with the very problem-atical notion of 'taste', is inadequate to the task of exposing for discus-sion aspects of medieval regimes of value.[19]

A classic instance of the conflict between style- and material-based appraisals of medieval art is posed by the use of marble and mosaic by high patrons in the late thirteenth century. Here the central English royal instance was the choice, entirely exceptional for a northern European Gothic church, of medieval Roman 'Cosmati' mosaics for the main floors, the shrine and the patron's tomb at Westminster Abbey, effected by both Henry III and Edward I.[20] The architecture of West-minster Abbey, certainly an important building for the subsequent development of English Gothic building, has normally been perceived as an outcrop of the French 'Court Style' first developed under Louis IX. Certain aspects of the building begun in 1245 – its plan, main interior elevations and window designs – are clearly dependent on prestigious French models like Reims Cathedral and Louis IX's Sainte-Chapelle, dedicated in 1248. The American architectural historian Robert Branner deduced from this that the English court had adopted

3. Westminster Abbey, Cosmati tomb of Henry III, completed *c*.1290. Reproduced by permission of the Royal Commission on the Historical Monuments of England, © Crown Copyright.

a self-conscious policy of modelling its major architectural enterprises on French court models, Louis' patronage acting as a kind of 'meta-patronage' for that of the Plantagenets. Through specific architectural conceits, notably its Reims cathedral-derived window tracery, Westminster Abbey signals its Frenchness. But Branner's deduction points to his agenda, since it totally ignored the Roman dimension of the building's most important fittings which are stylistically (and hence iconologically) incommensurate with the French aspects of the building's style. The agenda is simultaneously to base an account of Westminster on a bipolar nationalistic paradigm (French or English) and to reify the importance of 'modern' French Gothic architecture at the expense of a total view of the building's signifying works whose aesthetic character does not sustain the idea that modernity in this sense mattered to patrons.

The choice of Roman mosaics by English kings of course suggests a much more complex agenda, since such mosaics were not so fashionably Gothic as the building which enclosed them, but nevertheless carried with them an identifiable 'regime of value' precisely through their use of certain materials not commonly encountered in northern Europe in monumental decoration: porphyry, serpentine, glass mosaic and marbles. In both design and components, the sanctuary floor, shrine of St Edward and tomb of Henry III, works completed in the period 1268–90, are related directly to specifically papal commissions within the papal state itself, and to the work of contemporary artists like Arnolfo di Cambio implicated in such commissions. Marble, in which such mosaics were set, already formed an important part of English thirteenth-century cathedral building, and in this sense the material culture of Roman mosaics was tied to an already existing but very much older Romanesque, Byzantine and indeed ultimately antique Roman discourse of improvement, marble being simply 'better'. But the use of specifically papal decorative ideas suggests, at least to the present writer, that the visual policy of the Plantagenets was based in part on altogether more universalist, caesaro-papal, instincts. Whether or not such ideas existed in the form of some prior theoretical position – and this has been claimed for the 'policy' of Henry III – is not entirely germane: as with the 'imperial' dimension of Henry III's second Great Seal considered earlier, the signification of Westminster's *romanitas* inheres directly in the material culture of the works themselves.[21] They show something that is not independently evident in such evidence as we have from the period.

From this line of argument I would deduce the following points. First, we not only can, but should, see exceptional aesthetic choices in an ideological light: the use of a Roman art form and unusual materials in a Gothic context points to the conscious construction of a new set of significances by use, adaptation and ultimately appropriation. Westminster made that which was papal, royal; and such mosaics were not used in this way again because they had been enclaved to an entirely specialised ideological agenda. They were in effect spolia.

Secondly, the deployment of a caesaro-papal art form implies the establishment of new lineages – lineages, as it were, of aesthetic discrimination – which may be understandable in the light of the growing fashion in Western European royal and papal circles for ever more developed images of descent, continuity and filiation.[22] At precisely the same time in Rome, the occupation of the Holy See by members of significant Roman senatorial families brought about a conscious policy of redecorating the early Christian basilicas of Rome, in order to revive a sense of Rome's own *romanitas*.[23] As at Westminster, the product of this, in the sphere of the rebirth of fresco-painting in the generation of Giotto, was not a conservative but rather a radically new and perhaps unexpected aesthetic regime. Philip IV of France was the first French king to employ Roman painters at the French court after 1300. Philip also commissioned a sculpted genealogy of the kings of France from the earliest times for his major palace, the *Cité*, in Paris, strikingly resembling the new images of Apostolic succession then being executed in the Roman basilicas. Again, images and buildings linked directly to Edward I's patronage reveal exactly the same range of preoccupations, and we will consider those presently. In short, such policies indicate a much wider universalising consensus as to the value of certain art forms and images which transcended boundaries both of nation, style and of power-type.

Finally, we should note the complexity of these aesthetic regimes. To my mind this is a normal aspect of much medieval high patronage and its valuing of semi-precious materials and the essentially rhetorical value of *varietas* as the mark of outstanding patronage. But style analysis, seeking similarity and not difference, tends to obscure this point: royal patrons commanding great resources and responsible for the erection of great churches – and here there are obvious similarities between Henry III and the Luxembourg Emperor Charles IV's work at Karlstein Castle near Prague in the fourteenth century – proved to be natural *bricoleurs*, commanding artistic and material formulas of an entirely unique character, yet whose effects and constituents carried much more longstanding burdens of meaning.[24] Royal art is naturally eclectic, embodying what Appadurai has called 'semiotic virtuosity', that is the capacity to signal complex social messages.[25] I intend next to suggest that this virtuosity is linked more generally to the way the royal myths of power were themselves formed.

Necessary Fictions

There has been of late a resurgence of interest in the formation of royal mythology. In France this has occurred with special reference to the manipulation of texts and images in the 'official' royal chronicle continued at Saint-Denis, the *Grandes Chroniques*, and in England with reference to royal hagiography about St Edward the Confessor.[26] The field is a rich one, and attention has yet to be given to other formulations, notably of the coronation *ordines* of France and England, which might equally point to the subtle interaction of ideology and history in the shaping of royal myths of stability and continuity. In both France and England towards 1400 the claim that the coronation rite had effectively stabilised – a claim ultimately unsustainable given the character of all liturgies, especially rarely performed ones, to acrete symbolism and to mutate subtly – may help to explain why it was under Charles V of France and Richard II of England that 'definitive' illustrated coronation *ordines* were first produced.[27]

But this urge to stabilise that which was inherently fluid and manipulable was older, and in England we can examine it from the period in which it first becomes possible to identify the coherent formation of a mythology of kingship, namely the reign of Henry III. Under Henry, texts and images concerning St Edward are sufficiently commonplace for us to locate a distinct pattern or outlook on the part of the king and his immediate circle, notably the queen. To judge from Vauchez's account, St Edward was a latecomer to the stage of royal sainthood.[28] Like Louis IX, canonised in 1297, Edward offered an example of a certain type of virtuous rule.[29] But his cult was a local and not a popular one, in contrast to that of the 'opposition' figure Thomas of Canterbury, and it survived almost solely at the level of the interest of the political elite until the reign of Richard II who, like Henry, appears to have felt a special closeness to the saint king. At court, throughout the various residential palaces and castles, St Edward's image, as an icon or in narratives, was probably the most commonly seen. Notions of kingship were thus invested in royal biography, emphasising the continuing hold of the notion that right rule was identified not with a series of notional abstractions concerning good kingship, but rather in the cult of a certain type of royal personality.

So much was the implicit claim. But the specific ways in which Edward's own saintly reign were construed in the thirteenth century, most especially in the rewriting of his originally twelfth-century Latin hagiography in court French for Henry III and his queen, Eleanor, indicate the discrete operation of a manifesto. In a poem on the king composed and probably originally illuminated around 1240 by an author with distinct Benedictine interests – probably Matthew Paris – St Edward emerges as the representative of a kind of primitive claim, the claim to a primitive Golden Age of co-operative monarchy, harmonious barons and a united people.[30] This claim is substantiated by a brilliantly conceived literary and pictorial verisimilitude: the poem, *La Estoire de Seint Aedward le Rei*, is presented to us as history and not as a *roman*, a hagiographic genre also employed by Matthew. The text and illustrations are at one level 'naturalistic', brimming with an interest in ephemeral circumstantial evidence, and reportage-like anecdote. Offering a blow-by-blow narrative of the events of Edward's childhood, exile, miracles and rule, the text is also bolstered by liberal citations from papal bulls relating to the foundation by Edward of Westminster Abbey and the securing of its privileges. We find a detailed, as if eyewitness, account of the building of the abbey church under Edward's patronage, and lovingly attentive accounts of the goings-on at the papal curia.

The *Estoire*'s 'semiotic virtuosity' is thus based on two related strategies to form a voice of authority: its penchant for surface verisimilitude, carried forward into its naturalistic Gothic illuminations, establishes a voice of truth, while its citation of documents and other 'sources' establishes a note of authenticity. Both techniques are woven, though not without unevenness, into a narrative bricolage whose purpose is to put forward an absolutely persuasive, modern view of Edward's virtuous nature, while masking what is nevertheless disclosed throughout the text: a manifesto of right rule imposing certain norms of behaviour upon the king, namely that he should be co-operative, untyrannical and given to overwhelmingly generous patronage of the church (and Westminster Abbey in particular).

Fully-formed royal hagiography of this type, composed explicitly for the innermost royal circle of listeners and viewers, intertwines ideology and myth, a number of authenticating strategies, and the past and the present, in that form of pre-modern 'cold history' described by Lévi-Strauss.[31] And the aim of these strategies, many of them happily and self-consciously anachronistic (witness for example the attribution to Edward's Anglo-Saxon court of devotional practices absolutely typical of the thirteenth and not the eleventh century) is to establish a notion of *restoration* of a Golden Age. This tactic is markedly different from the impersonal notions of right rule and governance emerging in

neo-Aristotelian advice literature to princes at exactly this time, as in the work of Giles of Rome.[32] That which was to be restored was something essentially customary and local, something which could only be expressed in personal or mythic terms rather than ethical abstractions.

St Edward was of course displaced in the fourteenth century by St George, a foreign military saint to whom no notions of custom or peaceable tradition could accrue; whereas Edward represented an ideal notion of solidarity, George represented a martial, heroic mode of devotion free of national associations and the local constraints of relics, or history. By the reign of Edward III, George had been inscribed permanently into the pantheon of national saints represented on the Wilton Diptych. But this shift towards a more heroic stance had occurred earlier, under Edward I, who took warriors, whether kingly or not, as his public ideal of rulership. Under Edward we see for the first time an essentially late-medieval coalescence of romantic and biblical history, elevating new heroes – specifically King Arthur and the good leaders of the Old Testament like Judas Maccabeus, whose exploits were painted in the late thirteenth century on the walls of the Painted Chamber at Westminster – in such a way as to vaunt the active rather than the contemplative attributes of monarchy.[33] Edward's penchant, while similar to that of other aristocratic and royal patrons in France and the Low Countries towards 1300, was strikingly modern, and it was in this milieu that genres like the Nine Worthies – a selection of heroes including Arthur, Charlemagne and Judas Maccabeus – became popular forms of seigneurial interior decoration especially in tapestries.[34] This breaching of the conventional boundaries lying around biblical and romantic material is fundamental to the history of later medieval secular art, and emphasises the role of the secular in promoting unconventional alliances of ideas.

Central to Edward I's policy was also a form of universalism. Henry III, though bound to the myths of a local saint-king, had as we have already seen started the process whereby English royal patronage could assimilate caesaro-papal art forms by employing the Cosmati at Westminster, something continued by his son. Edward's policy was however more thoroughgoing, and more self-consciously imperialist. His

4. Life of St Edward, Cambridge University Library MS Ee. III. 59, *c*.1255. Edward in exile is told of his accession and returns to England. Reproduced by permission of the Syndics of Cambridge University Library.

masons erecting the castles in Wales invoked at Caernarvon the splendour of the striped masonry and polygonal towers of the Theodosian ramparts of Constantinople.[35] Edward I especially had a keen eye for what we might describe as British rather than English precedent. Arthur's cult was a central, if pragmatic, plank in his campaigns in Wales. In the course of Edward's campaigns in Scotland an illustrated genealogical roll was produced in courtly style at St Mary's Abbey York (for a while the home of the royal Exchequer), which substantiated the antiquity of the Plantagenet dynasty by tying it to the myths of Brutus, Troy and Jason, in effect generating a foundation-myth for the claim to Scotland.[36] Finally, Edward promoted a highly organised administrative search for written evidence for the claim, resorting, as Clanchy noted, to both myth and physical symbols.[37] Of the latter the Stone of Scone, the coronation seat of the Scottish kings taken by Edward in 1296 and installed by the shrine of St Edward in a special throne, was the most concrete. This installation is especially revealing. Though the Stone was tied as a trophy of Scotland's subjection to the relics of a national saint who had embodied an older vision of the personal character of power, Edward's action indicates the way that St Edward's shrine had now come to symbolise something essentially impersonal – the symbolic centre of the realm of England – at a time when the cult of St Edward himself had weakened decisively. The Coronation Chair, with the gilded representation of a seated king on its back, exemplified a purely symbolic presence in the manner of the Great Seals examined earlier; but the presence is that of the English state itself. The Stone of Scone symbolised territory, the movement of significant earth. Its life history was central to its authenticity and hence its value as a proof, and of it we might remark with Appadurai that 'the transfer of commodities in warfare always has a special symbolic intensity'.[38] Edward I was, like his father, a natural appropriator, and the way he gathered and displayed his booty is of importance to us in marking the first signs of the shift towards a late-medieval sense of nation and statehood.

Conclusion

From what has been said here, it will I hope be clear that the case for a purely aesthetic reading of royal art patronage is no more sustainable than a straightforward iconographic reading of court imagery; both are important, and the understanding of both is a prerequisite, but neither is adequate. The ideology – or, more simply, mythology – of the English medieval court's visual culture has to be sought less in the intersection of these forms of reading than in deeper structural issues. Aesthetic accounts are seldom ideologically neutral; some of the longest-established accounts of court art as the narrative of various 'Court Styles' disclose on analysis a deeper preoccupation with forms of modernity, with the court as one, if not the leading, agent of modernisation. What I have suggested here, through discussing images of order and hierarchy, notions of display, and the construction of mythologies, is that to understand court art is to take account not of modernisation, but rather of the ways that groups in power either remember, or choose to construct, their pasts, so as to substantiate claims for the future directly invested in the production of art. In doing so I have suggested that the material culture of court art was dominated by mythical thinking linked to the manufacturing of the court's sense of its own past and identity, and, above all, that art had a central role in constituting medieval regimes of order and hierarchy.

6

HERALDRY AND HIERARCHY: ESQUIRES AND GENTLEMEN

Maurice Keen

Francis Thynne, Lancaster herald, wrote in 1605 that 'in ancient time' heraldic arms were 'the peculiar reward and honour of military service'.[1] If one looks back to those beautiful products of heraldic art, the English rolls of arms of the thirteenth and early fourteenth centuries, they offer eloquent confirmation of this statement. A high proportion of them are occasional rolls – rolls, that is to say, recording the arms of warriors who mustered for particular hosts, or took part in particular and known tournaments. Thus we have the Falkirk Roll, blazoning the arms of English knights and bannerets present at the battle of Falkirk, 22 July 1298; the Galloway Roll, blazoning the arms of 259 knights who were with King Edward I on his Scottish campaign of 1300; the Stirling Roll blazoning the arms of knights present at the siege of Stirling in 1304; and the first and second Dunstable Rolls, blazoning the arms of those who engaged in two tournaments at Dunstable, a traditional tourneying site, in 1308 and 1334.[2] This is by no means an inclusive list of the 'occasional' rolls of this period. Taken all together, they emphasise vividly and visually the strong association of heraldic insignia with battle and tournament in this age, and the martial quality of secular aristocratic culture.

A striking feature of all these early rolls of arms is that none of them attributes arms to anyone of lesser status than that of knight bachelor. The history of the English tournament confirms that in the martial world this was regarded as a significant cut-off point. In Richard I's ordinance regulating tournaments (the first of its kind) the humblest figure to be admitted to tourney was the landless knight.[3] Edward I's *Statuta Armorum* (1292) likewise limited full participation in tournaments to knights: each knight was allowed to bring three armed squires to the combat, but the arms they were to wear in their caps were to be their lord's, not their own.[4] If, however, we look forward to the Tudor age of the heralds' visitations, we find a cut-off point that, in terms of the recognition of the capacity to bear heraldic arms, is quite different. The early rolls of arms divided the armigerous into two categories, the knights bachelor and the lords (earls, barons and bannerets, who were all of course themselves knights). By the time of Henry VIII there were four categories, lords (now subdivided by a more refined series of gradations: duke, marquis, earl, viscount, baron), and knights, esquires, and gentlemen below the rank of esquire. By no means all 'mere' gentlemen in the time of Henry VIII would have had their own armorial bearings, but in principle they were accepted to be potentially armigerous, provided they could satisfy certain requirements: that they had sufficient possessions and riches ('lands and possessions of free tenure to the value of £10 sterling or in moveable goods £300 sterling'), and that 'they be not issued of vile blood [nor] rebels to our Person nor heretics contrary to the faith'.[5] We are already well on our way to the point where John Selden, the seventeenth-century antiquary, when he stumbled across a reference to a witness in the Court of Chivalry dispute between Lord Grey and Sir Edward Hastings in the early fifteenth century who stated that he was a gentleman of ancestry but had no arms, would declare this to be something 'the like whereof or anything of that nature I have not elsewhere observed'.[6]

   This extension of the range and the greater refinement of the degrees of those capable of being armigerous reflects heraldically a growing preoccupation with gradation which was a striking feature of English social history in the later Middle Ages, and which is also evidenced in other ways. It is very marked, for instance, in the sumptuary legislation of Edward III and Edward IV. Edward III's statute of 1363 'against the outrageous and excessive apparel of divers people against their estate and degree' limited 'esquires and other gentlemen under the estate of a knight' to cloth worth four and a half marks the whole cloth for their vesture and hose; richer esquires were limited to cloth worth five marks, lesser knights to cloth worth six marks. Greater knights, with revenues of 400 marks and above, might choose cloth as they wished, but must not trim their robes with ermine.[7] Edward IV's statute of 1463 reserved cloth of gold to the lords, forbade knights to wear cloth of 'velvet upon velvet', unless they were knights of the Garter, and forbade damask and satin to esquires and gentlemen under the degree of knight.[8] The distinctions of these statutes may be compared with those of the Poll Tax of 1379, which graduated a descending level of fiscal charges designed to take account of the wealth and degree of those liable. At the top of the scale came the two dukes, John of Gaunt and John of Brittany, charged at 10 marks each; then came the earls, at £4; the barons and knights banneret (greater knights, entitled to raise a square banner in the king's hosts), at 40s; knights bachelor and those liable to be distrained to knighthood (that is with £40 per annum or more from their lands), at 20s; landed esquires, at 6s 8d; and esquires who were landless but who were armed or in service, at 3s 4d.[9] The same preoccupation with defining a man's degree or 'mystery' (his occupation), as constituting an essential element of his identity, probably also coloured the regulation of the Statute of Additions of 1413, that in all indictments (and writs of personal actions) 'additions' should be included, identifying the 'estate or degree, or mystery' of the person indicted.[10] It was as a result of that statute that the word 'gentleman' first found its way into official legal records as a title of 'estate or degree' clearly distinct from that of esquire and from other superior degrees of gentility.[11]

Set alongside the heraldic evidence, this evidence from fourteenth- and fifteenth-century legislation is significant, firstly, as illustrative of the preoccupation with precise social gradation which seems to be characteristic of late medieval England, and of which there is other witness too. When Chaucer, for instance, set out to describe his fellow pilgrims on the road to Canterbury, he felt that his first duty 'accordaunt to resoun' was

> To telle you al the condicioun
> Of ech of hem, so as it seemed me,
> And whiche they weren, and of what degree,
> And eek in what array that they were inne.[12]

The legislative record is significant, secondly, in that in each example it appears to confirm that esquires, and in the case of Edward IV explicitly 'mere' gentlemen also, were considered as belonging with knights and other persons of superior grade to that upper tranche of society that could be distinguished as *gentilz*.[13] That this had come to be considered to be a significant cut-off point is indicated by other legislative evidence. The next degree down after the gentleman in the descending scale of social gradation was the yeoman: the statute of 1445 which regulated eligibility to represent a shire in parliament bluntly rejected as ineligible any man 'which standeth in the degree of Yeoman and under'.[14] Yeomanry could include men who were distinctly substantial in economic terms: Sir John Fortescue believed that there were some who could lay out more than £100 in the year.[15] A yeoman was not, however, of sufficient status to speak for his shire in the community of the realm assembled in parliament. That was reserved for a different sort of people: knights, notable esquires and gentlemen.

Two further points need to be noted about the extension of the ranks of the aristocratic and potentially armigerous in late medieval England to include, beside and beyond knights, esquires and gentlemen. First, it really was an extension. The Parliamentary Roll of Arms, drawn up early in the reign of Edward II and so dating from the period when the rolls did not recognise as armigerous any of lower rank than knights bachelor, is the nearest that medieval England ever produced to a national armorial; there are some 1,100 names on the roll, with a blazon of arms given for each.[16] Careful scrutiny of other sources has recovered the names of up to some 150 to 200 knights not mentioned in the roll but who were probably alive at the time of its compilation; let us say some 1,250 lords and knights in all.[17] An estimate for the year 1500 suggests that at that date there were some 60 peers, 500 knights, 800 esquires and 5,000 gentlemen entitled to coats of arms.[18] Allowance needs to be made in the first case for a substantial number of land-owners of Edward II's day rich enough to take up knighthood but who had not done so, in the second for a still more substantial number of gentlemen who did not, as yet, boast a coat of arms. Figures for the late Middle Ages are inevitably imprecise and impressionistic, because the sources are not adequate for the purposes of numerical precision. Even allowing a handsome margin for error, however, it seems abundantly clear that the parameters of genteel aristocratic society, as measured heraldically (and that is no bad index of contemporary socio-cultural assumptions) had been extended very significantly. The perception of the shape of the upper echelons of the social hierarchy had clearly altered, substantially.

My second point concerns the nature of that perception, and is of particular relevance in the context of the focus of the present collection of essays. The Parliamentary Roll of Arms offers something approaching a directory of the Knights of England about the year 1310. In the traditional tripartite division of Christian society into three functionally related orders, the men who pray and the men who fight and the men who work, the knights – the chivalry – constituted the second estate, the secular warrior aristocracy. The Parliamentary Roll of Arms could thus be fitted comfortably into that framework, as a directory of the chivalry of England. The coats of arms blazoned by each name on it, and which the bearer would have worn at war and in the tournament, are ensigns of the functional, martial role of the chivalry. Looking forward to around 1500, though the (say) 5,000 armigerous gentlemen of the day undoubtedly belonged to a social group which had an important and influential part to play in the direction of English society, it would be impossible to categorise their role in a comparably straightforward functional manner. At the upper end of the aristocratic hierarchy, the peers did not now distinguish themselves from those of lesser rank by any special military significance (as of tenants in chief, with a right to raise their banner in the king's host), but rather by their position in parliament. At the other end of the scale, it would be hard to identify any special function identifying the gentlemen. Clearly, between 1300 and 1500 there had been something more – and much more – than a refinement and extension of the gradations of the aristocratic hierarchy: there had been a shift in the perception of their significance, and of the significance of coats of arms, the ensigns of gentility. Here is matter surely worth pursuing in a collection of essays dedicated to the history of orders and hierarchies.

* * *

Let us go back to the two 'new grades' added to the hierarchy of gentility in the late Middle Ages, the esquires and gentlemen who were not recognised as armigerous by the heralds of the time of the early rolls of arms, but who clearly were so recognised by their successors in the days of Henry VII and Henry VIII. What was it, my first question must be, that carried them forward into the charmed circle of the armigerous?

    The rise of the esquire is a subject which has attracted a good deal of attention recently. There seems to be considerable agreement that the position of the esquires 'crystallised' somewhere around the mid four-teenth century, and this has most commonly been explained in terms of what Peter Coss has called 'territoriality', the significance of the position

of lesser landowners, not of knightly rank, in local administration and
office holding and of the lateral and familial ties that gave this social
group, regionally at least, a degree of homogeneity.[19] This chronology
tallies well with the heraldic evidence: in the second Dunstable Roll of
1334, as in the Parliamentary Roll of Arms, esquires are notable by their
absence. The rolls of the later fourteenth century, however, like
Sir George Calveley's book, the County Roll, and the Norfolk and
Suffolk Roll, do blazon the arms of substantial numbers of men who
were not knights.[20] Sir Robert Laton's Roll (*c*.1370, now lost), which
according to his testimony in the *Scrope* v. *Grosvenor* dispute he wrote
down at his father's dictation, blazoned the arms of all the 'kings,
princes, dukes, earls, lords, knights and esquires' that his father could
remember.[21]

This heraldic 'rise' of the esquires, their recognition specifically as
armigerous, would however seem to have been connected not so much
with territoriality directly as with the very significant part that men
of their status had come to play in the great campaigns of the fourteenth century. In indentures of the mid fourteenth century the words
'esquire' and 'man at arms' are used more or less interchangeably,
denoting the mounted troops superior in military status to the archers;
and as Andrew Ayton has recently shown, very large numbers of such
men served in some of the greater hosts of the mid-century. There were
perhaps as many as 4,000 men at arms at the siege of Calais (1346–7),
and over 3,000 in the host that Edward III led to France in 1359.[22] In
the specific context of the recognition of the esquires as armigerous, it
would therefore seem, we are still very far from breaking away from the
traditional functional association between secular aristocratic status and
the martial calling. The very word 'esquire' (Latin *scutifer*, *armiger*) has
indeed strong military connotations: in origin it denoted a knight's
servant who cared for his arms and horses and was often used in the
romances to describe an apprentice knight.[23]

In 1389 Richard II granted a patent to one John Kingston, whereby
he received him into the estate of gentility and made him an esquire,
so that he might take up the challenge of a French knight to perform
'certain deeds of arms'; and at the same time he granted him a coat of
arms, argent, a *chapeau* azure, with an ostrich plume gules.[24] As this
patent illustrates, esquires were coming now to do martially just those
things which knights had traditionally done. Some among them, like
John Kingston, were coming to take a full part in jousts and tournaments; some were indenting as captains of companies (when they would

need a coat, and a pennon of arms). In war they were serving, in the larger companies, alongside knights in much the same armour and on much the same conditions, except in the matter of rates of pay.[25] As shown by the repeated references to the 'talk of old knights and esquires' in Court of Chivalry testimony,[26] in cases such as the disputes over armorial bearings of Scrope and Grosvenor or of Lords Lovel and Morley, esquires were just as steeped as those a notch above them in the military hierarchy in the lore of chivalry and heraldry. In heraldic terms they had earned their place in knightly company in the rolls of arms, by prowess and service; and that service may indeed have had more to do with the recognition of their standing, not only heraldically but in broader social terms, than is often allowed.

*   *   *

In the story of the fourteenth-century 'rise' of the esquires, the word 'rise' needs to be handled with caution. There is no hint in it of the *escuierie* seeking consciously as a social group to push themselves forward, or of there being any vested group interest that distinguished them from the knighthood. If anything, the initiative seems to have come from above rather than from below; the key seems to be the social recognition of the esquires by their superiors and such experts in precedence as the heralds – recognition made explicit in statutes and legal usage. We are not witnessing the 'arrival' of a new class or estate, but rather a shift in the line of demarcation separating the gentle from the non-gentle, expanding the ranks of the former to embrace a wider range of people whose way of living gave them something of the quality of a lesser knighthood or *petite noblesse*. The fourteenth-century esquires, for the most part, came of landowning families, as did the knights; they served and fought alongside knights in campaign retinues; locally and regionally, they played their part in administration as stewards, keepers of the peace and jurors, as knights did, though most often in somewhat humbler capacities. Their so-called rise does not belong to the model-world of revolutionary pressures, but seems rather to represent an adjustment of the hierarchical scales which can in many ways be viewed as a natural consequence of the rise in the social profile of knighthood in the preceding century (which saw a significant decline in the numbers of those taking up knighthood) and the essential comparability of the lifestyle and functional role of lesser knights and substantial esquires.[27]

* * *

By the end of the Middle Ages, as has been stated earlier, there was a
further recognised grade of the aristocratic hierarchy below that of the
esquires, the 'mere' gentlemen. By then they too were recognised as
armigerous: it was the idea of a gentleman of ancestry without coat
armour that, later, so surprised John Selden. What of them? What is the
story of their 'rise'? It would seem that it was very similar to the story of
the esquires: indeed, in many ways it looks as if it may be part of the
same story.

The word 'gentleman', as a title of degree distinct from and inferior
to 'esquire', came to be employed formally in legal instruments in
consequence of the Statute of Additions of 1413.[28] In fact, the history of
the usage goes back a little further. The 1363 sumptuary laws referred
to 'esquires and all manner of gentlemen under the estate of knight'.[29]
Among the humbler martial witnesses in the Court of Chivalry case of
Lovel v. *Morley* (1386/7), most of whom described themselves as esquires,
we find a small handful who described themselves simply as gentlemen
or as of gentle blood.[30] In 1384 we find Richard II granting to a servant
seven and a half pence a day to support the 'estate' of gentleman, to
which the king had advanced him (no mention of the rank of esquire,
or of entitlement to coat armour, as in the same king's comparable
patent to John Kingston).[31] Nevertheless, it is not misleading to begin
the story of the mere gentleman, as Sir George Sitwell did in a famous
article, with the Statute of Additions, for it was in the decades following
1413, in the first half of the fourteenth century, that use of the designa-
tion seems really to have caught on.

As we are reminded by the very large number of men who took part
in such campaigns as those of 1347, 1359 and 1385 and who could, in
military terminology at least, be called esquires, one of the troubles
about that category was that it covered such a wide spectrum. The
gradations of the 1379 Poll Tax make the same point: at one extreme
stand the esquires with sufficient income from lands to support knighthood (and who in most cases would have come from families with
knights in their ancestry); at the other, landless esquires who have been
armed or are in service, many of whom had presumably very little to
support their estate at all.[32] For an age preoccupied with niceties of
gradation this spectrum was uncomfortably broad and diverse. All the
aristocracy, kings, lords, knights and others, were alike *gentils*. That was
their common bond. But there was a need to distinguish, to grade, a

need now almost visibly acute in the expanded, lower reaches of the hierarchy. The result seems to have been to endow the word 'esquire' with a degree of upward mobility in the social vocabulary (the same thing happened to the word 'knight' in an earlier time and for different, if comparable, reasons). What was left behind to the lesser esquires, and some others, was their gentility; they were gentlemen. So the word 'gentleman', on its own, came to be used to describe men who might once have aspired to be counted among the lesser esquires and some more besides.

The word 'gentleman', unlike the words 'knight' and 'esquire', does not have a specifically military ring. It is nevertheless clear that in the period when gentlemen were coming to be recognised as armigerous, the name often carried strong military associations. The excuse given by the Yorkshireman William Tomlinson in 1419 to Henry V's recruiting agents, who put it to him that he was 'able of person' and wealthy enough to serve the king, makes the point nicely and negatively: 'says he is no gentleman'.[33] The orders given by Thomas Montagu, earl of Salisbury, to his soldiers for his sieges in Maine in 1424 actually seem to equate gentlemen with men at arms (as men at arms had earlier been equated with esquires): 'also every vii gentlemen or men at arms make themselves a good and sufficient ladder of xv rungs'.[34] When in 1437 Calais appeared to be threatened, orders went out from the council to 'array' gentlemen in each 'country' to be ready to succour the garrison.[35] Nearly a century later, the same sort of association underlies the certificate listing for Northumberland 'the names of thoes gentyllmen of Northumberland wyth a declaracion of what habyllitie they ar to doo the Kyng's hyghnes service'.[36] The context makes it clear that 'service' here means military service.

This association of gentility and the word 'gentleman' with martial function is, as one would expect, most clearly marked in heraldic contexts. *Chescun gentil est homme d'armes*, says Richard Strangeways' heraldic book (*c*.1450).[37] Thomas of Clarence, in his ordinance for heralds (*c*.1417, of which more anon), exhorted the officers of arms to 'have knowledge of all those of noble and gentle estate living and dwelling in [their] provinces, and know the names of all those of such degree . . . and principally of those who ought to bear coat armour in the service of our sovereign lord'.[38] In the first grant of arms made by a herald of which a full text has survived, Garter, in his patent for Edmund Mylle (1454), confirmed that he had been assured by 'common report of worthy men that Edmund Mylle had long followed the career of arms' and had borne himself so honourably as to be worthy 'that he and his posterity shall in all places be honourably admitted ... among the number and in the company of men of old gentility': wherefore, said Garter, he had granted Mylle arms.[39] A fifteenth-century heraldic tract transcribed by Thynne, on the 'discommodities that may growe to an army for lacke of ensignes', brings out nicely that the distinction between esquire and gentleman was not lost on its author. An esquire, it is here stated, should have a pennon of arms, a gentleman a *guidon* (a small forked flag), 'for an esquire, gentleman or captain to be known thereby, so that all his men do follow him'.[40] In all these texts, an assumed connection between gentility, heraldic arms and ensigns, and a military function is evident. This should not surprise: an association of gentility, high and low, with martial activities was traditional.

*   *   *

In Garter's reference in his patent to Edmund Mylle's admission 'among the number and company of men of *old* gentility', we can, however, see another consideration besides the military entering importantly into consideration. The same is true of three documents of Henry V's reign, which likewise have a predominantly military and armorial context, but likewise hint at something more that is significant. They are worth looking at carefully.

The first is a writ of Henry V of 2 June 1417, directed to the sheriffs of Hampshire, Wiltshire, Sussex and Dorset, in which counties his host for the invasion of Normandy was mustering. It runs as follows:

> Item, we will and strictly charge you shall make proclamation that no man, of whatever status, rank or condition he may be, shall take to himself arms or a tunic of arms unless he possess or ought to possess the same by ancestral right or by the grant of some person having authority sufficient thereunto, [and] that all, except those who bore arms with the King at Agincourt, shall on a certain day declare their arms, and by what grant they have them, ... under pain of exclusion from the expedition which is about to set out, loss of their wages, and defacement of the said arms and tunics called 'coate armures'.[41]

Two points of particular interest emerge from this text. One is that Henry seems to set special store by the service of men of 'arms and ancestry' – of old gentility that is – being even, apparently, prepared to dispense with the service of those who pretended to that condition without justification. This point is confirmed by a subsequent instruction of his, to the commissioners who in 1421 were raising archers for him, to seek especially among those who were *de prosapie generosa*, of gentle birth.[42] The second point is that he clearly expected people to be able to prove their right to arms by ancestral use or in consequence of a formal grant (presumably from the king, or from a major captain, or from one of his heralds, who we know were by this time making grants).[43]

The second document re-emphasises the first of these two points. On 29 December, 1419, in the effort to recruit reinforcements for Henry V's army in France, Humphrey Duke of Gloucester as Guardian of the Realm despatched writs on the king's behalf to the justices of the peace in the various counties of the kingdom:

> Commanding and firmly charging you that in all possible haste you shall choose and appoint from the knights and esquires of the county of Cambridge [I quote from the Cambridge writ] who bear arms of ancestry such as in your good discretion seem able and sufficient to serve us in their own persons to the number of twelve lances . . . the names of which persons we will that you shall certify explicitly and openly under your seals to our council.[44]

The writs are interesting in that they give an indication, through the number of lances requested, of what the comparative genteel military potential of various counties was seen to be. Thus Cheshire, for instance, was asked for 30 lances, Devon, Somerset and Norfolk (among others) for 20, Cambridge, Oxford and Wiltshire for 12, Rutland for a mere four.[45] What is important in the present context, however, is the repetition of the emphasis, already seen in Henry V's instructions of 1417 and 1421, on the recruitment for military service of men entitled to coat armour, of old-established gentility.

Returns to the writs of 1419 survive for 28 counties. From these it can be shown, by comparison with other documents, that although the writs asked for knights and esquires, the names returned included persons who were – or soon would be – identified as 'mere' gentlemen. The 1419 references may be compared, for instance, with the lists of 1434 of those of sufficient status in their county communities to have been sworn individually to uphold the peace. Thus the 1419 Essex return includes the names of 10 men who in 1434 were either themselves described as esquires or came of families who were of that degree, and two names of men who, below that line, seem in 1434 to be considered as mere gentlemen.[46] The Herefordshire justices in 1419 returned the names (amongst others) of nine men who were described as esquires in 1434 and two who were then classified among the gentlemen.[47] Christine Carpenter's exhaustive directory of Warwick gentry, derived from a number of sources, enables one to suggest a status for all the men of 1419 for that county, in their own right or *via* a close connection. 13 names in all are involved (10 lances were requested, but some were unwilling to serve and there are 13 names on the list). There are two knights, two esquires from established knightly families, four other 'etablished' esquires, four men whose degree seems to hover between gentleman and esquire (on the whole on a rising curve), and one who, appearing as an esquire early in the century, loses that degree (or seems to) by 1436.[48] Taken together, these county lists offer a useful glimpse at the process in operative development, whereby the once broad category of armigerous esquires was coming to be distinguished into two grades. Most of the men selected for martial service in 1419 were ranked, unsurprisingly, as esquires in the 1430s: but the poorer and humbler among them, by that time, were being associated rather with the large group of men of some local substance not ranked in that degree, and of varied background (including, no doubt, some of their fellow soldiers, but also others whose claims to gentility rested on other bases).

The third text of Henry V's reign that must claim attention is the already mentioned ordinance to the heralds, issued by Henry's brother, Thomas Duke of Clarence, as Steward of England and Constable of the king's host, some time between 1417 and 1421.[49] The association of established gentility, heraldic arms and martial service is stressed here again: heralds must know the names of those dwelling in their provinces 'who ought to bear coat armour in the service of our sovereign lord'. This instruction and further numerous references to the duties of Kings of Arms and heralds in their provinces or marches show, as Wagner puts it, 'a well developed system of provincial jurisdiction and visitation'[50] in operation, and long anticipating the recorded visitations of the Tudor period. True, the ordinances do not make any reference to the defacement of the arms of those not entitled by gentility to bearings, as the Tudor instructions do; but the process is clearly alluded to in Henry V's own instruction of 1417, quoted earlier.[51] The inhibition to the heralds, against granting arms to persons of 'vile blood', dishonest reputation or inadequate substance, that appears in, for instance, Henry VIII's commission for a visitation in 1530, does however appear in Clarence's orders.[52] The background to the Tudor visitations was the near obsession of gentlemen with their right to coat armour and with the precedence it gave them: here already, in Henry V's reign, we can see signs of the way things would go. We can also see that already, around 1419, there were experts whose business it was to register the names (and the names of the issue) of the sort of people who 'ought to bear coat armour in the service of the king' and from among whom, in that year, the justices of the peace were instructed to recruit lances.

In all these texts of Henry V's reign we see the same second preoccupation coming into prominence alongside the traditional military and functional implication of the right to coat armour: the anxiety that it should be limited to those with an established claim to arms, either (preferably) by ancestry or by official grant. What this ushered in for the heralds, as experts in precedence and registrars of honour and gentility, was a steadily growing concern with pedigree, with ancestral rank and the stake in the land that it implied. With passing time, moreover, this second preoccupation, as I have called it, seems steadily to advance toward pride of place in hierarchical thinking. Later medieval rolls of arms progressively became more rarely 'occasional' (recording arms displayed at a tournament or muster), more and more commonly regional. Long before the end of the fifteenth century, the heralds are beginning to be collectors of pedigrees.[53] Steadily, the signs become surer of a shift of emphasis in the perception of the significance of the hierarchical structure to which heraldry gave emblematic expression, away from its relation to martial function toward a relation with a genealogically established place in regional and national society. The shift is paralleled in the growth of claims, in the fifteenth century, for a functional title to gentility for other occupations beside the military. Robin Storey in a seminal article has examined the rise in that time of the 'gentleman' bureaucrats of the Chancery and other administrative offices.[54] To Chief Justice Fortescue, writing in the 1460s, it seemed that there was 'scarcely a man learned in the laws to be found in the realm, who is not genteel or sprung of gentle lineage', and he viewed the Inns of Court as schools of gentility as well as of legal learning.[55] Fortescue's father was a tried warrior: his claim is a nice indication of the way in which in his day the perception of gentility was shifting away from lineage and martial occupation toward magistracy, blood and patrimony.

*   *   *

Their military role, it would seem in conclusion, was probably the most potent force carrying the esquires and gentlemen of the English later Middle Ages into the ranks of the armigerous (which, as was pointed out earlier, is not precisely the same as gentility, though the two are closely connected). Once established, however, their armigerous right came to be seen in rather different terms of significance. Emblematic of old blood and ancestral dignity, it began to be viewed more and more in terms of the maintenance of the social status quo, and as expressing the value, not of function in relation to hierarchy, but of hierarchy itself. In an age which saw hierarchy as integral to the maintenance of social order, indeed to society itself, the extension of the grades of aristocracy facilitated the refurbishing of the strength of the hierarchical principle and its reinterpretation in broader terms. At the same time it worked for the absorption of social pressures which might otherwise have developed into tensions, and that without rendering the barriers against upward social mobility from a still lower level too inflexible. Pedigree looks like a more exclusive touchstone than function, but the appearance is superficial. As the splendid and often absurd saga of Tudor genealogical forgery makes plain, pedigree is not difficult for the *arriviste* to manufacture after the event. The Pastons had already pointed the way for that future in the fifteenth century. Thrift and drive carried them upward from husbandry through the law to squirearchy: once there they were not slow to find a pedigree that carried them back (spuriously) to coat armour that had been borne by an ancestor who was a fighting man in the time of the Norman kings.[56] What they were seeking, though, was not a martial connection, but old blood. That was what they felt they needed to give them a visible, heraldically attested niche in the hierarchy of status.

Long after the time when the Pastons rehearsed their descent for Edward IV, John Selden, musing on the ancestry of the title esquire, wrote:

As in those elder times of military action, such gentlemen as were employed in service . . . were frequently, it seems, for distinction from the rest, called esquire (into which title some were also created), so at length, especially in the times of peace, when military service could make but little distinction, those that by birth or other eminence were commonly thought worthy of some note of distinction above the ordinary rank of gentleman have had the same title given to them.[57]

The Pastons prove here, as so often, forward-looking. Aspirants to gentility (and thence to esquirey and thence to knighthood) they sought the evidences that they were so entitled through their county connections, their good marriages, their manorial lordship[58] – those 'other eminences' that defined their place in the hierarchy *per se*. To cap it all firmly, they understood that they must also claim eminence of birth, for they knew (as Nicholas Upton, the contemporary of William, the founder of their dynasty, put it) that 'he is gentyll that descendyth of gentyll stok'.[59] Though they remained significantly anxious to assert their right to coat armour by long descent, they do not seem to have felt any need to make play of martial scenes where ancestors of theirs (genuine or otherwise) had worn that coat armour. Their attitude nicely reflects here the shift of perception of their day in the matter of standing in the hierarchy as heraldically measured, away from function toward a newly sharp emphasis on pedigree.

7

THE RISINGS OF THE COMMONS
IN ENGLAND, 1381–1549

Michael Bush

A Tradition of Revolt

The Pilgrimage of Grace broke out in October 1536, affecting most of the north and raising nine armies manned by 50,000 men. Its threat to march on London extracted from the government a pardon for every rebel and the promise of a parliament at York to consider its grievances. It saw itself as a rising of the commons.[1] Each army was the commons militant; its leaders were called captains of the commons; its manifestos were issued with 'the consent of the commons'; its oath was 'to be true to God, the king and the commons'; its cause was seen as 'the business of the commons'; its complaints were described as 'the griefs of the commons'; the 24 articles it submitted to the government were referred to as 'the commons' petition'; and those resisting the uprising were regarded as 'traitors to the commons'. 'Commons' was the cry to raise revolt: not 'Dacre, a Dacre', not comrades, goodfellows, neighbours, brothers, liegemen. The term meant commonalty, not community, and designated that level of society below the gentlemen and the clergy.[2]

Idiomatically a rising of the commons, the Pilgrimage of Grace was by no means a new form of revolt. It subscribed to an insurrectionary tradition that reached back to 1381, when the rebels of Kent and Essex were described as 'the commons' by all the chroniclers (that is, Walsingham, Knighton, Froissart and the *Anonimalle Chronicle*), and presented as marching in hosts on London with the boast that 'ever they were the king's men and the noble commons of England' (Froissart). Having been taken by the rebels and obliged to carry a message to the king, Sir John Newton declared to him: 'Sire, the commons of this your realm hath sent me to you to desire you to come and speak with them on Blackheath' (Froissart).[3] According to Walsingham, a letter from the rebels in London was sent to the abbot of St Albans requiring him 'to come and answer the commons'. With typical prejudice, the same chronicler claimed that 'at that time they gloried in such a name' and 'according to their foolish minds there would be no lords thereafter but only king and commons'.[4]

The same idiom was used in the uprising of 1450. All three of its petitions employed the term. One was offered as the voice of the commons: 'These be the desires of the true commons of your sovereign lord the king'.[5] In one of its clauses the king's true commons required him to get rid of the affinity of the duke of Suffolk; in another, to punish false traitors. The same petition presented Jack Cade as 'captain of the commons'. According to another petition, the king's 'lords are lost, his merchandise is lost, his commons destroyed', all as a result of the bad advice he had received. Therefore, the king's liegemen of Kent had assembled to provide redress 'with the help of the king . . . and all the commons of England, and to die therefore'.

Forming part of the same tradition of revolt was the Yorkshire uprising of 1489. One of its muster proclamations read: 'all the north parts . . . shall be ready in their defensible array . . . for to gainstand such persons as is aboutward for to destroy [the king] and the commons of England', closing with the statement 'and all this to be fulfilled and kept by every ilk commoner upon pain death'.[6] The Cornish uprising of 1497 fell into the same category of revolt. A feature of the tradition was a march on London. The rebels of 1381 and 1450 reached their goal, apprehended the evil ministers taking refuge in the Tower and executed them; the Yorkshire rebels of 1489, like those of 1536, got no further than Doncaster. Amazingly, considering the distance they had to march, the Cornish rebels of 1497 reached Blackheath, camping where both the rebels of 1381 and 1450 had camped, only to be cut down by the king's army.[7] This was described in the *Great Chronicle of London*: 'in the latter end of May the commons of Cornwall gathered them in great numbers and chose unto them a blacksmith for their head captain'. The chronicler declared that behind the explicit aim of removing a number of evil ministers responsible for imposing a hated tax was the hidden agenda to do 'as Jack Straw (of 1381), Jack Cade (of 1450) and other rebels did before them'.[8]

The tradition culminated in the two huge rebellions of 1536, the Lincolnshire uprising and the Pilgrimage of Grace, soon followed by the Postpardon revolts of 1537 and the two large-scale uprisings of 1549, Kett's rebellion in East Anglia and the Prayer Book uprising in Devon and Cornwall.[9] The Prayer Book uprising produced a petition entitled 'sixteen articles of us the commoners of Devon and Cornwall in divers camps by east and west Exeter'.[10] Again, it planned to march on London so as to bring to the notice of the boy king the fact that the government was ruling badly. Its main chronicler, John Hooker, described a movement of the commons: 'the commons . . . having driven the gentlemen to flight, do openly show themselves traitors and rebels; and therefore assembling themselves do appoint out captains': a tailor, a shoemaker, a labourer and a fish-drier. He then identified another central feature of the tradition, declaring: 'howbeit, it was not long before that certain gentlemen and yeomen of good countenance and credit, both in Devon and Cornwall, were contented not only to be associates of this rebellion but also to carry the cross before this procession and to be captains and guiders of this wicked enterprise'.[11]

Kett's rebellion unequivocally presented itself as belonging to the same tradition. It camped on Mousehold Heath where the rebels of 1381 had camped, and its 29 articles closed with the demand that the king give licence under the great seal 'to such commissioners as your poor commons hath chosen . . . for to redress . . . all such good laws . . . which hath been hidden by your justices, sheriffs, escheators and other your officers from your poor commons since the first year of the reign of Henry VII'.[12] Two points were made here: that the rebellion was raised in the cause of the commons; that, although the grievances were agrarian and against the landlords of the region (some of whom were brought to trial before the oak of reformation), the rebels, in accordance with the tradition, were politicised by their conviction that the problem was rooted in bad governance. Thereafter, the tradition faded away.[13]

These examples of revolt – by no means a comprehensive tally but rather a selection of spectacular instances – project a phenomenon that was established in the late fourteenth century and came to a head between 1450 and 1550. They were remarkably alike: first, in organisation, forming large armies which in most cases planned to march on the seat of government. Each possessed a sophisticated structure of command and an impressive capacity to articulate grievances in bills, manifestos, proclamations or petitions. Secondly, each was highly politicised, objecting to the policies of the government, which were blamed on evil ministers and corrupt officials, but not usually on the king. A third resemblance lay in the broad social spectrum of support that they received. In most, but not in all, cases, the uprising expressed a confluence of protest from gentlemen, clerics and commons. Thus, aggrieved gentlemen contributed either by actual participation or by failing to take counteraction. The extent of gentle participation, however, very much depended upon the prominence of agrarian grievances. Thus, in 1381 and in Kett's rebellion it was inconsiderable. As a result, these uprisings appear predominantly popular. Otherwise, if driven by political grievances which could be shared alike by the whole range of society, gentlemen could figure as leaders and captains: such as Robert Poynings, the son of Lord Poynings, the esquires John Sinclair and Thomas Burgess and the gentleman John Gibbes in 1450; the minor gentleman John a Chamber and Sir John Egremont in 1489; Lord Audley, John Trevysall, William Antron and Thomas Trowe in 1497; the peers, Lords Darcy, Latimer, Neville, Lumley, Conyers and Scrope, the knights, Thomas Percy, Robert Constable, Oswald Wilstrop, Nicholas Fairfax, Richard Tempest and Stephen Hamerton, plus many other gentlemen in the Pilgrimage of Grace; and the knight Thomas Pomeroy, the esquires Humfrey Arundell and John Wynslade and the minor gentlemen, John Bury and one Coffin in the Prayer Book uprising of 1549.

Arguably, however, the gentlemen made their major contribution to the development of these rebellions not by directing them but by letting them happen. This resulted sometimes from fear but often from sympathy for the rebel cause. In fact, risings of the commons typically began as popular movements which got out of hand when nothing was done to resist them by the gentlemen of the region, largely because the grudges they held against the government left them unwilling to save it from an obvious source of embarrassment. And so they would lie low or flee. But for the rebels this was often not enough. Unless agrarian grievances rendered the rebels hostile to gentlemen or deeply suspicious of them, they were keen to obtain their leadership. By this time gentlemen usually had little choice but to submit since the size of the uprising and the extent of its support, especially when it included their tenantry and servants, had left them incapable of defending their properties and families. They could therefore flee and have their properties spoiled, or join the rebellion and hope for the king's forgiveness on the grounds that their participation had been enforced.

But the leadership in risings of the commons was never monopolised by the gentlemen; and the key leaders were not what the society of orders would lead one to expect. Wat Tyler, Jack Cade, John a Chamber, Michael Joseph, Robert Kett, Robert Aske, Robert Pulleyn, John Hallom, John Atkinson, William Stapulton, Nicholas Musgrave, Ninian Staveley represented a whole host of captains drawn either from the commonalty itself or from the grey zone that lay between the commonalty and the gentlemen: they were either wealthy yeomen verging on minor gentry or the younger sons of gentry families whom the rule of primogeniture had condemned to follow professional careers. In addition, the system of leadership did not follow the normal pattern but rested upon a principle of answerability to the commons. In this respect, risings of the commons never turned into baronial revolts.

The essential purpose of a rising of the commons was to denote that the body politic was out of joint. The rationale behind it was as follows: since the normal means of remedy no longer worked – that is, the designated ruling order had failed to fulfil its obligation of ensuring that the king and his ministers dispensed good governance – the commons would have to be released from their duty of obedience, not permanently but as a temporary emergency measure, in order to put things to right.

Finally, a rising of the commons, although deeply offensive to the society of orders as an expression of disobedience and a source of disharmony, represented in no way a repudiation of it. In fact, risings of the commons were a defence of the society of orders. Usually they alleged that bad governance had resulted from excluding the true nobility from the counsels of the king and from replacing them by men of base background. The remedy was to make the personnel of government accord with the notion of orders. Although beginning as an act of topsy-turvydom, risings of the commons sought to enact the society of orders in revolt by requiring gentlemen to be true to the commons – that is, to fulfil their obligation of protecting the commons' wealth by providing leadership. Nevertheless, countering the vertical belief in hierarchy that this implied was a horizontal belief in belonging to 'the commonalty of the realm'. Such risings urged the commons to 'stick ye together' and to make a pact with all the commons of the realm to put matters right.[14] This awareness of a common interest meant that 'commonalty' was a social force that transcended 'feudal' and local allegiances to create a belief that throughout the country there existed a social group, the commons, with a shared identity and cause. This made it easier for different localities and regions to join the same revolts.

The Notion of Orders

The theory of orders proposed an organic society of complementary parts which, under the rule of the crown, was directed by the gentlemen and clergy and sustained by the productivity and subservience of the commonalty. It posited a formal hierarchy comprised of three orders, defined by differential privileges and determined by function. It assumed that, because the orders complemented each other – with the religious function of the clergy, the political function of the gentlemen and the economic function of the commonalty all interlocking – social harmony would necessarily prevail and a true commonwealth would inevitably result.

The theory ran through a large number of sixteenth-century treatises, typical of which was Edmund Dudley's *Tree of Commonwealth*.[15] This work identified, as the basic components of society, the clergy, the chivalry (that is, peers, knights, esquires and 'other gentlemen by office or authority') and the communalty (that is, merchants, craftsmen, labourers, franklins, graziers, farmers, tillers and 'other generally the people of the realm'). Distinguishing the three groups from each other, it claimed, were their duties. Thus, the chivalry were obliged to serve the prince and to defend the church and commonalty, whereas commons were obliged to work diligently, not to presume above their own degree and not to be exploitative. The range of duty and variety of social groups that Dudley identified with the commonalty clearly indicated that it was not seen as a class, in the sense of containing both rich and poor. At the same time Dudley recognised that within the communalty were social distinctions created by wealth since he called upon the merchants and graziers to be charitable to 'their underlings'. But the point he was making was that in the society of the time there were primary and secondary distinctions and that, within a society of orders, the distinctions determined by function, privilege or birth had priority over those simply determined by merit or wealth.

This notion of orders was not, of course, post-medieval. There it was in a sermon of 1421 which described 'a great ship sailing in the sea of prosperity' – its name, 'The Realm of England'.[16] Up in the forecastle was the clergy. Up in the hindcastle was the barony. Down in the ship were the commons, described as merchants, craftsmen and labourers. All three orders, it was said, were essential to the working of the ship. But all three had to abide by virtue: with it 'we sailed the sea of wealth and prosperity'; without it 'we sailed into woe'.

The same notion was also evident in the late-fourteenth-century poem, Langland's 'The Vision of William concerning Piers the Plowman'. Thus, on a May morning in the Malvern Hills when the sun was soft, the poet rested on a bank by a stream and drifted off as he stared into the water. He dreamt of 'a fair field full of folk' and of a king appearing on the scene followed by his knighthood and supported by the commons.[17] The king, with his knights and clergy, decided that the commons 'should their commons [that is, provisions] find'. In response, the commons ensured that they practised all kinds of craft and that the ploughmen tilled the land 'for profit of all the people'.[18] The allocation of function surfaced again in book six when a knight offered to help Piers plough his plot of land, and Piers – the embodiment of the commons and Christ – said: 'I'll swink [that is, labour] and sweat and sow for us both'. However, he also insisted that the knight perform his duty to society: that is, to guard the Church and 'myself' from thieves and wasters, to protect Piers' farm from wild animals and birds and to avoid maltreating his own tenants and bondsmen.[19] In the course of the fifteenth century the notion of orders developed a step further as the term 'commonweal' (or commonwealth) gained currency: that is, the general community whose operation and promotion served as the society of orders' goal.[20] In this way, the notion of orders came to fruition.

There is no reason to regard the society of orders simply as an exercise in wishful thinking, an ideological, self-serving concoction created for the comfort of gentlemen and clerics, but otherwise meaningless. Reality fell short of the ideal, however. Not surprisingly, the former was far more complex than the latter proposed. For one thing, each order undoubtedly had its own interpretation of the theory: the gentlemen and clergy stressed the virtue of obedience and subservience, that is, the obligations the commonalty owed them; whereas the commonalty stressed the virtue of charity and hospitality, that is, the obligations the upper orders owed to commoners. These differing perceptions thus produced two opposed views of society. The upper view accepted that only the disobedience of clerics and gentlemen was permissible and that popular disobedience was, by its very nature, a rejection of the notion of orders. Thus the Pilgrimage of Grace was seen by Richard Morison, one of Thomas Cromwell's intellectual circle, as a popular revolt bent on destroying the existing society. In his *Remedy for Sedition*, written in response to the uprising, he solemnly declared: 'to my purpose, lords must be lords, commons must be commons, every man accepting his degree'. Since the rebels had appointed commoners as captains, he asked: 'whom can they refuse when smiths, cobblers, tilers, carters and such other gay Greeks seem worthy to be their governors?'[21] In contrast, the lower view proposed that if the higher orders were abusing their position – that is, if kings were behaving tyrannically, or if gentlemen and clerics were neglecting to nurture the commons or serve the king – then corrective devices were necessary.

Corrective Devices

Some of these devices were literary, imparting no more than a message and a threat. Thus the ballads of Robin Hood presented the picture of a social outsider (that is, an outlaw), intervening to remind the clergy and the gentlemen of their duties as laid down by the notion of orders. There was also the Piers Plowman literary tradition, with its perverse but compelling picture of the commoner leading society in search of St Truth, temporarily turning the world upside down to bring about its cure.[22]

Then there was the corrective mechanism of revolt itself. Just as the upper view accepted the legitimacy of baronial revolt, for curbing the tyranny of the prince, his favourites and ministers, in the same cause the lower view accepted the legitimacy of a rising of the commons. Both the Robin Hood legend and the Piers Plowman tradition had connections with the latter. True, the rebels of 1381 had a low view of Robin Hood or Hobbe the Robber. John Ball in his letter to the commons of Essex called for his chastisement.[23] An address from Jack Carter to an assembly of 20,000 Essex men made a similar point, accusing Robin of deception.[24] The Cottingham ballad of 1392 also objected: 'But hething [that is, scorn or derision] will we suffer none, neither of Hobb nor of John.'[25] In contrast, the Yorkshire rebels of 1489 presented Hobb as the commons' friend and leader, producing a muster proclamation 'in the name of Master Hobbe Hirst', who was identified as 'Robin Goodfellow's brother he is, as I trow'.[26]

If the rebels of 1381 objected to Robin, they were deeply appreciative of Piers. John Ball's letter to the commons called upon them to stand together in God's name 'and biddeth Piers Plowman go to his work'.[27] Moreover, Langland's poem served as the user's guide to revolt for the rebels of 1536. Books five and six of the poem presented 'a thousand men thronged together', appealing to Christ and his mother for grace. Their intention was to go on a pilgrimage in search of St Truth but they had no idea as to where to find him until the archetypal commoner, a ploughman, declared that he knew the saint well and would take them to his place on one condition: that he was allowed first, as Ball put it, to 'go to his work' which meant in practice, to plough and sow his half acre.[28] Later in the poem, in book 19, the allegorical figure of Grace 'began . . . to go' with Piers Plowman and advised him 'the commons to summon', offering to give them 'weapons to fight with that will never fail'. A battle was nigh, against the agents of anti-Christ: 'the false prophets, flatterers and glozers [that is, fawners]' who will 'make themselves the curators of kings and earls'.[29] The northern uprising of October 1536, then, was an enactment of Langland's poem. It even produced Piers Plowman as a rebel leader, in the form of Captain Poverty – like Piers an embodiment of Christ and the commons – who proceeded to raise North Lancashire, Cumbria, the North Riding, the palatinate of Durham and Northumberland with his stirring letters.[30]

Risings of the commons, then, were part of the corrective machinery associated with the society of orders, the purpose of which was to ensure that society abided by its basic ideals. That the Pilgrimage of Grace had such a purpose was vividly expressed in a ballad composed at the time, probably by a monk of Sawley Abbey:[31]

> Such folly is fallen
> And wise outblown
> That Grace is gone
> And all goodness.
> Then no marvel
> That it thus befell
> Commons to mell
> To make redress.

That the rebels of late 1536 abided by the society of orders was made evident in their social awareness, organisation, and declared aims.[32] Basic to the language of the rebels were the terms 'commons', 'clergy' and 'gentlemen' (alternatively, 'men of worship'), who were seen as coherent social groupings, each with its own distinctive ethos and role. The uprising, moreover, organised itself as a society of orders, with lords and gentlemen acting as captains and negotiators; and, since it was meant to be a pilgrimage, with clerics leading the way as crossbearers. Yet, although organised in this manner, the uprising did not cease to be a rising of the commons, for the genteel leadership was constantly seen as serving the commons and answerable to the commonalty. Clerics and gentlemen were respected, then, only so long as they proved themselves true to the commons. Any sign of non-cooperation was quickly charged with treachery.

Central to the pilgrims' complaint was the belief that the society of orders was in dire peril. Much of the complaint was couched in such a way as to accuse the government of showing contempt for the society of orders: first, through maltreating the royal family, especially Princess Mary whom an act of parliament had rendered illegitimate; second, through replacing nobles in the councils of the king by men of villein blood; third, through trying to undo the Church by plundering its wealth and by taking away its liberties and privileges; and fourth, through oppressing the commons with too much taxation.[33] The same charge of offending the society of orders was brought against the gentlemen in the upland north for acting as harsh landlords and for failing to provide an adequate defence of the northern border against the Scots.[34] The uprising, then, had two principal aims: on the one hand, to defend the old religion, in order to preserve Christ's faith; on the other, to defend the society of orders, in order to maintain a true commonwealth.

Yet at the time the pilgrims were accused of subscribing to another set of social beliefs. Richard Morison was not the only one to make this point.[35] The king, in answering the pilgrims' first petition, questioned their claim to be defending tradition on the grounds that their opposition to him was highly irregular, as was their willingness to follow Robert Aske, 'a common pedlar in the law'.[36] In Cumberland, Barnard Townley, rector of Caldbeck, thought the rebels' plan was, by placing restrictions upon manorial exactions and tithes, to 'have destroyed nobles and gentlemen'; and there were several reports that the rebels intended to establish 'a commonwealth': that is, a levelled society in which wealth was held in common.[37] Much of this represented a typical over-reaction to popular disobedience. But it did make the obvious point that the rebels' policy, no matter what their claim, offended the notion of orders, through resisting the crown and through awarding priority to the interests of the commons. The latter offence was made evident in the rebels' usage of the term 'commonwealth'. This term was of central importance to the Pilgrimage of Grace, whose full title was 'the pilgrimage of grace for the commonwealth'. As used by the rebels, it had several meanings, some of which were perfectly in keeping with the notion of orders. Thus they used it to imply 'the weal of all', or to distinguish the wealth of the realm from the personal wealth of the crown.[38] Yet, they also used it in ways not so consonant with the notion. Its usage to denote a society without hierarchy was undoubtedly the fantasy of fearful gentlemen and clerics, and nothing suggests that the pilgrims used the term in this sense; but they did use it to mean the wealth of the commons: that is, the wealth specifically and exclusively of the commons.[39] Used in this sense, the term implied the exploitation of the commons either by the crown or by the landlords, and proposed, quite radically, that the commonalty needed to look after itself rather than relying upon the virtue of kingship or the benevolence of lordship to maintain social justice.

This blatant assertion of interest presented the commons not as an organic part of society but as a party competing for power, and therefore acting contrary to the notion of orders as it was normally formulated. The Pilgrimage of Grace revealed a society not of complementary parts but of rival interests, which cohered only because of the way the rebels from one order sought to manipulate the rebels from another to further their own particular cause. This was as true of the commonalty as it was of the gentlemen and the clergy. But it did not mean a rejection of the notion of orders. It simply expressed yet another corrective device, designed to keep society as closely aligned with its ideals as was practically possible.

Popular Perceptions of the Hierarchy

Could it be said that, in spite of their general acceptance of the notion of orders, the commons who supported the Pilgrimage of Grace, or, for that matter, any other revolt of the commons, were, in reality, none too reverential of the higher orders, and that the concern such rebellions showed for them was, in fact, superimposed by the participating gentlemen and clerics?

The various statements of grievance produced by the pilgrims expressed alarm at what was happening to the Church as, placed in the hands of heretics, its wealth and privileges were being taken away. The pilgrims' first petition called for 'the maintenance of the church and the liberties of the same' and the second included seven (out of 24) articles in its defence. Aske's first proclamation had called upon men 'to preserve the church of God from spoiling'; his second claimed that the government's intent was 'to destroy the church of England and the minsters of the same' and his oath required men to take the cross of Christ before them 'to the restitution of his church and to the suppression of heretics and subverters of the just laws of God'.[40] But what did the commons actually think? On 21 October 1536 Lancaster Herald made his way from Scrooby to Pontefract on a mission to proclaim to the rebels that they should disperse, or else. Close to the town he met a group of armed peasants who told him that they rose 'for the commonwealth', reasoning that if they did not 'the commonalty and the church should be destroyed'.[41] Eleven days earlier, the commons of Beverley had uttered a similar sentiment. In a letter pledging support for the rebels of Lincolnshire, they had declared their opposition to 'councillors, inventors and procurers' who were seeking 'utterly to undo both the church and the commonalty of the realm'.[42] The commons, without a doubt, were deeply worried about what was happening to the Church, especially the spoliation brought about by the dissolution of religious houses and the threatened dissolution of parish churches. Among other things, this reflected their concern for the position of the clergy and their role not only in administering the faith but also in providing hospitality and charity. During the course of the revolt clerics were criticised and threatened by the rebels, but this was because they were felt not to be sufficiently committed rather than because of any rebel animus to their social position. Some demand was made by the rebels that clerics should serve as soldiers, and some fiery clerics were keen to do so. But it was generally accepted that, in keeping with the society of orders, clerics should rightfully participate only in a non-military capacity, serving as army chaplains, as secretaries for the composition of letters, as crossbearers, and as suppliers of money, carts, horses and provisions.

The uprising revealed that the commons saw their cause as closely involved with that of the clergy.[43] For the sake of the commonwealth, it was felt, both had to be safeguarded against government greed. Likewise, they believed that the wealth of the Church had to be protected for the sake of religion. As a commons' petition of January 1537 declared: it was vital 'to maintain the profit of holy church which was the upholding of the Christian faith'.[44] In other words, although the commons might express anti-clerical objections to the payment of dues and tithes, they basically believed that the clergy should retain their wealth and status, and that the commons' duty was to protect them against a gang of heretics led by Cromwell which, in the protestant manner, denied that any basic difference existed between the laity and the clergy, even to the extent of allowing a layman to have care of souls.[45]

What about the commons' regard for gentlemen? A major grievance of the pilgrimage was that mean men were in charge of the government to the exclusion of the nobility; and that the nobility was being defiled through the elevation into its ranks of men of base blood.[46] This grievance sprang from the fact that Thomas Cromwell appeared to control the king and the previous June had been made a baron. With the notion of orders offended in this manner, bad governance, it was felt, must ensue. Was it not natural that a shearman's son should seek to fleece the realm? Let him stick to shearing sheep. The rebels' solution was to get rid of Cromwell and revert to what was practised on the king's accession 'when his nobles did order under his highness'.[47] This complaint might be seen as the work of the aristocratic interest, looking after its own. But it was also the cause of the commons. Percival Cresswell, a government agent, gave a vivid account of meeting a group of commons at Temple Hirst, Lord Darcy's family seat, on 10 November 1536.[48] As Darcy read the letters that Cresswell had delivered in an inner room, Cresswell was able to talk freely with some commoners in the garden. By this time the pilgrim host had dispersed, a truce having been agreed with the government, but meanwhile these men had been left to mind the noble lord. In the conversation, the commoners predictably heaped abuse on the upstart, Thomas Cromwell, and angrily asked if the king had dismissed him from the council. Cresswell sought to mollify them, saying that Cromwell had been absent from court for the last two days and that close to the king were a number of nobles of ancient lineage whom he named. The information caused the commons ecstatically to declare their faith in the noble order: 'God save the king and them all', they said. 'For as long as such noblemen of the true noble blood may reign and rule about the king, all shall be well.' Substantiating this declaration of faith was a letter from Aske to Darcy. Reporting on the pilgrims' York council and the decisions it had made on how to proceed with the government, the letter stated that the primary concern of the commons was to receive from the government two assurances: first, the grant of a general pardon; second 'the nobility here to rule'. Only when such an assurance had been given would the commons, Aske said, be prepared to declare their other grievances.[49]

Sustaining the commons' belief in nobility was their extreme hostility to Thomas Cromwell, not just because he was a heretic but also because he was one of them, a man who, coming from a background unfamiliar with the mores of rulership, would destroy the commonwealth through a ruthless policy of exaction and expropriation. The favours showered upon him contrasted sharply with the government's aggressiveness towards certain noble families, notably the Dacres of the north, who had been disgraced and stripped of office in 1534, and the Percies, whose massive patrimony was undergoing annexation by the crown, the result of the 6th earl's childlessness and simplicity. Expressing sympathy for the latter, the commons of Howdenshire, at the very start of the uprising, went to Wressle Castle and shouted outside its gates: 'Thousands for a Percy'.[50]

The commons declared their faith in the society of orders not only by voicing a strong objection to the government's contemptuous treatment of nobility but also by placing gentlemen in charge of their armies. As with the clergy, some hostility was shown towards gentlemen in the course of the uprising, with rents withheld, houses spoiled, estate records destroyed, enclosures levelled. But none of this marked a disbelief in the special position gentlemen were awarded by the society of orders. The gentlemen the commons opposed were proceeded against for failing to live up to what the theory of orders expected of them. Their crime lay in remaining loyal to a government apparently bent on revolution; in acting as harsh landlords, thus neglecting their paternalistic duties; in aiding, rather than resisting, the government's plunder of the realm; in placing private interest before that of the commonwealth. Essentially, the gentlemen were seen as under obligation to serve the king and to protect the commons. By allowing Cromwell to rule, they had dealt crown, clergy, commonalty, as well as their own order, a terrible blow. The rebels' solution was to stop all this and ensure that the society of orders worked in compliance with its basic principles.

Without doubt, subscription to the society of orders could cause considerable social antagonism, as its component parts failed to live up to its ideals and objection was made. Intensifying this antagonism was the coexistence of different perceptions of how each part should behave. The commoner emphasis upon the duties of the rulers to the ruled generated both anti-clerical and anti-aristocratic sentiments whilst the genteel and clerical emphasis upon popular subservience, and the awful consequences thought to stem from the neglect of this duty, sustained a deep, over-reactive suspicion of the commons. In this respect, degree was not taken away and 'that string' was not untuned; yet discord followed. In practice, the social harmony preached by the theorists of the day was a response to a high degree of disobedience. Social discord was an integral feature of the society of orders, its occurrence neither disproving the existence of such a society nor revealing necessarily the hand of class.

The End of an Idiom

The Pilgrimage of Grace, then, belonged to a tradition of revolt. Arguably its social and political concerns, along with its proposed remedies, were replicated throughout the tradition; and what is true of the Pilgrimage of Grace is generally true of the other revolts operating in the same idiom. Within the tradition were two major strands of revolt: on the one hand, risings of the commons principally moved by agrarian grievances and therefore against the landlords; on the other, risings of the commons principally moved by political grievances and therefore against the government. The two strands not only possessed different specific complaints but also awarded different roles to the enlisted gentlemen, on the one hand making them passive passengers or prisoners, and, on the other, allowing them to serve as captains. Yet both subscribed to the same social perception and political goal. The grudge of the commons was the malfunctioning of a socio-political system and their aim was to ensure that it worked properly, essentially by insisting that the obligations assigned to the three orders were properly performed. In this respect, the risings of the commons revealed that the notion of orders was not a belief simply suspended from above but one upheld from below.

Why did popular disturbances and aristocratic protest abandon the 'rising of the commons' idiom after the mid sixteenth century? Essentially this was because the conditions that had allowed popular movements to escalate into large-scale rebellions disappeared. Risings of the commons had depended upon the existence of complaints against the government which different communities could share with each other and which different orders could hold at the same time. These complaints had mainly stemmed from attempts at fiscal and religious reform. In the late sixteenth century, however, such reforms became less agitative, with governments averse to making radical fiscal changes and with societies becoming more tolerant of reformations in religion.[51] Secondly, the attitude of the gentlemen towards popular revolt altered, partly as a result of the incentives they received to support the Tudor regime, the result of the government's policy of granting to them the wealth it expropriated from the Church, and partly because of a deep suspicion of the commons, generated by the conflicts and threats associated with the risings of early 1537 and 1549. Fearful of the commons, the gentlemen became much less capable of collaborating with popular revolts and, firmly attached by patronage to the government, they became much more prepared to assist in their containment and suppression. Without the gentlemen's support, it became much more difficult for popular rebels to establish themselves as a regional, as opposed to a local, movement. Thirdly, the commons lost the solidarity that the risings of the commons had depended upon. To the fore in this tradition of revolt were the substantial yeomen, capable of leading the rest of the local community and of uniting village communities in the same cause. Thanks to a growth in the prosperity of commercial farming and an increase in social mobility, the yeomen became increasingly removed from the village community. Promoting the same process of withdrawal was the alienating presence in the countryside of a growing landless element, spawned by the development of rural industries and the conversion of poor peasants into wage-labourers. As a result, the village, the basic building block in a rising of the commons, quickly lost its traditional homogeneity, becoming instead a society of social extremes fissured by class. The same development undermined the concept of the commonalty.

Arguably, the risings of the commons had derived their strength from the weakness of class divisions. But now from the late sixteenth century the local community was becoming seriously divided by the aversion of the gentleman to an 'untrustworthy' commonalty and by the aversion of the substantial yeoman to cottagers. Attendant upon the latter was a growing disbelief in a social theory which placed him and them in the same social category. Risings of the commons therefore were ruled out, with the old causes gone, with gentlemen keener to stamp out popular revolt than to promote it, and with the yeomen keener to establish alliances with the gentlemen than with the rest of the commonalty. Upholding these developments were late-sixteenth-century improvements in the government's means of dealing with popular insurgency, especially following the Marian and Elizabethan reforms of the militia, the riot legislation of 1549, and the spread to most counties of the lord lieutenancy. Consequently, a tradition of revolt which had created some of the major events of the late Middle Ages ceased to be valued as a practical means by which society could protect itself against the state.

8

TIDY STRUCTURES AND MESSY PRACTICE: IDEOLOGIES OF ORDER AND THE PRACTICALITIES OF OFFICE-HOLDING IN RAGUSA

David Rheubottom

The Mediterranean city-states of the late medieval/early Renaissance present a paradox. On the one hand they show a vibrant, somewhat chaotic, dynamism in commerce, politics and urban life. In Florence and Venice, for example, different factions of the elite battled for supremacy. These struggles were so sharply contested that defeat might mean banishment. Yet these same struggles took place within a framework of government and office that appeared so stable and ordered that it could, like the structure of government in Venice, be described in geometric metaphors. What was the reality? Political life might be portrayed in terms of a strong ideology of order, hierarchy and structure, but were offices and councils of government neatly arranged? Did office-holders move through them in a regular fashion? It is clear that people living at the time tended to think so. But what was their actual experience of politics and government and how did it relate to the images and ideals which they held?

Such questions are simple to pose, but very difficult to answer. The reasons for this lie in the size and scale of the city-states themselves. In this chapter we consider the case of fifteenth-century Ragusa (Dubrovnik), a small merchant city-state on the Croatian coast of the Adriatic Sea. While Ragusa was very small, it enjoyed an economic and

political significance that was out of proportion to the extent of its
territory or the size of its population. Yet even in this micro-state with
its relatively small ruling elite, there were several hundred men holding
political office in any given year and occupying about sixty different
offices. The elites of Venice and Florence were very much larger and
their governments very much more complex. It is because of their size
and complexity that it is almost impossible to reconstruct the reality of
day-to-day political life. In Venice, for example, the Great Council
elected men from its own ranks to over 800 posts.[1] With this number of
offices and the overlapping authority of many of them, it would be very
difficult to study the structure of Venetian government and the experience of office-holding. Because of Ragusa's small size and the richness
of its archival sources, we have an ideal laboratory in which to examine
the relationship between an ideology of governmental hierarchy and
the 'lived-in' reality of office-holding and political careers.[2] Furthermore, office in Ragusa was restricted to members of the patrician class.
There were other 'orders' such as commoners, peasants, and slaves.
While patricians had economic and other ties with many of them, the
other orders did not participate in government or have a voice in the
formulation of policy. Patricians only married amongst themselves and
so there were no ties of kinship linking patricians to other orders.[3]
Therefore, we can temporarily ignore the relationship between 'orders'
and concentrate our attention on hierarchy within a single order,
Ragusa's governing class.

The argument is divided into three major sections. In Section One I
sketch in some background on Ragusa in the late fifteenth century,
paying particular attention to its constituent councils and offices. There
are two important points. First, there was a great deal of competition
for offices. Much was at stake particularly over the higher offices.
Second, and somewhat paradoxically, there appears to have been some
uncertainty about the place of certain offices vis-à-vis one another. In
other words, the notion of 'hierarchy', with respect to office, seems
rather problematic.

In Section Two I show how the governing Great Council grew in size
and changed in composition from 1440 to 1490. We will see how the
Great Council changed 'shape' through time, and the profound consequences that this had for the likelihood of holding office. I argue that
differing cohorts of patrician men had differing experience of office
depending (among other things) on when their careers began and how
those careers developed.

Section Three takes the conclusions of the first two sections and relates them back to the main theme: hierarchy and indeterminacy. I argue that, while the structure of government and the hierarchy of office appear to be stable over time (both as seen by patricians of the fifteenth century and to historians or anthropologists examining it from the perspective of the late twentieth century), significant changes were in fact taking place. I then consider the relationship between the apparently stable ideology of office and government and the lived-in reality of patricians' office-holding experience.

I   Competition for Office

Ragusa presents a bit of a conundrum. It was small in terms of both territory and population. Venice and Genoa, its rivals in the world of Mediterranean commerce, were much larger. It had a total population of only 20,000 souls – an appropriate term for this most Catholic of states. Its territory consisted of a very narrow strip of coastline on the eastern shore of the Adriatic Sea. At its widest this territory only extended three kilometres inland. This land could not produce enough to feed even the local inhabitants and grain had to be regularly imported by ship from as far away as Sicily and Asia Minor. Yet Ragusa was both successful and wealthy. Her traders covered the Mediterranean world and beyond. A tremendous volume of goods flowed through her port or were shipped aboard her vessels. Her merchant navy at this time was far larger than England's. It is important to note that this trade was not underpinned by a strong economic 'base' of land and agricultural production. Rather it depended upon the adroit management of trade and the terms of trade. Most of this trade, and all of the levers of state power, were in the hands of a patrician elite that was endogamous (marriage, that is, took place only within the group).

The heart of government was the Great Council. Only patrician males could sit on this body. It was the principal legislative body and it made all the crucial decisions regarding trade and diplomacy. Members of the Great Council elected the head of state, or Rector, from their own ranks. They also elected members of the Senate (also known as the Council of Appeal), members of the Small Council who advised the Rector, the judges of the several courts, and all of the state's other office-holders. At the pinnacle of the government was the Rector followed by his Minor Council and the Senate. These were held by elderly men who had long experience of government. At the other end were very junior posts such as that of Scribe in the Customs House (*Scrivari over garcon dela dohane grande*) which were held by young men who were just beginning their political careers. In between was a broad swathe of about 60 other offices. Most of these had multiple incumbents. All of the incumbents for all of these offices and councils were selected from the ranks of the Great Council through a process of nomination and secret ballot. Therefore, the most common business of the Great Council was filling all these offices and councils. As we shall see, the number of elections actually held during the year was much greater than 60. Elections dominated council business and provided a never-ending agenda.

The structure of government appears remarkably stable. Year after year, the same posts were filled and elections were held about the same time each year. Whatever else may have been going on in the very turbulent world outside the council chambers, the routine inside was an unrelenting grind of elections. Outside there may have been war and plague, inside there was the unending round of nominations and ballots. I have studied patterns of office-holding over the half century extending from 1440 to 1490. This covers about 7,000 ballots. I have abstracted these, and much other information concerning the patrician population, from Latin and Italian archival sources and entered them into a computer database for analysis.

Elections to posts fill council minutes. At every one of the meetings of the Great Council held in 1470, there was at least one ballot and two-thirds of all of the agenda items for that year concerned elections. At an average meeting four ballots were held. For each vacancy the names of three candidates were put forward. Therefore, to fill an office with (say) three incumbents, the names of nine nominees would be put forward.

Elections were often bitterly fought. On 26 February 1450 the Great Council met to elect a new Rector for the month of March. At this particular meeting five ballots were held but no one was elected. At the following meeting on 5 March, two more ballots were held before Junius de Calich was finally elected with a vote of 63 in favour, 50 opposed, and three abstaining. In the seven ballots required for this election, 11 different names had been put before the Great Council and seven of these names appeared on more than one ballot. The name of the eventual winner had appeared on five.[4] This was not unusual. During the same year some judgeships on the Criminal Court became vacant. Filling these four vacancies required 65 separate ballots spread over 30 council meetings. A total of 35 candidates from 20 different patricians' 'houses' were put forward. The name of one of these candidates, Jacomo de Gondola, appeared on 34 ballots before he was finally elected with a majority of one! Hotly contested elections were a hallmark of the Great Council.

I have referred to a 'hierarchy' of offices. It seems clear from archival sources that the patricians of the period thought that there was one. We know that they were obsessed with order and precedence. And we are told that the officials processed in order on state occasions. On the feast of the patron saint of the city, St Blaise (or Sv. Vlaho), they made their way in order from the Rector's palace to the cathedral. There they were seated with the Rector first, followed by his Minor Council, members of the Senate, and then the other officials. Unfortunately, I cannot find a source which spells out the sequence for those other officials. The book of state ceremonies is full of other details, but does not tell us who was there or in what order.[5] Another important source, the Chancellor's Handbook, which is a very rich source of information, lists every one of the state's offices along with a summary of legislation affecting each office; but the offices are presented in alphabetical order.[6]

In order to investigate the hierarchy of offices, a prosopological perspective has been adopted.[7] Here I provide only the briefest sketch of the methods in order to get quickly to the results. The governmental careers of 406 men have been studied. These men entered the Great Council between 1440 and 1490. I have assumed that the order in which a man held particular offices would be related to his age and his length of service. It is known that a number of the offices had age qualifications attached to them. Since a man might hold a particular office several times during his career, it is important to determine the point at which he was elected to an office for the first time. This resulted in the creation, first, of a list of first-held offices. In other words, a career list was assembled for each of the 406 men. Then, moving from these individual lists, the next step was to determine when, on average, an office was held for the first time, for all men holding that office.[8] These average values provide an initial approximation of an office-holding hierarchy. See Table 8.1.

The offices in this table are ordered according to the *average* number of years after entering the Great Council that a post was held. The position of *Gatti Officiali* (literally 'Cats Officials', but apparently concerned with sewers), for example, was held about 16 years after entry

Table 8.1 Hierarchy of offices (in ascending order)

Rank	Office name[a]	Numbers of incumbents[b]	Years after entry
1	*Scrivari over garcon dela dohane grande* (recorder in the custom's house)	1	−1.5
2	*Biscoti officiali* (officials responsible for (military?) supplies of hardtack)	3	4.2
3	*Conte Lagoste* (Count, or administrator, of district of Lastovo)	1	7.0
4	*Cechieri* (officers of the mint)	4	7.1
5	*Castellan de Stagno* (commander of the fortress at Ston)	1	7.7
6	*Officiali de scritta de armamento* (recorders of workmen in the armoury)	2	7.7
7	*Officiali lavorieri de scrita in Ragusi* (recorders of workmen in Ragusa)	3	8.0
8	*Officiali lavorieri de pagamento in Ragusi* (paymasters of workmen in Ragusa)	3	8.4
9	*Salezo officiali* (officials for roads and public ways)	3	8.7
10	*Armamento officiali* (paymasters of workmen in the armoury)	3	9.8
11	*Fontigieri* (officials for weights and measures)	3	11.2
12	*Stime officiali* (official valuers)	4	11.8
13	*Advocati alla camara del arte della lana* (attorneys to the wool trade)	2	12.3
14	*Capitanio de la ponta* (captain of fortification at Janjina)	1	13.2
15	*Castellan de quelmar, Castello de sopra (also de suxo)* (commander of the upper fortress at Mali Ston)	1	13.3
16	*Castellan de quelmar, Castello de sotto (also dezoso)* (commander of the lower fortress at Mali Ston)	1	14.4
17	*Conte de isola de Mezo et de Calamota* (Count, or administrator, of district of Koločep)	1	15.8
18	*Raxone officiali* (overseers of public accounts)	5	16.1
19	*Gatti officiali* (officials for sewers)	3	16.4
20	*Officiali lavorieri de scrita in Stagno* (recorders of workmen at Ston)	2	16.6
21	*Camerlengi del comone* (registrars)	4	16.7

Table 8.1 *continued*

Rank	Office name[a]	Numbers of incumbents[b]	Years after entry
22	*Procuratori de San Francesco* (trustees of a religious foundation)	3	16.8
23	*Vicario del rector* (magistrate of small claims court)	1	16.8
24	*Judicieri del comone* (judges of the Municipal Court)	5	17.0
25	*Castellan de Sochol* (captain at the fortifications of Sochol in Konavli)	1	17.8
26	*Massari de le biave* (officials responsible for the state's grain supply)	3	18.4
27	*Procuratori del Monasterio de San Jeronimo* (trustees of a religious foundation)	3	18.7
28	*Aqueducto de la fontana officiali* (officials for water supplies and fountains)	3	18.8
29	*Officiali Hospedal de Misericordia* (supervisors of the city orphanage)	3	18.9
30	*Procuratori de Sancta Crose de Grauosio* (trustees of a religious foundation)	3	19.0
31	*Officiali lavorieri de pagamente in Stagno* (paymasters of workmen at Ston)	2	19.0
32	*Doanieri* (customs officials)	4	19.4
33	*Conte de Zupana* (Count, or administrator, of district of Šipan)	1	19.8
34	*Advocati del proprio* (attorneys in the Civil Court)	6	20.2
35	*Procuratori del hospedal de Misericordia* (trustees of the orphanage)	3	20.9
36	*Salinari* (officials responsible for the salt trade)	3	21.1
37	*Procuratori de la Croma* (trustees of a religious foundation)	3	22.4
38	*Procuratori de Sancta Georgio de Canal* (trustees of a religious foundation)	3	22.5
39	*Advocati del comone* (municipal attorneys)	3	22.6
40	*Conte de Canale* (Count, or administrator, of district of Konavli at Pridvorje)	1	22.8
41	*Lane officiali del arte della lana* (supervisors of the wool trade)	3	22.9

Table 8.1 *continued*

Rank	Office name[a]	Numbers of incumbents[b]	Years after entry
42	*Conte de Slano* (Count, or administrator, of district of Slano)	1	24.4
43	*Procuratori de Sancta Maria Angellorum* (trustees of a religious foundation)	3	24.5
44	*Procuratori de Sancta Chiara* (trustees of a religious foundation)	3	24.5
45	*Procuratori de San Domenego* (trustees of a religious foundation)	3	26.2
46	*Cazamorti* (officials concerned with the plague and public health measures)	5	27.2
47	*Procuratori de San Piero, Lorenzo et Andrea* (trustees of religious foundation)	3	27.5
48	*Procuratori de San Blasio* (trustees of a religious foundation)	3	29.0
49	*Consoli de le cause civil* (judges of the Civil Court)	6	29.2
50	*Judici del criminal* (justices of the Criminal Court)	5	29.7
51	*Pregato* (members of Senate, or Council of Appeal)	varies	30.1
52	*Consereri del menor conselo* (members of the Rector's Small Council)	6	31.2
53	*Rector* (head of state)	1	33.1
54	*Conte de Stagno* (Count, or administrator, at Ston)	2	34.5
55	*Proveditori de la terra* (overseers of elections, monitoring conduct of public officials)	5	34.8
56	*Procuratori del hospedal Grande* (trustees of the hospital for the poor)	3	35.8

Notes:
[a] Names of offices as given in Specchio, fos. 1–309. The *Texorieri de Sancta Maria* and the *Collegio de le Appellatione* are not included in this listing. The former held office for life. The latter body was not established until 1490.
[b] The number of incumbents are those holding office at any one time. This ignores changes in the arrangements for some offices.

(and ranks number 19 in the ordering). The *Officiali Hospedal de Misericordia* was held about 19 years after entry (and ranks number 29). As seen in the rank order, these two offices would appear quite far apart, yet the first was held only about three years before the second. It must be remembered that there is considerable variation from one person to the next in when they held a particular office for the first time. This can be expressed in terms of the standard deviations about the mean values. In the case of the *Gatti officiali* and *Officiali Hospedal de Misericordia*, these are quite large (6.9 and 6.7 respectively).

To illustrate this variation, we can examine the office of *Armamento officiali*. Figure 8.1 is a scatter diagram showing when this office was first held over the period. The vertical axis indicates the number of years which had elapsed between entry in the Great Council and the point when this post was first held. The horizontal axis shows the period from 1440 to 1490. On average this post is held 9.8 years after entrance. But

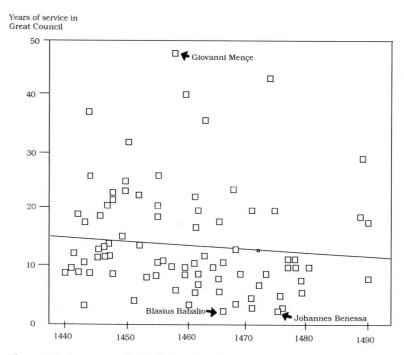

Figure 8.1 *Armamento officiali*, by length of service

as one can see from the scatter diagram there is considerable variation. To point to the extremes: Giovanni Mençe held the post for the first time in 1458. In that year he had been in the Great Council 48 years. On the other hand, Blasius Babalio first held the post in 1466 when he had been in the council only two years (as had Johannes Benessa in 1475). An analysis of the shape of the Great Council will help us to understand this situation.

II The 'Shape' of the Great Council Over Time

For this study I begin at 1455 because, from that year, we know exactly when patricians entered the Great Council and began their political careers. Before 1455 that beginning date has to be estimated. If the Great Council grew enormously from 1455 to 1490, that growth was not uniform. Nor was it accomplished through a gradual increase of the youngest segment of the council. It depended both upon the addition of new members and the loss of older ones. In the ten years from 1455 to 1464, for example, the number of new entrants into the council scarcely offset the yearly toll of deaths. As a result the council's size remained almost constant. It was only after 1465 that numbers began to increase dramatically. In 1470, for example, nine new members entered. In that same year four members died, a net increase of five. In the following year there were 15 new entrants which more than compensated for the single death. Again in 1472 there were 23 new entrants and two deaths. This pattern continued. Indeed, from 1470 until the end of the period there were only two years in which the number of new entrants did not exceed the number of deaths. One of these was the terrible plague year of 1482 when 42 council members died.

These two processes, the entry of new members and the death (or political incapacity) of old members, were largely independent of one another although not completely so. Since the age at entry varied independently from the age at death, the composition of the Great Council changed from year to year. Reflecting these various additions and subtractions to the total membership, we might say that the 'shape' of the Great Council changed significantly throughout the period. In order to examine these changes and their effects in greater detail, I have sampled the Great Council at five-year intervals from 1455 until the end of the study period in 1490. These have resulted in eight quinquennial 'censuses' of council membership.[9]

For each of these census years, I have examined the internal composition of the council in, as it were, cross-section. These cross-sections were derived by considering members' length of service. Members who entered the council within the same five-year period were treated as constituting a single cohort. Thus, the Major Council in 1455 consisted of several cohorts: those who had less than five years of membership, those who had less than ten years but more than five years, and so on. A cohort, therefore, is a group of men who have had about the same amount of experience in the Great Council. In any of the various census years, the council would consist of a number of cohorts. The number of cohorts might vary from one census year to the next, and the number of men within a cohort would almost certainly vary. Thus, the composition of the Great Council can be studied along two dimensions: through time from 1455 to 1490 at five-yearly intervals, and cross-sectionally by comparing cohort with cohort.

One example will make the procedure clear: the quinquennial 'census' of 1455. In this year the Great Council was very heavy with senior men. Over half of the members had been in the council for over 20 years (see the first column in Figure 8.2). In this year there is also a noticeable dip or 'trough' in the middle of the distribution. This is the cohort of men which had been in council between 15 and 19 years. It was unusually small with only 20 members. In this same year the council was also bottom-heavy with large numbers of relatively new entrants. We might say, therefore, that the distribution of the council in 1455 was thin in the middle but rather heavily weighted at both ends. It did not remain so.

Five years later in 1460 (see the second column in Figure 8.2) the council had become less top-heavy. Yet, paradoxically, the most senior cohorts of the council, that is those with more than 30 years of service, had grown. This would make the council appear more gerontocratic. Yet the next two cohorts had actually decreased in numbers. The third cohort is the same 'trough' noted in the 1455 council, but it has now shifted upward in the distribution as its members have aged. Thus, in the interval between 1455 and 1460, the overall shape of the council had altered with the middle cohorts of the 1460 council containing two crests.

Therefore, examined sequentially from 1455 to 1490, we can see that the proportion of junior members increases as we would expect from

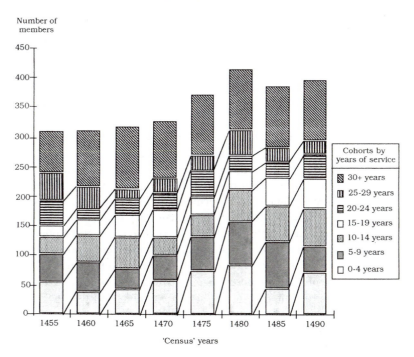

Number of
members

Figure 8.2 The Great Council 1455–90: membership by length of service

the overall growth of the council, but this increase is not very uniform and the distribution of Great Council members by years of service reveals some striking peculiarities. How are these changes to be regarded?

The changing shape of the Great Council has significant structural implications. Note has already been made of the 'trough' in the middle of the 1455 Great Council. Following through the changes in the council's composition, there is also a 'crest' of young entrants in the council of 1480, that is the cohort of men who had served 4 years or less. As the use of the terms 'troughs' and 'crests' implies, there appear to be regular changes which move, wave-like, through the composition of the Great Council. These troughs and crests have a periodicity of approximately a quarter-century. This is very similar to a phenomenon first noted in nineteenth-century Norwegian marriage data by Eilert Sundt and which now bears his name, Sundt's Law.[10]

In the Norwegian case, the crests were understood as the result of an unusually large number of births within a short period of time. Such baby-booms occurred in the aftermath of epidemics which decimated large sections of the population. However, more recent demographic research has shown that quasi-cycles of about thirty years are characteristic of pre-industrial populations and that such cycles do not depend, as Sundt suggested, on catastrophic shock for their occurrence.[11] I suggest that the crests and troughs represent quasi-cycles moving through the Great Council from 1455 to 1490.

These Ragusan quasi-cycles are also the results of an unusual number of weddings and subsequent births. While Ragusan kinship and marriage bears upon politics and government in interesting ways, there is not scope to examine them within the confines of a single chapter. Rather than examine the causes of the successive crests and troughs, I shall explore their consequences especially for the conduct of Ragusan politics. While the increasing numbers of patricians were seen as a boon for the city, it also led to increasing competition for office. More men were available to compete for the same number of offices. Generally, nominees for office were usually of similar experience and length of service. It thus follows that the more men that there are of similar experience, the less likely it is that they will hold office. The converse is also true. But there are some important exceptions. One exception is the gerontocratic domination of government by the most senior men. The second exception concerns the uneven distribution of men within the Great Council in terms of length of service.

So far as gerontocracy is concerned, senior men tended to monopolise the more senior and prestigious offices. Therefore, the likelihood of holding office is not only inversely related to the number of similarly aged competitors, but it is also inversely related to the number of more senior men. The number of offices held by the more senior cohorts (that is those with over 30 years' service in the Great Council) is not related to their proportion of the total Great Council membership, but to the absolute size of the cohort itself. In periods when there were many more of these senior men, they simply held more offices. Moreover, they also tended to monopolise the most prestigious ones. These posts, and the men occupying them, constituted the 'inner circle' of government.

After a man had been in the Great Council for about thirty years and had served in a number of different offices, he would have gained sufficient stature to be elected to one of these key positions of government, like the Rector, a member of the Senate, one of the Small Council, or one of the judges of the Criminal or Civil Courts (the *Judici del criminal* or *Consoli de le cause civil*). Movement into this inner circle came slowly and only after a man had served in many elected offices. Most men who were elected to one of the inner-circle posts had served in about 15 previous offices before they were elected. In any single year there were approximately 56 men in the inner circle although the number fluctuated somewhat from year to year. Once elected into the world of these *sapiens* (as they were known), a man was seldom out, even though a completely unbroken record of inner-circle offices is rather unusual. Most men who finally achieve one inner-circle position thus occasionally hold other offices. When they do it is most likely to be as one of the *Procuratori* of a church or monastery, or to be as *Advocati del proprio*, *Advocati del comone*, *Conte de Slano*, *Cazamorti* or *Conte de Stagno* – all senior, prestigious offices.

A person's rate of advancement up through the office hierarchy into the inner circle might reflect his experience and growing expertise. But this movement also depended in part upon the numbers and types of men within the inner circle itself. Because of the nature and number of posts at the top of government, there was an upper limit on the number of men who could be routinely elected.

Inner-circle posts carried both power and prestige, but the number of such posts available each year was (relatively) fixed. The number of senior men, however, was not. In periods when there more senior men, more of them held inner-circle posts. In such periods, more of them were also holding the occasional junior post outside of the inner-circle. When they could not hold an inner-circle post, senior men tended to monopolise the next most senior offices. Their immediate juniors, now being deprived of their customary offices, would assume posts normally occupied by *their* juniors. Since the total number of government posts available in a year was fairly constant, this effect 'cascaded down' from the most prestigious and senior posts to the most junior. The impact of this cascading effect depended, in the first instance, on the number of men in the inner circle and also on the number of those who were their immediate juniors. Further effects would depend upon the relative numbers of those juniors and those who were, in turn, their juniors, and so on.

Thus, in periods when there were many senior men, they tended to hold more inner-circle offices. The same holds true for the next most senior cohort, the one after that, and so on down the ranks of the Great

Council. Therefore, while there was an approximately constant 'volume' of offices to be filled, in periods when there were relatively more senior men, there were consequently relatively fewer offices left for the more junior men to hold. Competition for offices, therefore, can be understood in terms of pressures emanating from the top down. But this is only one part of the picture. Another part is the distribution of offices and councils. For while there were many inner-circle offices, there were relatively few offices which served as stepping-stones to them.

The most common route into this select world of the inner circle was through the offices of *Advocati del proprio* and *Cazamorti*. Both of these were held about one year prior to election into the inner circle. Other common routes were through the offices of *Massari de le biave*, *Advocati del comone*, and *Doanieri*. There were relatively few posts available at a level just below that of the inner circle. This paucity of posts created a serious bottleneck in the route to high office. Many offices were available to (say) those with 15 to 19 years of service in the Great Council, fewer for those with 20 to 24 years service, and still fewer for those with 25 to 29 years – the threshold of the inner circle.

The 'bottleneck effect', however, had another restricting dimension. Offices like that of *Cazamorti* which served as stepping-stones into the inner circle were precisely the same offices which were most likely to be held by members of the inner circle at those times when they were not holding an inner-circle post. This increased the bottleneck effect and made it particularly difficult for men to break into the ranks of the inner circle.

Gerontocractic domination did not penetrate through all offices. Some were simply thought too junior and demeaning for a senior man to hold. None of the most senior men was ever elected to be *Scrivari over garcon dela dohane grande*, for example. Other junior posts such as that of *Biscoti officiali* or *Cechieri* were also inappropriate for the elderly grandees. There were thus 'floors' associated with particular age and status cohorts, and these established thresholds below which it was unseemly to seek, or accept, office.

Therefore, in the competition for office, senior men took the most powerful and prestigious posts. In periods when there were more of them, they took posts which in other times might have gone to more junior men. This, as we have seen, had a knock-on effect down through the hierarchy of offices. If we ask who were a particular man's competitors for political office, we do not find a simple answer. They were, other things being equal, his contemporaries. The more near-contemporaries he had, the less likely it was that he would hold office. Similarly, their relative scarcity would increase his chances. But his chances depended not only on his contemporaries, but also on the numbers and relative seniority of more experienced men. It depended, in other words, on his place in the distribution of Great Council members and on the shape of that distribution at particular moments in time.

Men of differing cohorts, entering the Great Council at differing periods, experienced differing amounts of competition over their political careers. Their experience depended not only on the size of their own cohort, but also on the the size of the next most senior cohort. This was a result of the 'cascading' effect. Not only are the members of larger cohorts less likely to hold office, but their experience is of the lower offices.

III Hierarchy and Indeterminacy

In outlining the structure of Ragusan government, it was noted above that while offices could be ordered in a hierarchy, there was also considerable variation in the point where particular offices were held for the first time. This raises the question of how much hierarchy there was, and the extent to which that hierarchy remained stable over time. Let us consider the second question first. Throughout the period from 1440 to 1490, most of the offices and councils maintained their position in the hierarchical order. For example, if we plot the number of years after entry into the Great Council that each incumbent holds an office, the resultant trend is essentially flat or slightly negative. The office of *Armamento Officiali*, which we have already examined, illustrates this point (See Figure 8.1).

But not all offices retained the same relative position within the hierarchy. The office of *Cechieri* shows a very marked drop over time. In the early part of the period it was held (for the first time) about twenty years after entry. But by the end of the period, it was being held about ten years after entry. Relative to other offices, therefore, it dropped down the office hierarchy. The post of *Conte de Canale* also shifted its position. But here, as time progressed, the office was held later and later. Therefore, it could be said to have moved up the office hierarchy. The net effect of these changes over time was to slightly reduce the number of middle-range offices.

The remaining question is: just how much hierarchy was there? In discussing the ranking of offices and councils, I pointed to the very considerable variation that existed. The standard deviations about the mean are quite large. We can now explain some of that variation as being the result of the changing shape of the Great Council and of the 'cascading' and 'bottleneck' effects. Does this mean that the idea of a 'hierarchy' is a mirage?

One way of answering this is to examine whether pairs of offices are actually held in a determinant order. While there might in some cases appear to be an ordering, that ordering might merely be an artifact of posts being held in individual careers of office-holding. Alternatively there might have been for some posts a cultural notion that Post 'A' should be held before Post 'B'. The evidence indicates that when two offices were held at about the same point in career patterns, there appears to have been no preference about whether Post 'A' should be held first or Post 'B'. But in cases where there were usually several years between the holding of one office and the other, the one regularly preceded the other. Indeed, we can say that the greater the difference in years, the more determinant the appearance of ordering. Even so, ordering clearly existed at each stage in a career. Preferential ordering indicates determinant relationships between particular pairs of offices, and if we accept a determinant relationship as one in which there were at least ten pairings and where one of the pair preceded the other in at least 90 per cent of the pairings, then determinant relationships existed, for example, between the following pairs of offices: *Scrivari over garcon dela dohane grande* and *Biscoti officiali* (both held early in a career), *Biscoti officiali* and *Cechieri* (also early), *Biscoti officiali* and *Armamento officiali* (also early), *Cechieri* and *Advocati alla camara del arte* (early to middle), *Raxone officiali* and *Doanieri* (middle), *Officiali lavorieri de scrita in Stagno* and *Massari de le biave* (middle), *Judicieri del comone* and *Advocati del proprio* (late middle), and *Advocati del comone* and *Consoli de le cause civil* (late). The importance of these cases, and others like them, is that they clearly indicate that patricians thought that a hierarchical relationship existed between particular pairs of offices which could in fact be held at about the same point in a career. Furthermore, such pairings were to be found in various parts of the office hierarchy from very early in political careers to very late. The hierarchy had a characteristic shape which certainly retained some degree of stability throughout the period. But how real was this stablity?

Conclusion

In this work, explained briefly here, I am intent upon examining the governing of a historical city-state. The work not only refers to a particular *period* of a half-century, but attempts to chart the significance of the *passage* of time. The point of this can be simply stated. Although it was buffeted by major events, throughout the period from 1440 to 1490 the government of Ragusa appears remarkably stable. Year after year, and at about the same time every year, ballots are held to elect the same number of incumbents to the same offices. This tedious repetition would be ample proof, if proof were needed, that Ragusa enjoyed a remarkably stable government throughout the period. But proof is not needed. The same pattern of balloting for the same offices and councils pre-dates our chosen period by at least one century and follows it for several more.

But I wish to suggest that this appearance of stability is something of a mirage both for the observer of the late twentieth century and, most likely, for the patricians who participated in the electoral process itself. Let me begin by suggesting reasons why it was a mirage. They are (1) the shifting numbers of men available to serve in particular offices at particular times, (2) the changing shape of the Great Council, (3) the movement of troughs and crests of men through it, (4) the changing amount of competition at differing points in time and for differing sections of the Great Council, and (5) the movement of some offices within the hierarchy.

If these kinds of shifts and alterations can be discerned in the data, why might the patricians of the period have been unaware of them? I suggest three reasons. First, the office-holding experience of men was greatly different even for age mates who entered the Great Council at the same time. A cohort, a set of men entering the Great Council within a five-year interval, is a useful analytical device, but these cohorts do not necessarily have much sociological significance. Not all the members of a cohort, for example, would have been of the same age and experience. Georgius Polo de Poça and Marcus Andreas de Zrieva both began their political careers in June 1474. Georgius, however, was 31 years old

while Marcus was just 20.[12] Georgius began to hold office almost immediately. Marcus, however, waited for six years by which time Georgius
had already held four offices. Therefore, while cohort members may
have similar length of experience in the Great Council, the nature of
that experience could be very different.

Some cohort members also held many offices, others held none.
Further, and what is probably the more telling point, some cohort
members could become rapidly differentiated from their fellows. Certain men moved rapidly up through the offices of government so that
after the passage of a few years they were competing with men who had
had much longer service. In terms of their political standing, such
men could be said to have left their entrance cohort and become
de facto members of more senior ones. There are great differences
between men in their rate of rise through the offices and councils of
government.

The second reason why patricians may have been unaware of subtle
changes in the structure of government concerns the variations in
career patterns. There is no single road through the offices. Indeed, it
is not even possible to speak in the plural of 'paths'. Men who have
reached the top will have done so in quite different ways. Some will
have held dozens of different offices. Others, while holding office
dozens of times, will have served in relatively few offices on multiple
occasions. Still others may have combined both, moving rapidly for a
time through a succession of offices and then apparently stagnating for
a period when only a few were held and these being held repeatedly.
Not only this. We find that some offices shift position in the hierarchy
over time. Therefore two men may have held the same post at about the
same point in their career, but when one man held it the post may have
been regarded as quite senior, and his holding it an indication of great
potential. At a different time holding the same post might have been
regarded as a matter of little merit. While these variations in cohort and
office-holding have been discussed separately in this chapter, the effects
are not so much different as additive. What they reveal is great variation
in the experience of patrician men rising through the offices. But in the
midst of all of this, there were also forces at work which maintained a
fiction of continuity and constancy in government.

Crucial among these forces was the broad pattern of order we have
already discussed such as the undoubted seniority of such offices as that
of *Proveditori* or the juniority of the *Biscotti officiali*. We have also noted
the ordering within particular pairs of offices. They would have been

enforced by the framework of legislation which imposed an ordering on some offices such as that which set out age criteria for the holding of particular offices. All of these devices would have added conviction to an ideology of stability in government. There is another, less obvious, feature to which I wish to draw attention. This is the authoritative voice of the more senior men in representing the nature of government.

Great deference was paid to the views of the most senior and experienced. The elderly were living embodiments of a glorious past. They could testify to what they had heard and observed, particularly from those who were already very elderly when they themselves were young and inexperienced. They could also speak from great personal experience. Few younger men would be in a position to gainsay their views, and no one would be inclined to give public voice to such views given the great veneration for age.

Two points need to be made about the authoritative opinions of seniors. The first is that they were likely to support and buttress one another in the very unlikely event of a challenge from below. It was in their common interest that the primacy of age be maintained and that they defer to one another in terms of broad principles. Second, in points where they might disagree, such disagreement would be interpreted as the irascibility of age and personal rivalry, rather than placing any doubt on the authoritativeness of gerontocratic opinion. Furthermore, within each household and set of close kinsfolk, the personal experience of the most senior men was likely to inform the views of younger men. While domestically transmitted views might gainsay the publicly stated views of the most gerontocractic and respected men, self-interest and deference were unlikely to let such private knowledge intrude into public discourse in governmental councils. Further, the very great range of personal experience even within a small group of kinsmen would present sufficient ambiguity about the nature of the cultural world of government to disguise its ongoing changes while at the same time preserving the fiction of stability and continuity.

The Weberian view of office which has dominated classical accounts, treats office as a position which serves particular (governmental) functions. An array of such positions, defined in terms of their rights and duties, can be taken to constitute the structure of government. Such a view can often be expressed in diagrams or geometrical metaphors which suggest both orderliness and stability. An alternative view, and the one which has characterised this study, looks not to the rights and duties which define particular positions, but rather at the progress of office-holders moving through a succession of posts and, conversely, at posts as they are held by a succession of office-holders. This is a prosopological view which totalises in that it attempts to discern general patterns in what is a collection of individual careers. This perspective, while unconventional in terms of the analysis of politics in nation-states, is nevertheless classically anthropological. In this respect, offices, like *kula* valuables or pearl shells in Melanesian ceremonial exchange systems, may also be regarded as tokens of esteem which represent the 'value' of the incumbent at a point in time. Ragusan offices, as tokens, circulate rapidly. Most could only be held for a year or less and an office-token cannot be exchanged for itself. Indeed, if a person is not bestowed with another office-token in the meantime, two years must ordinarily elapse before the same token can be bestowed again. A person may therefore be regarded as accumulating value according to the number of office-tokens they have held and the period in which they have held them. A person accumulates value through the succession of offices he has held.

But this view is one-sided. Offices, as we have seen, are not fixed. They are not fixed points with an associated amount of (fixed) value. They, too, may be said to have value according to the quality of persons who have passed through them. Office-holding, therefore, is a two-way dynamic process. People change in value as they hold a succession of offices, but offices too may change in value as they are held by a succession of incumbents.

9

'THREE ORDERS OF INHABITANTS': SOCIAL HIERARCHIES IN THE REPUBLIC OF VENICE

Brian Pullan

Many scholars would agree without difficulty on the abstract character-istics of an ideal society of orders. But they would debate other ques-tions more fiercely. Did any actual society bear a close relation to the stark outlines of this model or pattern? Does the simple notion of a society of orders throw light on the historical reality, or does it merely distort and obfuscate it? A society of orders is generally conceived as one which is hierarchically arranged, consisting of large social groupings which are charged with performing quite different functions for the benefit of society and the body politic, and hence are treated in distinc-tive ways by the law, the fisc and the representative system. The upper orders – usually identified as the nobility and the clergy – are not (at least not primarily) social classes, because their social position does not derive principally from their material wealth, their roles in the produc-tion of material goods, or their shared life-chances.[1] Rather, it springs from the value attributed by some kind of social consensus (how this arises is seldom clear) to the duties they perform – by praying for the common weal, by administering the sacraments, by fighting for king and country, by dispensing justice. It would be foolish to suppose that their status has nothing to do with their material possessions or with the

147

rents and dues they derive from their property, but it is possible to argue that these things are secondary to the functions which they carry out, for which their wealth merely provides support. A relatively low value is placed upon the generation, rather than the enjoyment, of wealth: indeed, the duty to labour may well be regarded as a curse, or a penalty for sin, which confers only vileness and bestows no honour. Moreover, it would be quite possible for groupings whose wealth derived from similar sources to be members of different orders on account of the different functions expected of them. After all, the nobility and clergy formed separate orders, even though both relied to a large extent on incomes from the land, the most valued commodity of all.

Among the rewards of the upper orders are legally recognised privileges, which differentiate each order from the rest of society. These may be positive, guaranteeing exclusive access to prestigious positions and profitable offices, or negative, bestowing immunities from normal legal processes or from the obligation to pay taxes associated with plebeian status. Members of orders share similar notions of honourable and shameful behaviour, for orders are defined partly in terms of what they must not do, and each has its own taboos – as the clergy may be forbidden to have sex or shed blood, the nobility be barred from trading or stooping to manual labour. Indeed, the nobility and clergy are of a different species from commoners. For they have stamped on them at birth, or by ceremonies such as ordination or dubbing, a deep-seated quality which cannot be obliterated save by some penalty so drastic as the attainder of a traitorous nobleman and his descendants or the unfrocking of a criminous clergyman. At least in theory, social and legal standing are separable from wealth; a nobleman who begs is still a nobleman, and the moral influence of a friar may depend upon his choice of poverty, his renunciation of material things, as well as upon his eloquence in the pulpit. In practice it may be hard for a nobleman to command respect without having the means to live in suitable style, but there is also a profound distrust of new money, which does not command social acceptance: titles and rank can be bought, but genuine social status – as distinct from legal recognition – takes much longer to acquire.

So long as the system works properly, conflict should not arise, for orders, as the limbs or organs of the body politic, do different things, and should not compete, as classes do, for shares in the profits of economic enterprise. Ideally, since it aspires to harmony and equilibrium, the society of orders contains no dynamo for structural change.

Where conflict does break out, its professed aim is to restore balance, remove abuses, recover or destroy dishonest gains, remove oppressive ministers, bad advisers or favourites, defend violated privileges, rather than to redistribute wealth and power or introduce rule by a previously subjugated social class. Structural change may be precluded, but social mobility is not. However, advancement into a privileged order can only be achieved by the formal consent of superiors, and there is often a prolonged interval, extending over perhaps three generations, between acquiring a new legal position and being socially acknowledged.[2]

All such things may be seen by critics as mere expressions of a conservative ideology, contrived by churchmen and aristocrats or by their sycophantic supporters in order to defend their entrenched positions. Naturally, historians approaching past societies are entitled if they choose to employ the vocabulary of a later age, the language of class, to expose the exploitative relationships concealed behind the façade of the society of orders and its smug pretence of social concord. Class struggles might not at the time have been recognised for what they were, but that is not to deny that classes existed, representing a grimmer and more deep-rooted version of reality. In defence of orders, however, it should be said that they were not merely figments of the imagination of powerful people, not just the cardboard creations of propagandists, for they were embodied in fiscal systems, in regional and national parliaments, in patents of nobility, in registers of honourable citizens, and officially recognised in numerous other ways. The language of orders often overlapped confusingly with the language of estates, the term 'estate' being sometimes used to denote an order or other grouping in so far as it took part in government, either directly or through representatives. But the meaning of 'estate' was not always so exact. For the word could refer to any social condition or way of life, privileged and honourable or not, within an order or outside it – as a petition in the name of the poor people of London in 1552 spoke of 'that wretched and vile estate' of beggary brought on by idleness, the condition of the vagabond or strumpet bound for the house of correction at Bridewell.[3]

One familiar version of the society of orders rests it upon three bodies, clergy, nobility and people, those who pray, those who fight and those who labour, arranged hierarchically according to the importance of the functions they perform. In societies consciously dedicated to the pursuit of salvation for the largest possible number of souls, the clergy stood highest, although in France in 1614–15 there was a move to recognise as paramount the magistracy of the nobles.[4] Such threefold visions of society gained especial sanctity from analogies with the triune God, as though human organisation were attaining unity in diversity and becoming three in one and one in three, through the sense of reciprocal obligation, the charity and deference that cemented the different orders into an idyllically harmonious relationship.[5] Or society might be seen as an earthly mirror, a parallel version or a continuation, of hierarchies created in heaven.[6] Hence to think of shaking its founda-tions would be an act of near blasphemy, a blatant defiance of God. It was true that both twofold divisions of society (into clergy and laity) and fourfold divisions (in which the people became not one entity but two, consisting of townspeople and country-folk) were put forward. Other schemes split up the ecclesiastics and exalted monks above secular clergy. But the classic threefold division sat well with a monarchy which traced its authority to God and was devoted to conquest and the de-fence of its inheritance by force of arms. It was especially appropriate to a Catholic monarchy, since Luther's famous declaration that 'all Christians are truly of the spiritual estate and there is no difference among them save that of office'[7] promised to undermine the clergy's status as a privileged order and transform them into, at best, a learned profession.

Arguably, however, when projected on to the vast canvas of an ag-gressive monarchical state, the concept of a society of orders threatens to decay into a cliché, embodying commonplace notions but explaining very little. It may be, however, that if transposed to the microcosm of a much smaller society, to the narrower space of a town or city-state, this concept will take on a more exact meaning, every community having its own more refined and subtle version of the society of orders. The idea of orders may persist, even if the orders themselves are differently constituted and directed towards different ends. To test the proposi-tion, this essay will explore the concept of the society of orders within the context of the Venetian Republic – a state and society devoted to the pursuit of wealth through commerce rather than of prestige through military prowess; a Catholic commonwealth which became famous, at least in the seventeenth century, for its resistance to clerical domination and its defiance of papal censures.

The contrast between an absolute monarchy and a republic was not entirely clear-cut. For the Doge of Venice was a prince and no mere burgomaster. Though scarcely a priest-king, he was in minor orders, and had something of Venice's patron, St Mark, about him or even a touch of the divine.[8] But the Doge of the later Middle Ages and the early modern centuries was an elected and not a hereditary ruler. Never surrounded by a resplendent court and supposedly constrained by an ever-lengthening coronation oath, he wielded authority by personifying the collective absolute power of the hereditary Venetian aristocracy over its subjects, within the city and outside it.[9] Collective rule was assured by rotating magisterial offices, and places on the most important councils and committees, among members of a legally defined, numerous but exclusive, political nation. Few individuals held any particular magisterial post for more than a year or two at a time, unless there were grave difficulties in finding a successor.[10] Foreign ambassadors and papal nuncios of the sixteenth century little doubted that they were dealing with a many-headed monster, and professed themselves unhappy at constitutional changes that made the situation even worse – for example, at the shifts of power in the 1580s from the inner circle surrounding the secretive Council of Ten to the much more numerous body which met in the Senate.[11]

Unlike the Dutch Republic, the Venetian was not a military union. Nor was it a federation of towns and provinces which enjoyed, at least formally, equal standing and equal representation through deputies to a central parliament. Venice was very much the dominant city, whose native corps of rulers exercised power over two empires of subject provinces and cities. They were lords of a number of island colonies and coastal strips extending to the eastern Mediterranean and forming the seaward dominions, and over a more populous and prosperous landward empire on the northern Italian mainland. The seaward dominions formed the senior empire; westward expansion across the peninsula to the borders of the state of Milan took place for the most part in the fifteenth century. It fell to the Venetian nobility to provide the great subject cities with governors and supply most of the bishops to the principal mainland sees. Local elites controlled many of their own affairs, their institutions surviving their capitulation to Venice even if their princes, such as the Carraresi of Padua, did not. Each city and province had its own social hierarchy, there being no single, unified nobility recognised throughout Venetian possessions. Only at certain periods of the seventeenth and eighteenth centuries, between 1646 and 1718, and after 1775, were individual noble families from the mainland generally permitted or encouraged to join the Venetian nobility. By the late eighteenth century they seemed to have lost enthusiasm for doing so.[12] There was no central representative institution or Estates-General at which the prince consulted with his subjects, although at least one province, the Friuli, had its own parliament, which appeared to recognise the traditional three estates. For it was attended by prominent ecclesiastics, nobles who occupied castles, and representatives of certain towns.[13] Between 1537 and 1541 the peasants of the Friuli gained separate representation of their own, and in other regions there were some elected rural councils, known as *corpi territoriali* and chosen by the headmen of village communities.[14] In effect, however, the Republic of Venice consisted of the city of Venice, the Dominante, a body politic complete in itself; the remainder of the state was not part of the Republic of Venice so much as subject to it, and cast in the role of petitioner.

Though far from being a traditional monarchic state, Venice recognised legally defined orders, for a society dominated by commerce was not necessarily a fluid one, disposed to believe that money automatically conferred status and poverty diminished it. The state's public image was agreeably tinted by a political myth which was eventually presented in the form of a handy book by the noble Venetian churchman, Cardinal Gasparo Contarini. By 1530 Venice had been forced to curb her aggressive, land-grabbing instincts, and Contarini stressed her serener qualities by portraying the harmony and stability of her social order rather than her capacity for conquest.[15] For the city's achievement, or so he argued, lay in contriving a 'mixture of all estates' – by which he meant a blending of monarchic, aristocratic and popular elements, which would also reconcile the claims of youth and age and of rich and poor.[16] These 'estates', however, were all found within the nobility, for when he spoke of popular government he was referring not to the common people of the city but to the ordinary run-of-the-mill male adult nobles, two or three thousand strong in a city of well over 100,000 inhabitants.[17] If he believed in democracy, it was democracy only for noblemen, who were free of the need to become artificers or shopkeepers.

Contarini wrote of a binary division of the residents of Venice into noblemen, who were free, and people, who were servile, without leisure, and enslaved by the need to earn a living.[18] But others, before and after him, preferred to recognise a three-tiered ranking into nobles (also called gentlemen or patricians), citizens, and artisans, otherwise called the 'mean people' (*popolo menuto*) or simply 'the people'. In a descriptive work eventually dedicated to the Doge of Venice in 1493, Marin Sanudo, a noble historian soon to become an indefatigable dia-

rist, spoke tersely of three *generationi* in Venice, meaning three different
sorts or species of person.[19] An exile from Florence, Donato Giannotti,
elaborated on the point in the 1520s.[20] Between the late sixteenth and
the late seventeenth centuries other writers expressly referred to these
social categories as orders; Antonio Milledonne, a senior civil servant
composing an edifying dialogue in the 1580s, associated the concept
of orders with the harmonious social relationships which arose from
everyone knowing his place and being contented with his lot. He had
one of his actors remark that

> Venice has three orders of inhabitants, nobles, citizens and people.
> Suitable provision has been made for all of them according to their
> condition or rather capability, and hence everyone is contented with
> his position and existence, and does not attempt to advance any
> further by disturbing the universal peace.[21]

Even Contarini eventually admitted that there were people and people,
and that there were some 'of the honester and best respected sort' who
deserved to be distinguished from the 'very base common people'
engaged in manual work as craftsmen or labourers.[22] However, he was
reluctant to concede the name of 'citizen' even to respectable commoners, since he firmly believed that the only true citizens, enjoying full
political rights, were the nobility, who almost constituted a complete
social system by themselves.[23]

None of these accounts made mention of the clergy – whether because their authors had determined to isolate Venetian lay society and
concentrate on that alone, or because they believed that the secular
clergy and the male and female religious of Venice were not really part
of the civic commonwealth. The concept of orders did not account for
everyone in Venice; like most social models it was too simple to be
comprehensive. Census-takers, who knocked on the doors of houses
and institutions, and did have to count all heads, made use of some
additional categories – the servants who dwelt in noblemen's and citizens' houses, the clergy and religious of both sexes, the inmates of
hospitals, the beggars (probably the homeless ones who slept in door-
ways and under arches), and the Jews who lived apart from Christian
society in the Ghetto, which had been a place of compulsory residence
for them since 1516.[24] Some of these represented social degrees or
qualities, but were not clearly placed within a recognised system of
orders.

Secular clergymen, however, were not marginalised. They were heavily involved in the routine administration of the city, and the government called upon their services as upon those of lay social orders. In Venice, as in other towns, arrangements for poor relief, designed to involve representatives of all the more respectable and independent 'conditions' or 'degrees' within the community, offer a guide to the social categories acknowledged by the government itself when pursuing good order in the city. By Senate legislation of 1529, the administration of a wide-ranging relief scheme was entrusted to the parish priest in each parish, with the assistance of four lay deputies elected by the parishioners – two noblemen, one citizen and one artisan. In such an important domestic enterprise, these were the groups that counted.[25]

To some extent the clergy were recognised as a distinctive social order, serving the community and yet separated from it by the posses-sion of privileges and immunities in recognition of their sacramental powers.[26] But they were not a first order entitled to take part in and exercise supreme moral authority over government. In the mid four-teenth century, a lay religious brotherhood had pronounced unequivo-cally that 'it is not lawful for any lay or secular person to admonish, correct or demand obedience of any priest or clerk', and had even thought it unseemly that laymen should wash and lay out the corpse of a priest. These scruples did not last for long, for priests were, by the end of the century, being employed as chaplains to the brotherhood, subject to dismissal for derelictions of duty or moral lapses.[27] But at least in theory the clergy enjoyed traditional privileges. They could not easily be taxed without papal permission, and were often alleged to be getting off lightly; their liabilities to tax were recorded on special registers, separated from those of the laity and not generally overhauled between 1564 and 1769, whilst many special exemptions were allowed.[28] There was some government recognition of the right of the clergy to be tried in church courts, accompanied by complaints that clerical justice, as administered by the papal nuncio, was not severe enough.[29] However, a clerical tonsure would not confer immunity from punishment for any offence defined as a heinous crime, and the Venetians were able to claim papal privileges entitling them, at the very least, to punish ordi-nary clergymen (not prelates) who committed such atrocities in the city of Venice itself.[30]

Clerical immunities were violated occasionally, if the time seemed ripe. Clergymen were forced without papal permission to lend to the state in 1527, the year in which Rome was sacked by imperial troops.[31] One implacable Patriarch, the Dominican Gerolamo Querini (1524–54), excommunicated a magistracy which had condemned a priest and refused to hand him over to the Church.[32] In 1606, the government's alleged attacks on the 'liberty of the Church' were to bring down upon it the most famous of several papal interdicts, the pope contesting its right not only to punish high-ranking clergymen who had committed crimes on the mainland, but also to pass laws restraining the right of laymen to leave landed property to ecclesiastical institutions.[33] The concept of clerical privilege, though not always respected, was a force to be reckoned with, and had its defenders, both within and outside Venice.

Some attempts were made to emphasise the special standing of the clergy by detaching them from worldly concerns. These moves came partly from within the Church, Pope Eugenius IV forbidding Venetian clergymen to act as notaries in 1433,[34] and partly from the Venetian state, which was bent on ensuring that the profits of office were fairly distributed, and did not want noblemen who pursued ecclesiastical benefices to be entitled to hold government offices as well.[35] But, as a papal nuncio commented ruefully in 1536, the Venetian government was anxious to wield both the spiritual and the material sword, to exercise control over ecclesiastical as over secular affairs, as though the state would otherwise be no sovereign state.[36] It wished to curb clerical influence over government, whilst using clerics as instruments of government, and subjecting ecclesiastical institutions, at least in their material aspects, to the state. Venetian nobles and citizens were notorious in clerical eyes for their desire to use convents for social rather than religious purposes, placing in them daughters for whom they could not afford marriage portions, and the government was eager to control convents by exploiting its power to supervise their resources through an important magistracy established in 1521.[37] Attitudes were influenced by having the pope as a close neighbour, prone to employing his spiritual powers to gain advantages for his temporal state – hence the conviction, on the part of some noble purists, that those who pursued high office in the Church were in danger of allying themselves with a foreign power, especially as Venice had no concordat entitling the state to make its own appointments to the lucrative sees on the Italian mainland and one could obtain preferment only with papal favour.[38] Such scruples, however, were not shared by the whole ruling order, for some families established effective control over bishoprics for several generations, treating them almost as hereditary property.[39] Venetian anti-clericalism was in part the product of rivalries within the nobility, those without access to ecclesiastical patronage envying and despising those who profited from it.

However, there was a strong inclination to believe that the clergy were most useful when they could be subordinated to the state and to lay agencies, rather than allowed to claim the status of a privileged order. Venetian parish clergy were used as minor civil servants by the sixteenth century, employed not only to help administer poor relief but also to notify noble births, inform on baptismal ceremonies, report plague suspects, and take censuses.[40] Although the clergy had a distinctive status and there were some stout defenders of their privileges, they were not a corporation separated from the rest of society or immune from state power. When the Jesuits were manoeuvred into upholding papal authority against the state's demand for total obedience during the interdict of 1606–7, their reluctant defiance of Venice earned them expulsion from the state for a period of fifty years.[41]

By contrast the nobility were not merely the first estate but the only full members of the Venetian polity. From the early fourteenth century to be noble was, for a man or boy, to be 'of the Great Council or capable of being of it'; for a female, it was to be the legitimate daughter of such a person.[42] For grown men it was to be entitled, usually by virtue of one's birth, to enter an assembly of adult males, mostly over the age of twenty-five, which always numbered at least a thousand and sometimes – certainly in the early sixteenth century – exceeded 2,500.[43] This body's main function, as a sovereign gathering of all full citizens, was to choose, from its own ranks, the smaller councils, the Senate and the Ten, which did the real work of governing, and to elect to most of the offices defined as magistracies. In the late thirteenth and the fourteenth centuries, the Great Council had been enlarged but at the same time formally closed to newcomers, a group of Venetian families combining to exclude those whom they defined as outsiders, although it took several decades to determine who should enter the Council and who should not.[44] In the fifteenth and sixteenth centuries, other such formal closures were to follow in the Venetian dominions, both in Italian subject cities of the Venetian Republic and in those of Dalmatia and the Ionian islands, towns erecting their own exclusive clubs of hereditary rulers and generally denying access to power to those born outside these circles.[45] In Venice the general principle was that noble status should pass to legitimately born descendants in the male line of the men who had formed part of the Great Council in the late thirteenth and fourteenth centuries. Some importance, however, attached to the standing of a nobleman's wife. Indeed, Francesco Barbaro, a fifteenth-century humanist, held that since mother's milk shaped character the quality of the wife was almost more important than that of her husband.[46] From 1506 there was an obligation to register the births of noble sons with the principal law officers of Venice, if they were to enjoy the privileges of their rank, and from 1526 a duty to register noble marriages.[47] Most weddings joined noblemen to the daughters of other nobles, but marriages to citizen girls were acceptable, even if some forms of misalliance, with slave women from 1422 and with courtesans or the descendants of manual workers from 1589–90, would deny noble status to the children of the union.[48]

Closure of the noble order had the effect of excluding newly rich commoners from direct participation in government, though some of their wealth could be transferred to nobles through marriage, by means of the dowries bestowed on their daughters by rich citizens seeking prestige and influence from noble sons-in-law.[49] Venetian humanists were quick to defend the traditional notion that nobility was not, in essence, a quality of the soul attached to virtuous individuals, but one transmitted by blood and acquired by descent from illustrious ancestors.[50] As Contarini explained, it was 'nobility of lineage' rather than 'greatness of wealth' that conferred the right to participate fully in public life, since the accumulation of fortunes often went with ignoble qualities, with plebeian parsimony rather than patrician generosity, aspirants 'never sparing the toilsome and careful wearing out of their lives, but with an intolerable saving, defrauding themselves of the comforts of life, thereby to increase their substance'.[51] It was true that the closure was not absolute, and a small number of new admissions were made, especially in 1381. But the nobles made a conscious decision in 1403 not to replace extinct noble families by recruiting new ones.[52] Only over the years 1646–1718, when the Republic was heavily involved in protracted warfare for the defence or reconquest of possessions in the eastern Mediterranean, did the nobility openly violate on a large scale the principle that rank could not be bought. Large cash contributions to the Venetian state, in the form of outright payments and investments in public loan funds, generally established a strong claim to be admitted to the Great Council, though petitioners were still scrutinised for signs of unworthy qualities, and the newest nobility took time to penetrate to the higher offices of state.[53]

For Venetian noblemen the most significant privilege lay in access to magisterial offices and to many minor offices of profit which came to be reserved for them. They were liable to pay the ordinary taxes levied on the population at large, and indeed heavy expenditure on certain forms of office, where the need for ostentation outstripped the official stipend, often acted as a form of supertax on the well-to-do. But they did enjoy some judicial privileges. From 1571 onwards cases involving noblemen were discreetly despatched behind the closed doors of the Council of Ten rather than be exposed to public view. Noble criminals were more likely to suffer exile or imprisonment than public execution. And until 1633 they could expect to escape the humiliation of being sentenced to forced labour at the oars of a Venetian galley.[54]

Though lineage, birthright and privilege were dear to them, Venetian nobles departed in several respects from traditional notions of what was proper to noblemen. They could well have been taxed with that tight-fistedness which Contarini deplored, for at least in Venice itself they spent little on large retinues, lavish hospitality or extravagant clothing, though they did invest heavily in jewellery for their wives and in such durable assets as family palaces and villas. Most heretical, perhaps, was their direct involvement in commerce, their seeming confusion of the roles of the captain and the justice with that of the self-seeking merchant. In the late Middle Ages and for much of the six-teenth century they were a 'thalassocracy',[55] ruling by virtue of their command of the sea and of the profits drawn from maritime commerce, rather than by their control of land, rents and dues, though many enjoyed an income from these sources as well. When they fought they fought as sea-captains and admirals, rather than as army officers com-manding troops in the field. This tradition could be justified, when it had to be, by invoking necessity: Venice's barren site had always forced the leaders of its community into trade, because honest commerce was more honourable than pillaging or plundering.[56] Nobility was thought compatible with wholesale international trade in goods of high quality – spices, glass, broadcloth, silks, precious metals – as well as more basic commodities such as salt, timber or stone. Such trade was one thing, ignoble shopkeeping quite another. It could be said that trade was public-spirited, a form of service to the state which was readily taxable through the customs and excise duties which enhanced the prince's revenue: the Venetians, being traders, wrote Giovanni Botero, had become rich as a community, whereas the Genoese, being bankers and financiers, had become rich as individuals.[57]

As Venice's mainland territories expanded, her nobles invested a greater proportion of their fortunes in landed possessions, though without destroying their character as urban nobles or investors in commerce. They were not merely seeking rural pleasure-grounds or convenient bolt-holes from a city that might be ravaged by plague; many were interested in farming for profit, and the products of manufacturing, financed by Venetian nobles in mainland towns such as Bassano, could well be sold abroad.[58] It was perfectly possible in the seventeenth century to invest in commerce as a sleeping partner, and to join forces with, for example, a Jewish merchant, even when the noble merchant travelling with his goods on board ship had become a distant memory and noblemen had largely disappeared from the Venetian colony in Constantinople.[59] Fifty to sixty per cent of new families recruited into the Venetian nobility between 1646 and 1718 had drawn their fortunes from trade.[60]

In theory, Venetian nobles were all equal, with no layering into dukes, marquesses, counts and barons, and no system of primogeniture to distinguish between elder and younger sons. In practice, though, there was a huge gulf between great families that married into foreign princely houses and pursued cardinals' hats,[61] and obscure, impoverished ones that scrambled for minor offices of profit. Venetian and other observers recognised certain strata within the nobility, sometimes a mere three and sometimes as many as five, defined either in terms of wealth, or in terms of ability to obtain access to certain councils or offices – the civil and criminal lawcourts known as the Quarantie or Forties being a well-known preserve of the poorer, if not of the poorest, nobility.[62] The paradoxical term 'noble plebeians' was coined in the 1730s to describe the most bedraggled members of the ruling order, without independent income or landed property, who seemed culturally different from their superiors, especially in their tendency to wed and breed freely in the hope of attracting offices and pensions, rather than restrict marriage in the hope of preserving the family patrimony from division.[63] In practice there were many reasons why wealth should contribute to advancement and power, if only because private means were necessary in order to hold prestigious unpaid offices, and the abuse of bribing mercenary noblemen to vote for their richer peers was already rife in the early sixteenth century.[64] Arguably, however, even in the late seventeenth and eighteenth centuries, Venice was an oligarchy rather than a plutocracy, in that the families most successful in pursuing high office were not necessarily the richest ones, and even very poor nobles could in practice become senators or ducal councillors.[65] With its huge range, from wealth to 'indescribable' poverty, the Venetian nobility displayed the characteristics of an order, like a shaft sunk through the economic pyramid and passing through all levels from pinnacle to base, rather than those of a class; it was shared privileges, and the possibility of participating in government, rather than similar economic roles or life chances, that bound them together.

Below the nobles in the social hierarchy were the 'citizen commoners' or *cives populares*, as they were called in a law of 1443.[66] There were several types of citizenship which identified their holders as Venetians, vowed to Venice and to no other homeland, and conferred privileges which distinguished them from foreigners, natives of subject territories, or birds of passage. Some notions of citizenship, as of nobility, were officially shaped during the fourteenth century, by legislation or other means. Already, in those years, for one to prove himself a genuine native Venetian, an *originario*, it was good to be able to show that his father and grandfather, as well as himself, had been born in the city.[67] In the fifteenth and sixteenth centuries this status, increasingly narrowly defined, was to become a vital qualification for entry to the higher civil service, which served councils and embassies, and an important one for entry to the middling bureaucracy, which attended to law courts and government offices. Other forms of citizenship, known as *de intus* ('at home') and *de intus et de extra* ('at home and abroad'), were concerned with minor offices and trading rights. Immigrants could acquire them by keeping houses in Venice, by marrying Venetian wives, and by paying Venetian taxes for a specified length of time. Usually fifteen years residence was required for citizenship within the city, and twenty-five to acquire the right and duty to trade abroad as a Venetian, paying Venetian customs duties at a lower rate than did foreigners. However, requirements were modified at times when Venice was especially anxious to attract new settlers, and citizenship of certain cities in the dominions would at once bestow citizenship *de intus* of Venice herself, though immigrants would have to apply in due course for citizenship *de intus et de extra* if they wished to trade directly with the Middle East.[68] According to Milledonne's discourse of 1580, citizenship *de intus* would qualify its holder to be a minor servant of a government office or lawcourt (at the level of a messenger or summoner, rather than a notary, clerk or accountant); to exercise any craft for which he possessed the necessary skill; and to become an officer of one of the smaller religious confraternities.[69]

Citizenship was of vital importance because the government was determined to restrict full enjoyment of the benefits and opportunities afforded by Venice to residents of long-standing and proven loyalty. The conviction that these should not be open to newly arrived foreigners (especially not to Protestant heretics from England or the Dutch Republic) would, in the seventeenth century, gravely hinder Venice's capacity for competing with free ports such as Livorno, which were prepared to admit aliens on much easier terms.[70] It should be said, however, that in some circumstances the term 'citizen' could be used more loosely, with reference to a person's occupation rather than his legal status. Those who conducted the census of 1607 received instructions to count as citizens 'advocates, physicians, notaries and other professional men, and also priests who are not noble, when they are heads of households'.[71]

All legally recognised citizens were deemed to be Venetians,[72] but not all were believed to form a social order. This category seemed most appropriate to the *cittadini originari*, whose status qualified them to staff the permanent civil service. They were sometimes described in the fifteenth century as an *ordo scribarum*, or order of secretaries.[73] Between 1419 and 1539, 'ministerial' offices designed to support councils and magistrates in their functions were reserved in increasing numbers to citizens of some kind or to 'men of our people', as distinct from foreigners. From 1478 the Chancery was clearly reserved to *cittadini originari*.[74] This was now organised as a professional civil service, its members being educated in the composition of quasi-Ciceronian prose and subjected to on-the-job training, with the chance of progressing from a novitiate as 'extraordinary' notaries to high rank and advanced initiation as Secretaries to the Council of Ten. They served at home and abroad, supporting noblemen or undertaking missions of their own, even acting as residents at the courts of uncrowned heads such as Dukes or Viceroys.[75] Responsible for maintaining continuity in government, in a system based on noble amateurism and the circulation of magisterial offices, they were capable of wielding considerable informal influence, and were sometimes suspected of self-aggrandisement by proxy, through encouraging their magistrates – especially the Ten – to assume excessive powers.[76] Contarini represented such arrangements as a gracious extension of authority to subjects, designed to compensate citizens for their exclusion from the ruling order.[77] In fact they were probably intended as a security measure, to ensure that state secrets rested in the hands of persons firmly identified as Venetians, and believed to contribute to a republican system of balances and checks, designed to forestall over-concentrations of power, by ensuring that policymaking and bureaucratic functions rested in the hands of members of different orders.[78]

Many positions in the middling bureaucracy which serviced the law courts and fiscal and administrative offices were steered towards *cittadini originari*, while the senior supervisory posts in the huge government shipyard, the Arsenal, were reserved to them. Whereas the Council of Ten controlled the Chancery from 1462 onwards, and with it a maximum of about a hundred posts (there were 88 in 1631), the Courts of the Forty exercised similar authority over a much larger number of less prestigious jobs, between four and five hundred in 1636. In theory these should have been rotated, changing hands every four years, but with time increasing numbers of them came to be held for life.[79]

Parallels between the nobility and the citizen bureaucrats became more marked during the sixteenth century. The *cittadini originari* claimed to be gentry of the second order and later rejoiced in their superiority to the nobles of the mainland, who were much farther from the centre of affairs; perhaps they were duly flattered by the suggestion (made in 1671) that under an absolute monarchy they could have boasted of being 'old nobility of many centuries' standing'.[80] From 1569 onwards they were required to prove their status formally to the law officers, their own register, known as the Book of Silver, corresponding to the Book of Gold in which the names of nobles' sons were recorded at birth. From about this time they were regularly called upon to show that neither their fathers nor their grandfathers had exercised manual trades or served personally behind shop counters, though not legally required to prove this point until well into the following century.[81] It could be argued, after all, that some ancient and worthy Venetian families had been overlooked or arbitrarily excluded from the nobility at the time of the closing of the Great Council. Indeed, one old citizen family, the Dolce, justified claims to noble status on these grounds in 1647 when the Council's doors had been reopened.[82]

Arguably the more well-to-do *cittadini originari* belonged to the same class as many prosperous and respectable nobles, since their economic interests and style of life were very similar. But they were members of a different order in that they performed different functions in government and enjoyed different privileges. Whereas the nobility were for long stretches of time a closed order, almost a caste, recruitment to the citizenry was a continuous process, and it was once suggested that the accessibility of citizenship was a way of emphasising citizens' lower standing.[83] Enemies of Venice occasionally professed to believe that an intelligent and literate group of persons accustomed to promotion on merit, their ambitions for advancement blocked at a certain point, must needs hate the nobility and would therefore be the natural allies of any foreign invader who promised to overthrow the closed regime.[84] In fact the secretaries seemed to aspire upwards, seeking informal power through their association with individual noblemen and the noble institutions which they serviced, rather than developing a distinctive ethos of their own or planning revolt against the prevailing order. In every century some prominent citizens married their daughters to noblemen, and secretaries recorded with pride the presence of high-ranking noblemen at parties for the betrothal or marriage of their daughters to bridegrooms of their own rank.[85] Blood ties between nobles and citizens could be strong, since it was customary for the illegitimate sons of noblemen and their descendants to become *cittadini originari*.[86] As keeper of the state seal and head of the permanent civil service, the venerable Grand Chancellor might be called the Doge of the People, but he was scarcely the people's choice.[87] For his election, often hotly contested, was the business of the Great Council, and at least from the early sixteenth century he was chosen from among the secretaries, a narrow section of the populace closely identified with the patrician regime.[88] It was almost unheard-of for citizen secretaries to assemble and transact business on their own account, and when they for once did so in 1629 they excited disapproval, albeit discreetly expressed, from the Council of Ten.[89] In a certain sense Venice did possess a middle class, in that there were identifiable groups of people half-way up the ladders of wealth, status and power, but the city was little troubled by a homogeneous and organised bourgeoisie capable of tenaciously pursuing its own interests, even to the point of overthrowing noble domination.

In schemes of social classification, third orders or third estates tend to become overpopulated residuary categories, huge ragbags into which one stuffs everyone not part of the privileged upper orders. To represent the peasantry as an order is notoriously difficult. But more meaning attaches to the concept of a third order, given institutional form in crafts, guilds or fraternities, within the narrower compass of an urban society: the ordinary townsman was a corporate man as the countryman was not, his position in society being registered by his inscription on the rolls of an occupational organisation. In sixteenth-century Venice guilds had clearly defined functions, as an order should have: to supply consumers with properly made goods and wholesome foods, and to contribute to the defence of the state by supplying oarsmen for the galleys of the reserve fleet. It was true that the status of a guildsman could not always be distinguished from that of a citizen, for citizenship *de intus* was a necessary qualification for office-holding in guilds, and there were citizens *de intus et de extra*, merchants or wholesalers, in several of the more important guilds, such as that of the mercers. But the vast majority of guildsmen were manual workers or retailers, small masters, assistants or journeymen, and it was they who dominated the ranks of the artisanate or 'mean people', census-takers confining the use of the term 'artisan' principally to them.

The word 'guild', which does not correspond exactly to any single Venetian word, needs some explanation. Venetian guilds were composed of two organisations which were distinct in principle but usually had a common membership – the Arte or craft, which regulated the trade, and the Scuola, a religious brotherhood which united fellow-craftsmen in devotion to a saint and, by acting as a friendly society and burial club, offered them and their widows a little social security.[90] Scuole could exist quite separately from any particular trade or profession, and there were religious brotherhoods whose members were mostly merchants or businessmen.[91] There was no guild exclusively for merchants, but merchants could be members of particular guilds, such as the silk guild or that of the drapers.[92]

Despite this mercantile presence in some guilds, it could also be said that one of the aims of guilds was to preserve the independence of craftsmen against the merchants who offered to supply them with raw materials and market their products. Much government regulation seemed designed to frustrate the development of large-scale industrial capitalism and to keep manufacturing in the hands of small operators best defined as 'craftsmen-managers' – hence the provision for the silk industry that a man could not own looms unless he knew how to work them himself and could not keep more than a few such machines.[93] Some guildsmen, such as the tanners in 1591, complained of being dominated by half a dozen merchants striving to control the entire trade.[94]

Concerned with manufacturing, victualling, retailing of new and second-hand goods, and with the supervision of other trades, Venice's guilds were very numerous. In the sixteenth century there were 100 Venetian guilds to a mere 21 in Florence, and eight in the Venetian building trade to only one in Florence.[95] These apart, there were several boatmen's co-operatives or ferry-stations, known as *traghetti*.[96] At least one organisation regulated both a series of occupations and a territory within the city, as did the community of fishermen in the parishes of San Nicolò dei Mendicoli and the Angelo Raffaele, which exerted control over the fishmarkets, over some fruiterers, and over hunters and fowlers who pursued their quarry in the lagoon.[97] Guilds had no political role within the state at large, in that – given the noble monopoly of authority – guild membership did not bestow any political franchise as it had once done in republican Florence. During the sixteenth century, however, the guilds had a clearly defined function with regard to the state, in that the burdensome responsibility for raising galleymen for the reserve fleet was laid upon them and upon the ferry-stations and the greatest religious brotherhoods. Hence there was every incentive to extend the guild organisation to include as many trades as possible, and to capture newer trades, such as printing, within its net.[98]

Officially, there was no hierarchy among the guilds, no division as there often was in other cities into major and minor guilds enjoying different privileges. But some occupations, those of a glassmaker, a goldsmith, a jeweller or a furrier, were recognised as so refined, or as involving such 'noble' substances, that they did not bar their practitioners or their descendants from seeking the status of a *cittadino originario*.[99] A snobbish sense of hierarchy undoubtedly began to arise during the 1590s, stimulated by the question of which guild members were obliged to serve personally in the galleys when the reserve fleet was called out, and which were not. Exemptions from this demeaning and strenuous duty were granted in 1594 to drapers and to wool and silk merchants, and in 1596 to goldsmiths and to mercers; ten years later, vintners and leather-workers staked claims to similar privileges.[100]

Apart from hierarchies between guilds, there were naturally hierarchies within them. In the late Middle Ages at least, the gulf – in some industries which required capital and heavy plant – between the master craftsmen who organised production and the underlings who actually did the work, was probably greater than that between noblemen and rich commoners. Master craftsmen long resident in Venice were alone entitled to vote in many, if not all, of the guilds.[101] By the 1540s, relationships were very tense between the master bakers and their German assistants, who were accused of plotting violence and strike action, and of using their separate religious brotherhood to influence the management of the trade in a way never intended when the brotherhood was established in 1422.[102] In the early seventeenth century journeymen cloth-shearers complained that they could never hope to rise to the rank of master; it was as though they were condemned to be employees forever, never setting up in business on their own account.[103] Within the huge retailing guild of the mercers in the late sixteenth century there was a different kind of hierarchy, based not upon qualifications or ethnic divisions, but mostly on the volume and value of business, and to a small extent on gender. In 1586 a list of 964 mercers was arranged in five separate books, devoted respectively to wholesalers, retailers, 'juniors', 'poor' and women.[104]

Guilds were not trades-unions in the making; they were more or less hierarchical associations of small bosses and their employees under state supervision, expected to contribute, as any order should, to the wellbeing of society and the state. If an embryonic proletariat existed among those journeymen who would always be journeymen, they were too much fragmented by the guilds and by differences of language and culture to develop the collective consciousness that could have made them a working class 'for itself', capable of sustained action to promote its own interests. More characteristic of Venetian workers were violent but short-lived protests against the declining quality of bread or deteriorating conditions of employment at the Arsenal.[105]

It was not that Venice was free of conditions favourable to working-class solidarity – of large work-places, of industrial zoning, or of districts in which manual workers chose to live in order to be close to their work. Glass-furnaces clustered on Murano, tanneries on the Giudecca. In 1589 the parish of San Nicolò dei Mendicoli did not consist only of fishermen and fowlers. But it seemed like a quarter of the poor rather than a socially mixed district, a place where rents were very low and many households were headed by women and widows.[106] In the late Middle Ages even Arsenal workers did not live close together near to their yard, but by the mid seventeenth century they had begun to do so, and to form something resembling a company town in the district of Castello, close to the Arsenal itself.[107] By that time Arsenal workers had much in common with factory workers: they were concentrated *en masse* in a vast work-place, they had some obligation to clock in and out, and they performed relatively simple and repetitive tasks, since the warships they constructed were more highly standardised than were the products of the privately-owned yards.[108] But neither Arsenal workers nor fishermen, both highly conscious of their own traditions, would have been likely to merge with a mass of other workers in pursuit of a common interest – save for sporting reasons in the organised fist-fights which ritually divided the people of Venice on several occasions every year into the two rival factions of the Castellani and the Nicolotti. Shipwrights and fisher-folk were very much aware of themselves as privileged bodies, and were treated as such by the state.[109]

*   *   *

This essay has concentrated on the particular social hierarchy that seemed most visible to literate commentators on Venice and was most clearly embodied in institutions – in the Great Council, the Chancery, the guilds, and the carefully regulated concessions of commercial privileges. There were other hierarchies in existence, which were less often the subject of comment, such as the hierarchy by which all Venetians were superior to all foreigners merely resident in the city, or the hierarchy by which all good Catholics in Venice were superior to all Jews and infidels, the Ghetto's walls testifying to official determination to keep the Jews in the place proper to a defeated and superseded religion. It can well be said that the society of orders was a purely masculine construct, which carried the assumption that wives could at best take up the status of their husbands, and that the transmission of status to children was a male prerogative. Perhaps the hierarchies that existed within orders were more oppressive, and of more everyday importance, than the hierarchical arrangement of orders, which placed nobles above citizens, and citizens above artisans.

It would in principle be possible to cut across these lines and analyse Venetian society in terms of classes, employing a language unfamiliar to Venetians themselves. It might be argued that the more prosperous nobles and citizens formed a single class, united by similar economic interests and partnerships in common enterprises, sharing the same style of life, wearing similar clothing, drawn together by intermarriage and by collaboration in the performance of administrative tasks at national, civic, or parochial level. To find evidence of sustained and organised class conflict, of an entrepreneurial bourgeoisie ranged against a landowning nobility, or of a working class drawn from all trades systematically asserting its own interests against either merchant capitalists or small bosses, would be far more difficult – although there are examples of disputes and upheavals within particular trades. As Weber once argued, a different kind of class conflict often broke the surface in societies of the more distant past, one concerned with the prices of vital commodities rather than with wage levels,[110] and attacking, not employers, but grain speculators, taxfarmers, usurers, or the government that had failed to control them. Venice sometimes encountered grain riots in which the people united in fury against alleged governmental incompetence, although its victualling policies were usually efficient enough to prevent such disturbances from breaking out frequently, and the city was more troubled by influxes of starving peasants than by savage and angry crowds. Societies, however, can have more than one substance, and they need not be perceived solely in terms of classes or in terms of orders; nor do classes, in all definitions of the term, have to be openly antagonistic towards each other all the time.

That said, the legal distinctions prominent among Venetians were of undoubted practical importance. Their function was to define various levels of citizenship (of which nobility was the highest form) and to establish Venetian-ness, distinguishing the loyal Venetian (including some persons born outside Venice but granted naturalisation) from the alien who ought to be denied the full benefits of living in the city. On all its various levels, citizenship conferred one of two things, and generally both of them: the right to compete for certain kinds of office, and the right to engage in certain kinds of economic activity. Legal status was used to restrict competition for different kinds of office to different kinds of people, and to forestall the domination of the Venetian economy by foreigners who might withdraw their capital and connections at very short notice indeed. Venetians thought and wrote of a society of three orders, but they did not do so in the traditional terms of those who pray, those who fight, and those who labour to produce wealth for the benefit of the first two.

NOTES AND REFERENCES

INTRODUCTION (*pages 1–5*)

1. See G. Constable, 'The orders of society', in *Three Studies in Medieval Religious and Social Thought* (Cambridge, 1995), p. 252.
2. Translated by A. Goldhammer from *Les trois ordres ou l'imaginaire du féodalisme* (Paris, 1978).
3. See O. G. Oexle, 'Tria genera hominum: zur Geschichte eines Deutungsschemas der sozialen Wirklichkeit in Antike und Mittelalter', in *Institutionen, Kultur und Gesellschaft im Mittelalter*, ed. L. Fenske *et al.* (Sigmaringen, 1984), esp. p. 494 n. 94; and G. Constable, 'The orders of society', esp. pp. 279–88.
4. See the discussion in E. A. R. Brown, 'Georges Duby and The Three Orders', *Viator*, 17 (1986), 57–8.
5. Peasants were occasionally represented in assemblies (as in Sweden and Denmark) but election was by a peasant elite; for a general study of European parliaments, see A. R. Myers, *Parliaments and Estates in Europe to 1789* (London, 1975).
6. On nobility and religion, see A. Murray, *Reason and Society in the Middle Ages* (Oxford, 1978), pp. 317–82.
7. For a survey of the late medieval Church, see F. Oakley, *The Western Church in the Later Middle Ages* (Ithaca and London, 1979).
8. See *The Cambridge History of Medieval Political Thought c.350–c.1450*, ed. J. H. Burns (Cambridge, 1988), esp. pp. 520–87.
9. A. Black, *Political Thought in Europe 1250–1450* (Cambridge, 1992), pp. 14–18.
10. *Cambridge History of Medieval Political Thought*, ed. Burns, pp. 540–2.
11. P. Rorem, *Pseudo-Dionysius. A Commentary on the Texts and an Introduction to their Influence* (New York and Oxford, 1993).
12. *Giles of Rome On Ecclesiastical Power*, trans. R. W. Dyson (Woodbridge, 1986).
13. John of Paris, *On Royal and Papal Power*, trans. J. A. Watt (Toronto, 1971); and John of Paris, *On Royal and Papal Power*, trans. A. P. Monahan (New York and London, 1974).
14. Ibid., ch. 3.

169

1   APPROACHES TO PRE-INDUSTRIAL SOCIAL STRUCTURE

I would like to thank Joe Bergin, Richard Davies and, in particular, Rosalind Brown-Grant who suggested a number of improvements to an earlier draft of this paper.

1. For these terms, see S. Ossowski, 'Old notions and new problems: interpretations of social structure in modern society', in A. Béteille (ed.), *Social Inequality* (Harmondsworth, 1969), pp. 79–89; and S. Ossowski, *Class Structure in the Social Consciousness* (London, 1979).
2. For references, see S. H. Rigby, *Marxism and History: A Critical Introduction* (Manchester, 1987), chs 2–3.
3. Rigby, *Marxism*, pp. 19–21; R. H. Hilton, *Class Conflict and the Crisis of Feudalism* (London, 1985), ch. 9.
4. For references, see Rigby, *Marxism*, chs 9, 11, 12. For Marx's most famous use of the 'base and superstructure' metaphor, see K. Marx, *A Contribution to the Critique of Political Economy* (London, 1971), pp. 20–1.
5. K. Marx and F. Engels, *Collected Works*, vi (London, 1976), 505; F. Engels, *The Origin of the Family, Private Property and the State* (Moscow, 1968), p. 168; F. Engels, *The Peasant War in Germany* (London, 1977), p. 42.
6. S. H. Rigby, 'Marxism and the middle ages', in A. Ryan *et al.*, *After the End of History* (London, 1992), pp. 14–18.
7. S. H. Rigby, *Engels and the Formation of Marxism: History, Dialectics and Revolution* (Manchester, 1992), pp. 7–8; S. H. Rigby, 'Making history', *History of European Ideas*, 12 (1990), 827–9.
8. K. Marx and F. Engels, *Selected Correspondence* (Moscow, 1975), pp. 390–1, 393–402, 433–5, 441–3.
9. J. Breuilly, 'The making of the German working class', *Archiv für Sozial Geschichte*, 27 (1987), 444–52.
10. S. H. Rigby, 'Historical causation: is one thing more important than another?', *History*, 80 (1995), 227–42; S. H. Rigby, 'Marxist historiography', in M. Bentley (ed.), *Companion to Historiography* (London, 1997).
11. For an extremely sophisticated version of this approach, see C. Middleton, 'Peasants, patriarchy and the feudal mode of production in England', *Sociological Review*, 29 (1981), 140–1, 146–52.
12. K. Svalastoga, *Social Differentiation* (New York, 1965), pp. 9, 59–60; P. Worsley *et al.*, *Introducing Sociology* (Harmondsworth, 1973), pp. 283–7; W. G. Runciman, 'The three dimensions of social inequality', in Béteille, *Social Inequality*, pp. 45–54.
13. T. B. Bottomore, *Classes in Modern Society* (London, 1967), p. 26; R. K. Kornhauser, 'The Warner approach to social stratification', in R. Bendix and S. M. Lipset, *Class, Status and Power* (London, 1954), pp. 225–31; F. Parkin, 'Social stratification', in T. Bottomore, and R. Nisbet, *A History of Sociological Analysis* (London, (1979), pp. 601–4; R. J. Holton, and B. S. Turner, *Max Weber on Economy and Society* (London, 1989), pp. 134–5.
14. J. Westergaard and H. Resler, *Class in a Capitalist Society* (Harmondsworth, 1976), p. 2; G. E. M. De Ste Croix, *The Class Struggle in the Ancient Greek World* (London, 1981), p. 45.

15. R. A. Nisbet, *The Sociological Tradition* (London, 1967), pp. 212–17; A. J. Reiss *et al.*, *Occupations and Social Status* (New York, 1961), pp. 240–50; R. Murphy, *Social Closure* (Oxford, 1988), p. 29; Kornhauser, 'The Warner approach', *passim*; E. Digby Baltzell, '"Who's Who in America" and the "Social register": elite and upper class index in metropolitan America', in Bendix and Lipset, *Class*, p. 173.

16. P. S. Cohen, *Modern Social Theory* (London, 1978), pp. 98–105; P. Hamilton, *Talcott Parsons* (London, 1983), pp. 96–7; T. Parsons, 'A revised analytical approach to the theory of social stratification', in Bendix and Lipset, *Class*, pp. 93, 97, 101, 105, 115, 120, 123; T. Parsons, *Essays in Sociological Theory* (Glencoe, 1958), pp. 56, 70–1, 232, 325–9; A. W. Gouldner, *The Coming Crisis of Western Sociology* (London, 1977), p. 287.

17. J. Blum, *The End of the Old Order in Rural Europe* (Princeton, 1978), pp. 3–6 (emphasis added), 440–1; R. Mousnier, *Social Hierarchies: 1450 to the Present* (London, 1973), *passim*; G. Fourquin, *The Anatomy of Popular Rebellion in the Middle Ages* (Amsterdam, 1978), pp. 37–8; P. Crone, *Pre-Industrial Societies* (Oxford, 1989), ch. 6. See also M. Keen, *English Society in the Later Middle Ages* (Harmondsworth, 1990), pp. 3–5; C. Given-Wilson, *The English Nobility in the Later Middle Ages* (London, 1987), pp. ix, 14.

18. P. A. Sorokin, 'What is social class?', in Bendix and Lipset, *Class*, p. 88; S. Giner, *Sociology* (London, 1972), pp. 150–1; A. Giddens, *Sociology* (Cambridge, 1989), pp. 208–9.

19. See, for instance, S. Reynolds, *Kingdoms and Communities in Western Europe, 900–1300* (Oxford, 1984), p. 2; E. Britton, *The Community of the Vill* (Toronto, 1977), pp. 167–71, 271 n.12; A. R. De Windt, 'Peasant power structures in fourteenth-century King's Ripon', *Medieval Studies*, 38 (1976), 257. For a critique, see Z. Razi, 'The Toronto School's reconstitution of medieval peasant society: a critical view', *Past and Present*, 85 (1979), 152–7.

20. Keen, *English Society*, p. 1. For this approach applied to medieval urban society, see S. Thrupp, *The Merchant Class of Medieval London* (Ann Arbor, 1962), pp. 14–27; and S. Reynolds, 'Medieval urban history and the history of political thought', *Urban History Yearbook*, 1982, pp. 14–23.

21. Mousnier, *Social Hierarchies*, pp. 10–11, 20. For social inequality as 'an unconsciously evolved device by which societies insure that the most important positions are conscientiously filled by the most qualified persons', see K. Davis and W. E. Moore, 'Some principles of stratification', in C. S. Heller (ed.), *Structured Social Inequality* (New York, 1969), pp. 496–503; Parsons, *Essays*, pp. 70–86, 232, 325–9; R. K. Kelsall and H. M. Kelsall, *Social Stratification: An Essay on Class and Inequality* (London, 1974), ch. 3.

22. Fourquin, *Anatomy*, pp. 140–5, 149; R. Mousnier, *Peasant Uprisings in Seventeenth-Century France, Russia and China* (London, 1971), pp. 305–48; R. Mousnier, 'Research into the popular uprisings in France before the Fronde', in P. J. Coveney (ed.), *France in Crisis 1620–1675* (London, 1977), pp. 136–68.

23. P. Burke, 'The language of orders in early modern Europe', in M. L. Bush (ed.), *Social Orders and Social Classes in Europe Since 1500* (London, 1992), pp. 1–2, 12.

24. Crone, *Pre-Industrial Societies*, ch. 6; M. I. Finley, *The Ancient Economy* (London, 1979), pp. 47–62; P. Zagorin, *Rebels and Rulers, 1550–1660*, i (Cambridge, 1982), ch. 3.

25. Fourquin, *Anatomy*, p. 37; Mousnier, *Social Hierarchies*, p. 10.

26. S. H. Rigby, *English Society in the Later Middle Ages: Class, Status and Gender* (Basingstoke, 1995), ch. 8.

27. K. Marx and F. Engels, *Collected Works*, v (London, 1976), 62.

28. Crone, *Pre-Industrial Societies*, p. 102 (emphasis added).

29. Mousnier, *Social Hierarchies*, pp. 67–8, 76.

30. Fourquin, *Anatomy*, pp. 37–8, 53–60.

31. G. Duby, *The Three Orders: Feudal Society Imagined* (Chicago, 1980), *passim*.

32. J. E. C. Welldon (trans.), *The Politics of Aristotle* (London, 1901), p. 281 (bk 6, ch. 11).

33. Thrupp, *Merchant Class*, pp. 291–5; *Rotuli Parliamentorum* (London, 1783), iv, 419.

34. Mousnier does, however, admit that social consensus often has to be 'imposed', which suggests that it is not actually a consensus in the first place (Mousnier, *Social Hierarchies*, p. 25). See also, A. Arriaza, 'Mousnier and Barber: the theoretical underpinning of the society of orders in early modern Europe', *Past and Present*, 89 (1980), 39–57.

35. Blum, *Old Order*, p. 4 (emphasis added).

36. C. C. Dyer, 'A redistribution of incomes in fifteenth-century England?', in R. H. Hilton (ed.), *Peasants, Knights and Heretics* (Cambridge, 1981), pp. 192–215.

37. T. H. Marshall, 'The nature of class conflict', in Bendix and Lipset, *Class*, p. 86.

38. R. Brenner, 'Agrarian class structure and economic development in pre-industrial Europe', *Past and Present*, 70 (1976), 50–60.

39. A. Giddens, *The Class Structure of the Advanced Societies* (London, 1978), pp. 44, 94; A. Giddens, *Capitalism and Modern Social Theory* (Cambridge, 1979), pp. 166–7; R. Dahrendorf, *Class and Class Conflict in Industrial Society* (London, 1972), pp. xi, 206; Parkin, 'Social stratification', 604, 608.

40. M. Weber, *Economy and Society*, ii (Berkeley, 1978), 926–8, 932, 935, 938; F. Parkin, *Max Weber* (London, 1982), p. 97.

41. M. Weber, *Economy and Society*, i (Berkeley, 1978), 43–4, 302–7, 342–3, 639–40, 930, 935; J. Freund, *The Sociology of Max Weber* (Harmondsworth, 1972), pp. 154–6.

42. G. Neuwirth, 'A Weberian outline of a theory of community: its application to the "Dark Ghetto"', *British Journal of Sociology*, 20 (1969), 148–63; R. Collins, *Conflict Sociology* (New York, 1975); R. Collins, *The Credential Society* (New York, 1979). Murphy, *Social Closure*, provides a full bibliography.

43. The account of Parkin's social theory offered here is based on F. Parkin, 'Strategies of social closure in class formation', in F. Parkin (ed.), *The Social Analysis of Class Structure* (London, 1974), pp. 1–19; F. Parkin, *Marxism and Class Theory: A Bourgeois Critique* (London, 1979); and Parkin, *Max Weber*, pp. 100–4.

44. E. Searle, *Lordship and Community: Battle Abbey and its Banlieu 1066–1538* (Toronto, 1974), pp. 188–94.

45. Parkin prefers the distinction between individualist and collectivist modes of exclusion to the more traditional sociological distinction between 'ascribed' and 'achieved' statuses or roles; see Svalastoga, *Social Differentiation*, p. 11.
46. Murphy, *Social Closure*, pp. 219–20.
47. R. B. Dobson (ed.), *The Peasants' Revolt of 1381* (London, 1983), pp. 374–5.
48. Weber, *Economy and Society*, i, 342.
49. Rigby, *English Society*, ch. 8.
50. Parkin, *Marxism*, pp. 112–13. This approach is a common one amongst sociologists; see G. E. Lenski, *Power and Privilege* (New York, 1966), pp. 75, 79, 86–7; and Giner, *Sociology*, pp. 68–72. It also had its medieval antecedents; see J. Swanson, *John of Wales: A Study of the Works and Ideas of a Thirteenth-Century Preacher* (Cambridge, 1989), pp. 65, 107, 142–58.
51. Marx and Engels, *Collected Works*, v, 77. See also Weber, *Economy and Society*, i, 342.
52. Murphy, *Social Closure*, pp. 11–12, 126–7, 131 n.20.
53. C. Roth, *The Jews of Medieval Oxford* (Oxford Historical Society, New Series, vol. 9, 1951 for 1945–6), pp. 5–6, 44–5, 151–2.
54. G. Rudé, *Paris and London in the Eighteenth Century* (London, 1974), pp. 17–34; S. H. Rigby, 'Urban "oligarchy" in late medieval England', in J. A. F. Thomson (ed.), *Towns and Townspeople in the Fifteenth Century* (Gloucester, 1988), p. 73.
55. Parkin, 'Strategies', 8–9; Parkin, *Marxism*, pp. 60–71, 85.
56. W. G. Runciman, *A Treatise on Social Theory*, ii (Cambridge, 1989), 2–3, 12–17, 20–4; Parkin, *Marxism*, p. 67. M. Mann, *The Sources of Social Power*, i (Cambridge, 1986), 2–6, suggests that there are *four* types of social power: economic, ideological, political, and military. Runciman rejects this claim (Runciman, *Treatise*, ii, 14–15) because although military *institutions* are distinguishable from political ones as a means through which coercive power is exercised, they do not in themselves constitute a fourth *kind* of power.
57. Runciman, *Treatise*, ii, 20–4.
58. Parkin, *Marxism*, pp. 84–5, 138; Lenski, *Power*, pp. 74–5; Runciman, *Treatise*, ii, 20–4.
59. Parkin, 'Social stratification', 626–9.
60. W. J. Goode, *The Family* (Engelwood Cliffs), p. 80; F. Parkin, *Class Inequality and Political Order* (St Albans, 1973), pp. 14–15; R. Lockwood, 'Class, status and gender', in R. Crompton and M. Mann (eds), *Gender and Stratification* (Cambridge, 1986), pp. 19–20; M. Keen, *Chivalry* (New Haven, 1984), p. 160; J. J. Parry (ed.), *Andreas Capellanus: The Art of Courtly Love* (New York, 1990), p. 36.
61. J. West, 'Women, sex and class', in A. Kuhn and A. Wolpe (eds), *Feminism and Materialism: Women and Modes of Production* (London, 1978), pp. 223–5.
62. J. M. Bennett, *Women in the Medieval English Countryside* (Oxford, 1987), pp. 5–6, 178, 185–9.
63. R. McDonough and R. Harrison, 'Patriarchy and relations of production', in Kuhn and Wolpe, *Feminism*, pp. 14–40.

174

64. Runciman, *Treatise*, ii, 3, 20, 24, 110.
65. C. M. Barron, 'The "Golden Age" of women in medieval London', *Reading Medieval Studies*, 15 (1989), 47–9.
66. M. K. Whyte, *The Status of Women in Preindustrial Societies* (Princeton, 1978), pp. 107–16, 168–79.
67. N. Z. Davis adopts this metaphor in *Society and Culture in Early Modern France* (Stanford, 1975), p. xvii. See also C. R. Friedrichs, 'Urban politics and urban social structure in seventeenth-century Germany', *European History Quarterly*, 22 (1992), 207–8.
68. The following account of Murphy is based on R. Murphy, 'The structure of closure: a critique and development of the theories of Weber, Collins and Parkin', *British Journal of Sociology*, 35 (1984), 547–67; and Murphy, *Social Closure*, pp. 70–82.
69. Murphy, *Social Closure*, p. 72.
70. Rigby, *English Society*, pp. 123–5.
71. Murphy, *Social Closure*, p. 72.
72. Rigby, *English Society*, pp. 257–62.
73. Parkin, *Marxism*, pp. 5, 113.
74. Rigby, *English Society*, pp. 84–7.
75. Duby, *Three Orders*, *passim*; S. H. Rigby, *Chaucer in Context: Society, Allegory and Gender* (Manchester, 1996), pp. 11–13, 20–2.
76. Rigby, *English Society*, pp. 215–20, 239–40; Blum, *Old Order*, p. 4.
77. W. Doyle, 'Myths of order and ordering myths', in Bush, *Social Orders* (London, 1992), p. 221.
78. Duby, *Three Orders*, pp. 162, 355.
79. Burke, 'The language of orders', 12; W. M. Reddy, 'The concept of class', in Bush, *Social Orders*, p. 18; Doyle, 'Myths', 223–4.
80. Historians are less likely to be interested in the charge made against closure theory by a number of sociological critics that its social analysis overprivileges action and agency at the expense of the social structures which underlie them. See A. Giddens, 'Classes, capitalism and the state', *Theory and Society*, 9 (1980), 887; N. P. Mouzelis, *Post-Marxist Alternatives* (London, 1992), pp. 58–60; J. M. Barbalet, 'Social closure in class analysis: a critique of Parkin', *Sociology*, 16 (1982), 485–9; C. Hamnett, L. McDowell and S. Sarre, *The Changing Social Structure* (London, 1990), pp. 94–5; Murphy, *Social Closure*, pp. 50–2, 108–22, 128 n.3. Parkin himself rejects the charge that he overemphasised the role of agency in social closure. See F. Parkin, 'Reply to Giddens', *Theory and Society*, 9 (1980), 892–3. For other criticisms of closure theory, see Rigby, *English Society*, pp. 17, 57, 301.
81. Murphy, *Social Closure*, pp. 11–12, 50, 73, 166, 178–9, 189, 219–20; Parkin, *Marxism*, pp. 47, 60–71.
82. K. B. McFarlane, *The Nobility of Later Medieval England* (Oxford, 1973), p. 269; Thrupp, *Merchant Class*, pp. 305–6; J. R. Lander, *Conflict and Stability in Fifteenth-Century England* (London, 1971), pp. 173–5; Given-Wilson, *Nobility*, pp. 56–8, 65; F. B. Palmer, *Peerage Law in England* (London, 1907), ch. 10; Rigby, *English Society*, pp. 195–203; M. L. Bush, *The English Aristocracy* (Manchester, 1984), pp. 7, 35–6; M. L. Bush, *Rich Noble, Poor Noble* (Manchester, 1988), pp. 3, 56, 111–15, 157.

83. Parkin, *Marxism*, p. 61.
84. McFarlane, *Nobility*, p. 143; Given-Wilson, *Nobility*, pp. 14, 64–5. See, however, Given-Wilson's cautionary comments on McFarlane, *ibid.*, p. 60.
85. Given-Wilson, *Nobility*, pp. 13–14, 56–7.
86. Rigby, *English Society*, ch. 6.
87. G. L. Freeze, 'Between estate and profession: the clergy in Imperial Russia', in Bush, *Social Orders*, pp. 51–3.
88. Parkin, 'Strategies', pp. 8–9; Parkin, *Marxism*, pp. 60–71, 85; Murphy, *Social Closure*, pp. 11–12, 126–7, 131 n. 20.
89. Marx and Engels, *Collected Works*, vi, 211.
90. J. R. Lumby (ed.), *Chronicon Henrici Knighton*, ii (London: Rolls Series, 1895), 189.
91. S. McSheffrey, 'Women and Lollardy: a reassessment', *Canadian Journal of History*, 26 (1991), 221–3.
92. Rigby, *Chaucer*, ch. 4.
93. G. Rosser, *Medieval Westminster 1200–1540* (Oxford, 1989), p. 243; C. Phythian-Adams, *Desolation of a City* (Cambridge, 1979), p. 89.
94. R. H. Hilton, *The English Peasantry in the Later Middle Ages* (Oxford, 1979), pp. 63, 106; P. Franklin, 'Peasant widows' "liberation" and remarriage before the Black Death', *Economic History Review*, 2nd ser., 39 (1986), 197.
95. See, for instance, G. R. Elton, *The Practice of History* (London, 1989), pp. 52–3. J. Tosh, *The Pursuit of History* (Harlow, 1991), ch. 6, replies to some of these objections.
96. Hamnett, *Social Structure*, pp. 94–5; G. Mackenzie, 'Review' of Parkin, *Marxism*, in *British Journal of Sociology*, 31 (1980), 582–4; Barbalet, 'Social closure', p. 495.
97. K. R. Popper, *Conjectures and Refutations* (London, 1989), p. 36; J. Monod, *Chance and Necessity* (London, 1974), pp. 48–9; W. G. Runciman, 'Towards a theory of social stratification', in Parkin, *Social Analysis*, pp. 22, 65; Parkin, *Marxism*, pp. 42, 114; Parkin, *Max Weber*, p. 96.
98. G. C. Homans, *The Nature of Social Science* (New York, 1967), pp. 7–18.

2   EUROPEAN AND MIDDLE EASTERN VIEWS OF HIERARCHY AND ORDER IN THE MIDDLE AGES: A COMPARISON (*pages 26–32*)

1. J. Schacht, *The Origins of Muhammedan Jurisprudence* (Oxford, rev. edn 1953).
2. F. Mernissi, *Women and Islam* (Oxford, 1991).
3. Bat Ye'or, *The Dhimmi: Jews and Christians under Islam* (London, 1985).
4. B. Lewis, *Race and Slavery in the Middle East* (Oxford, 1990).
5. W. Kölmel, '"Freiheit–Gleichheit–Unfreiheit" in der sozialen Theorie des späten Mittelalters', *Miscellanea Mediaevalia*, ed. A. Zimmermann, xii pt i (Berlin, 1980), 390–407, esp. 399, 402.
6. *Islamic Jurisprudence: Shafi'i's Risala*, trans. Majid Khadduri (Baltimore, Maryland, 1961), pp. 81–2.

7. Halil Inalcik, 'Comments on "Sultanism": Max Weber's typification of the Ottoman polity', *Princeton Papers in Near Eastern Studies*, 1 (1992), 57; I. Metin Kunt, 'The development of the Ottoman state to 1600' (unpublished paper, p. 13).

8. Halil Inalcik, *The Ottoman Empire: The Classical Age 1300–1600* (London, 1973), pp. 65–9, 173–8; S. J. Shaw, *History of the Ottoman Empire and Modern Turkey*, i (Cambridge, 1976), 284–97.

9. L. Rockinger (ed.), *Briefsteller und Formelbücher des 11. bis 14. Jahrhunderts* (Aalen, repr. 1969), esp. pp. 447–50, 727–8; Ashtiany Julia *et al.* (eds), *Abbasid Belles Lettres* (Cambridge, 1990), p. 119.

10. R. Brunshvig, 'Métiers vils en Islam', *Studia Islamica*, 16 (1962), pp. 41–62.

11. J. L. Kraemer, 'The jihād of the philosophers', *Jerusalem Studies in Arabic and Islam*, 10 (1987), 297–8; Naṣīr ad-Dīn Tūsī, *The Nasirean Ethics*, trans. G. M. Wickens (London, 1964), pp. 215–16, 230.

12. G. E. von Grunebaum, 'The body politic: the social order', in von Grunebaum, *Medieval Islam* (Chicago, 2nd edn, 1953), p. 203.

13. I would like to thank Dr I. Metin Kunt for this information.

14. Inalcik, 'Comments on "Sultanism"', 54–5; E. I. J. Rosenthal, *Political Thought in Medieval Islam* (Cambridge, 1958), p. 220.

15. B. Lewis, 'Ottoman observers of Ottoman decline', *Islamic Studies*, 2 (1954), 78–81; Inalcik, 'Comments on "Sultanism"', 68–9; Rosenthal, *Political Thought*, p. 229.

16. S. D. Goitein, *Studies in Islamic History and Institutions* (Leiden, 1966), chs 11–12; M. Rodinson, *Islam and Capitalism* (London, 1974).

17. A. Lambton, *State and Government in Medieval Islam* (Oxford, 1981), p. 137.

18. *The Cambridge History of Medieval Political Thought*, ed. J. H. Burns (Cambridge, 1988), pp. 307–9.

19. E. Lewis, 'Organic tendencies in medieval political thought', *American Political Science Review*, 32 (1938), 849–76.

20. *Summa Theologiae*, 1.96.3 (Aquinas, *Selected Political Writings*, ed. A. P. d'Entrèves (Oxford, 1954), p. 102).

21. See C. Fleischer, *Bureaucrat and Intellectual in the Ottoman Empire: The Historian Mustafa Alī 1541–1600* (Princeton, New Jersey, 1986), p. 7.

22. Aristotle's *Politics* was untranslated and virtually unknown in the Arabic-speaking world: S. Pines, 'Aristotle's *Politics* in Arabic philosophy', *Israel Oriental Studies*, 5 (1975), 150–60.

23. A. Black, *Guilds and Civil Society in European Political Thought* (London, 1984), pp. 88–9; for bibliography, see I. Lapidus, *A History of Islamic Societies* (Cambridge, 1988), p. 937.

24. *Encyclopaedia Islamica*, s.v. *ikta*; Lapidus, *Islamic Societies*, pp. 148–52.

25. Black, *Guilds*, p. 79 (citing Aquinas); Kölmel, '"Freiheit"', 401 (citing Ockham).

26. P. Crone, 'The tribe and the state', in *States in History*, ed. J. A. Hall (Oxford, 1986), pp. 48–77.

27. Black, *Guilds*, pp. 38–40, 103–4.

3 DANTE: ORDER, JUSTICE AND THE SOCIETY OF ORDERS
(*pages 33–55*)

1. On Dante's family and social background, see J. Catto, 'Florence, Tuscany, and the world of Dante', in *The World of Dante: Essays on Dante and His Times*, ed. C. Grayson (Oxford, 1980), pp. 1–17.
2. See F. Schevill, *History of Florence from the Founding of the City through the Renaissance* (New York, 1961), p. 172.
3. For the Blacks and the Whites and the career of Boniface VIII, see Schevill, *History of Florence*, pp. 161–78; and G. Holmes, 'Dante and the popes', in *The World of Dante*, ed. Grayson, pp. 18–43.
4. See *Purgatorio* 24.82–7; *Inferno* 19.46–78; *Purgatorio* 20.70–8. The edition from which passages from the *Divina Commedia* are taken is Dante Alighieri, *The Divine Comedy*, trans. C. Singleton (Princeton, 6 vols, 1970–75).
5. On the Guelf–Ghibelline conflict and relations between Church and Empire, see Schevill, *History of Florence*, pp. 103–18, 133–44; J. K. Hyde, *Society and Politics in Medieval Italy: The Evolution of the Civil Life 1000–1350* (London, 1973), pp. 132–41; and G. Tabacco, *The Struggle for Power in Medieval Italy: Structures of Political Rule* (Cambridge, 1989), pp. 182–320.
6. See the chapter on the nobility in J. Larner, *Italy in the Age of Dante and Petrarch 1216–1380* (London, 1980), pp. 83–105.
7. *Paradiso* 16.67–8.
8. Giovanni Villani, *Cronica di Giovanni Villani*, ed. F. Gherardi Dragomanni (Florence, 4 vols, 1844–5), i. 38; see *Inferno* 15.61–9. Fiesole is a town of Etruscan origin situated on a hill just to the north of Florence.
9. 'La gente nuova e i sùbiti guadagni | orgoglio e dismisura han generata, | Fiorenza, in te, sì che tu già ten piagni', exclaims Dante the pilgrim in *Inferno* 16.73–5; see also (once again) 15.61–9.
10. *Dantis Alagherii Epistolae: The Letters of Dante*, ed. and trans. P. Toynbee (Oxford, 2nd edn, 1966), 6.6 and 6.2. Subsequent references to the *Epistolae* are to this edition.
11. On Dante's unfavourable comparison of the present with the past, see C. T. Davis, '*Il buon tempo antico* (The Good Old Time)', *Dante's Italy and Other Essays* (Philadelphia, 1984), pp. 71–93.
12. See *Paradiso* 17.69.
13. See *Purgatorio* 7.113, 124–9; Villani, *Cronica*, vii.1.
14. *Paradiso* 8.31–84; see *Purgatorio* 20.67–9.
15. See Andreas Capellanus, *Andreas Capellanus on Love*, ed. and trans. P. G. Walsh (London, 1982).
16. Dante's high opinion of the Sicilian court is expressed in his treatise on the vernacular tongue, *De vulgari eloquentia*; see W. Welliver, *Dante in Hell: The De Vulgari Eloquentia: Introduction, Text, Translation, Commentary* (Ravenna, 1981), 1.12.4.
17. *De vulgari eloquentia* 1.18.4, 5.
18. See K. Foster, 'Chivalry and Dante', in *God's Tree: Essays on Dante and Other Matters* (London, 1957), pp. 150–68; C. T. Davis in 'Dante's Italy', *Dante's Italy*, pp. 1–22.

19. See *Convivio* 4.11–13. The text referred to is that published as Dante Alighieri, *Opere minori*, tomo i, parte ii, ed. C. Vasoli and D. De Robertis (Milan/Naples, 1988); all translations of passages from the *Convivio* are taken from Dante, *The Banquet*, trans. C. Ryan (Saratoga, 1989).
20. *Convivio* 4.20.5.
21. See *Convivio* 4.21.7–8.
22. *Convivio* 4.16.4.
23. See *Convivio* 4.16.10.
24. See *Convivio* 4.7.
25. *Convivio* 1.9.5. On Dante's public, see M. P. Simonelli, 'Pubblico e società nel Convivio', *Yearbook of Italian Studies*, 4 (1980), 41–58.
26. See *Convivio* 3.11.10–11; 1.9.2–3.
27. See *Convivio* 1.9.8 and 1.1.1–4.
28. *Epistolae* 10.15.
29. *Epistolae* 10.8.
30. Larner, *Italy in the Age of Dante and Petrarch*, p.170; see *Inferno* 24.1–15; 26.25–30; 32.32–3; *Purgatorio* 4.19–24; 26.67–70; 27.76–87.
31. *Paradiso* 17.133–42.
32. *Purgatorio* 4.132.
33. *Convivio* 1.11.6–7.
34. *Convivio* 4.17.9; see Aristotle, *Ethics* 10.7: 1177a12–1178a8.
35. *Convivio* 1.1.4.
36. Dante, *Monarchia*, ed. and trans. P. Shaw (Cambridge, 1995), 1.3.4. All references to the *Monarchia* are to this edition.
37. *Monarchia* 1.4.1.
38. *Convivio* 4.4.1; see Aristotle, *Politics* 1.2: 1253a1–3; 3.6:1278b19; *Ethics* 1.5: 1097b11; 9.9: 1169b18–19.
39. *Paradiso* 8.115–26; see the whole conversation, 8.49–148.
40. *Paradiso* 8.142–8. The king referred to is the original subject of the conversation, Charles Martel's brother Robert, who was given to writing sermons: see Villani, *Cronica* xii.10.
41. See in particular G. Duby, *The Three Orders: Feudal Society Imagined* (Chicago/London, 1980).
42. On labour consciousness and the changing attitudes to work in the later Middle Ages, see J. Le Goff, 'Trades and professions as represented in medieval confessors' manuals', in *Time, Work, and Culture in the Middle Ages* (Chicago/London, 1980), pp. 107–21.
43. Of the 59 instances of the use of *ordino* and *ordo* listed in E. K. Rand, E. H. Wilkins and A. C. White, *Dantis Alagherii Operum Latinorum Concordantiae* (Oxford, 1912), 47 occur in the *Monarchia*.
44. *Paradiso* 1.103–5. For Dante's views on the structure of the created universe, see P. Boyde, *Dante Philomythes and Philosopher: Man in the Cosmos* (Cambridge, 1981), pp. 112–31, 248–69.
45. *Convivio* 3.7.6.
46. See *Monarchia* 1.12.4.
47. *Monarchia* 1.4.2.
48. *Monarchia* 3.3.8.
49. Thomas Aquinas, *Summa Theologiae* (London/New York, 61 vols, 1964–81), xxxvii, 20 (2–2.58.1, responsio).

50. *Purgatorio* 6.97–105.
51. *Convivio* 4.3.6.
52. See Schevill, *History of Florence*, pp. 167–8; but also Holmes, 'Dante and the popes', pp. 19–24.
53. See *Inferno* 19.46–78.
54. *Paradiso* 22.73–84.
55. *Monarchia* 3.10.17; see also 2.10.1–3.
56. *Matthew* 10.9–10; quoted by Dante, *Monarchia* 3.10.14.
57. *Monarchia* 1.11.11–12.
58. *Monarchia* 1.14.7, 5.
59. See *Monarchia* 1.9.
60. *Monarchia* 3.16.7–8.
61. See *Purgatorio* 16.88, where Marco Lombardo speaks of the arrival in this world of 'l'anima semplicetta che sa nulla', 'the simple little soul, which knows nothing'.
62. *Monarchia* 3.16.10.
63. See *Monarchia* 3.16.17.
64. *Purgatorio* 16.106–14.
65. See *Monarchia* 3.4, where Dante argues against the inferences usually drawn from the 'two lights' metaphor.
66. Duby, *The Three Orders*, p. 59.
67. For Dante's political philosophy in general, see E. Gilson, *Dante the Philosopher* (London, 1952), pp. 162–224; A. P. d'Entrèves, *Dante as a Political Thinker* (Oxford, 1952); and P. Armour, *Dante's Griffin and the History of the World* (Oxford, 1989).
68. *Convivio* 4.6.17.
69. *Monarchia* 3.16.17.
70. See *Convivio* 4.17.9.
71. Thomas Aquinas, *Summa Theologiae*, xxx, 164 (1–2.113.1, responsio). There are a great many points of contact between Dante and Aquinas, whose *Summa* and commentaries, especially that on Aristotle's *Ethics*, he clearly knew very well. Dante was not, however, a Thomist – least of all in his political philosophy.
72. On freedom as concurrence with one's essential nature, see *Monarchia* 1.12; *Purgatorio* 16–18; and P. Boyde, *Perception and Passion in Dante's Comedy* (Cambridge, 1993), pp. 193–214.

4 FROISSARDIAN PERSPECTIVES ON LATE-FOURTEENTH-CENTURY SOCIETY (*pages 56–73*)

1. See K. Fowler, 'Froissart, chronicler of Chivalry', *History Today*, 36 (1986), 50–4; F. S. Shears, *Froissart, Chronicler and Poet* (London, 1930); and P. F. Ainsworth, *Jean Froissart and the Fabric of History: Truth, Myth, and Fiction in the 'Chroniques'* (Oxford, 1990).
2. J. Froissart, *Chroniques*, ed. S. Luce, G. Raynaud, and L. and A. Mirot (Paris, Société de l'Histoire de France, 15 vols in progress, 1869–); J. Froissart, *Oeuvres*, ed. K. de Lettenhove (Brussels, Académie Royale de Belgique, 28 vols, 1867–77).

3. First presented as a paper to the J. K. Hyde Centre for Medieval Studies, University of Manchester. I am grateful to my former colleagues at Manchester for their suggestions; also to Dr Tom Scott and Dr Godfried Croenen of the Univeristy of Liverpool; and to Tim Ainsworth and Nicola Pinder who kindly read this essay in draft.

4. See P. F. Ainsworth, 'Froissart the writer and Walter Scott: chivalry and its inheritance in the *Chroniques* and *Old Mortality*', in R. Wakely and P. E. Bennett (eds), *France and Germany in Scotland: Studies in Language and Culture* (Papers from the centenary celebrations of the Departments of French and German at the University of Edinburgh 1994–1995; Edinburgh, 1996), pp. 65–80.

5. See my review of J. Blanchard, *Commynes et les Italiens* (Paris, 1993), in *Medium Aevum*, 64 (1995), 147–9.

6. J. J. N. Palmer (ed.), *Froissart: Historian* (Woodbridge, Suffolk, and Totowa, NJ, 1981).

7. *Froissart Across the Genres* (First International Colloquium devoted to the works of Jean Froissart, University of Massachusetts at Amherst, USA). The proceedings, eds D. Maddox and S. Sturm-Maddox, are soon to be published, and will include my keynote paper, 'Intimations of *(Old) Mortality*, or: The configuration of transience in Jean Froissart'.

8. J. Froissart, *Chronicles*, trans. and ed. G. Brereton (Penguin Classics, Harmondsworth, 1968), pp. 162–3. (And see the fine translation and edition of the Chronicles in P. E. Thompson (ed.), *Contemporary Chronicles of the Hundred Years War* (The Folio Society, London, 1966), pp. 85–256.)

9. Such as the tale of 'Orton' the familiar spirit, in *Chronicles*, ed. Brereton, pp. 295–302.

10. J. Froissart, *Chroniques. Livre I. Le Manuscrit d'Amiens. Bibliothèque municipale n° 486: Tome IV. Depuis l'offensive anglaise dans le Toulousain jusqu'à une mobilisation préparée par le duc d'Anjou dans le Bordelais (1367–1377)*, ed. G. T. Diller (Droz 'Textes littéraires français' 429; Geneva, 1993), pp. 165–6. See my review in *French Studies*, 49 (1995), 325–6.

11. See Ainsworth, *Jean Froissart and the Fabric*, pp. 100–6. Also *Chronicles*, ed. Brereton, pp. 201–10.

12. Ainsworth, *Jean Froissart and the Fabric*, esp. pp. 180–1.

13. Ibid., p. 300, and n. 139.

14. Ibid., bibliography (pp. 309–10).

15. See P. F. Dembowski, *Jean Froissart and his 'Meliador': Context, Craft and Sense* (Lexington, KY, 1983).

16. Ainsworth, *Jean Froissart and the Fabric*, pp. 32–50.

17. Ibid., p. 77 and n. 24. See also my forthcoming 'Heralds, heraldry and the colour blue in the *Chronicles* of Jean Froissart', to be published in *The Medieval Chronicle* (Proceedings of the Utrecht Conference of July 1996, 1997).

18. 'I introduced myself to this knight, for I found him both courteous and temperate in his speech. I asked him for news, especially concerning the capture of the Constable, about which I was most anxious to learn the truth' (*Chroniques*, Book III, ed. Mirot (Société de l'Histoire de France, xiv), p. 4; my translation).

19. See, for example, J. Froissart, *Chroniques. Livre I. Le Manuscrit d'Amiens. Bibliothèque municipale n° 486: Tome II. Depuis l'expédition du duc de Normandie en Hainaut jusqu'à la campagne d'Edouard III en France (1340–1346)*, ed. G. T. Diller (Droz 'Textes littéraires français' 415; Geneva, 1992), pp. 196–253 and 308–31. See my review in *French Studies*, 48 (1994), 314–16.

20. Ainsworth, *Jean Froissart and the Fabric*, pp. 115 and n. 7, 117, 118 n. 13, 121, 233.

21. Discussed in my forthcoming 'The image of the city in peace and war in the Breslau MS of Froissart's *Chronicles*, Book II', first given as a paper at the Colloquium 'Au carrefour des époques: la ville bourguignonne sous les ducs Valois', University of Edinburgh May 1996, held under the joint auspices of the Department of History and the Centre de Recherches Francophones Belges.

22. *Chroniques*, Book III, ed. Mirot (Société de l'Histoire de France, xiv), p. 148; my translation.

23. See, for example, ibid., pp. 215–16 (a nocturnal raid); cf. *Chronicles*, ed. Brereton, p. 265 (Froissart at the court of the count of Foix).

24. J. Froissart, *Chroniques. Livre I. Le Manuscrit d'Amiens. Bibliothèque municipale n° 486: Tome III. Depuis la bataille de Crécy jusqu'au mariage du duc de Bourgogne avec Marguerite de Flandre (1346–1369)*, ed. G. T. Diller (Droz 'Textes littéraires français' 424; Geneva, 1992), p. 406. See my review in *French Studies*, 49 (1995), 184–5.

25. *Le Manuscrit d'Amiens, Tome II*, ed. Diller (see above n. 19), p. 72; my translation.

26. *Chroniques*, Book III, ed. Mirot (Société de l'Historie de France, xiv), pp. 159–60; my translation.

27. *Chronicles*, ed. Brereton, pp. 461–2.

28. On the importance of metonymy in narratives dealing with royal or comital succession, see my 'Knife, key, bear and book: poisoned metonymies and the problem of *translatio* in Froissart's later *Chroniques*', *Medium Aevum*, 59 (1990), 91–113.

29. See esp. M.-Th. de Medeiros, *Jacques et chroniqueurs: une étude comparée de récits contemporains relatant la Jacquerie de 1358* (Paris, 1979); also, Ainsworth, *Jean Froissart and the Fabric*, pp. 51–9 and 89–90.

30. The allusion is to the near-contemporary (1337–9) fresco painted for the Civic Palace Hall at Sienna by Ambrogio Lorenzetti (active 1324–48), 'The Effects of Good Government'. See G. Duby, *Le Moyen Age. Fondements d'un nouvel humanisme, 1280–1440* (Geneva, 1984), pp. 48–9.

31. For more references, see Ainsworth, *Jean Froissart and the Fabric*, index, p. 325 s.v. 'Good Government'.

32. J. Froissart, *Chroniques. Dernière rédaction du premier livre. Edition du manuscrit de Rome Reg. lat. 869*, ed. G. T. Diller (Geneva and Paris, 1972), prologue, p. 37; my translation. Cf. *Chroniques*, Book I, ed. Luce (Société de l'Histoire de France, i), p. 5. Cf. C. Marchello-Nizia, 'L'Historien et son prologue: forme littéraire et stratégies discursives', in D. Poirion (ed.), *La Chronique et l'histoire au Moyen-Age* (Paris, 1984), pp. 13–25.

33. *Chronicles*, ed. Brereton, pp. 211–30.

34. J. van Herwaarden, 'The war in the Low Countries', in Palmer (ed.), *Froissart: Historian*, pp. 101–17.
35. *Chroniques*, Book II, ed. Raynaud (Société de l'Histoire de France, ix–xi).
36. D. Nicholas, *The Metamorphosis of a Medieval City. Ghent in the Age of the Arteveldes, 1302–1390* (Lincoln, NA, and London, 1987), pp. 4–5.
37. Van Herwaarden, 'War in the Low Countries', p. 108.
38. Nicholas, *Metamorphosis*, pp. 158–9.
39. Van Herwaarden, 'War in the Low Countries', p. 105.
40. Van Herwaarden, however, reminds us that 'any idea that we are here confronted with proletarian rule is completely untenable': ibid., p. 108.
41. Van Herwaarden also refers to the frescoes at Sienna depicting Good and Evil Government: ibid., p. 116.
42. *Chroniques*, Book II, ed. Raynaud (Société de l'Histoire de France, x), p. 221. A small proportion of the material which follows was first published in my article, 'Du berceau à la bière : Louis de Mâle dans le Deuxième Livre des "Chroniques" de Froissart', in *Dies Illa: Death in the Middle Ages. Proceedings of the Manchester Colloquium, 3–6 May 1983* (*Vinaver Studies in French*, 1), ed. J. H. M. Taylor (Liverpool, 1984), pp. 125–52.
43. *Chroniques*, Book II, ed. Raynaud (Société de l'Histoire de France, ix), p. 216.
44. *Chroniques*, Book II, ed. Raynaud (Société de l'Histoire de France, x), pp. 213–14.
45. Ibid., p. 216.
46. Ibid., pp. 217–18.
47. Ibid.
48. Ibid., pp. 221–2.
49. John vi, 32–3 (New King James Version).
50. *Chroniques*, Book II, ed. Raynaud (Société de l'Histoire de France, x), p. 223.
51. I Corinthians xi, 17–34.
52. *Chroniques*, Book II, ed. Raynaud (Société de l'Histoire de France, x), p. 223.
53. Even this detail acquires symbolic overtones here: there was a guild of coverlet weavers at Ghent (Nicholas, *Metamorphosis*, pp. 171–6). It is interesting to note also that there was a guild of blue dyers or *blauwers*, at Ghent; this may put a fresh gloss on material discussed in the article mentioned above (my note 17) referring to a 'blue woman' of Friesland. 'Dyeing is the only branch of the textile industry in which large numbers of women were found': ibid., pp. 165–6.
54. Ainsworth, 'Du berceau à la bière', p. 134 for full details.
55. Ibid., p. 133.

5 HIERARCHIES AND ORDERS IN ENGLISH ROYAL IMAGES OF POWER (*pages 74–93*)

1. See, for example, M. Camille, 'Labouring for the Lord: the ploughman and the social order in the Luttrell Psalter', *Art History*, 10, no. 4 (1987), 423–54 for a critique of the 'illustrated social history' syndrome.

2. The central documentary survey of English royal palaces remains H. M. Colvin (ed.), *The History of the King's Works: The Middle Ages*, 2 vols (London, 1963); see also my remarks in P. Binski, *The Painted Chamber at Westminster* (London, 1986), pp. 34–5, 105–12. In general, see G. Duby (ed.), *A History of Private Life, II: Revelations of the Medieval World* (Cambridge, Mass., and London, 1985).

3. A. D. Hedeman, *The Royal Image: Illustrations of the Grandes Chroniques de France 1274–1422* (Berkeley, 1991); C. R. Sherman, *Imaging Aristotle: Verbal and Visual Representation in Fourteenth-Century France* (Berkeley, 1995).

4. Colvin, *King's Works*, i, 369–95, 479–85, 527–33.

5. A. S. Minnis and A. B. Scott (eds), *Medieval Literary Theory c.1100–1375* (Oxford, rev. edn, 1991), p. 250.

6. For what follows see P. Binski, *Westminster Abbey and the Plantagenets: Kingship and the Representation of Power 1200–1400* (New Haven and London, 1995), pp. 84–6.

7. J. J. G. Alexander and P. Binski (eds), *Age of Chivalry, Art in Plantagenet England 1200–1400* (Royal Academy of Arts, London, 1987), no. 275.

8. F. Wormald, 'The Throne of Solomon and St Edward's Chair', in M. Meiss (ed.), *De Artibus Opuscula XL: Essays in Honour of Erwin Panofsky* (New York, 2 vols, 1961), pp. 532–9.

9. *Liber de Antiquis Legibus*, ed. T. Stapleton (Camden Society, 1846), p. 43.

10. N. Rash, 'Boniface VIII and Honorific Portraiture: observations on the half-length image in the Vatican', *Gesta*, 26, no. 1 (1987), 47–58; M. Camille, *The Gothic Idol: Ideology and Image-Making in Medieval Art* (Cambridge, 1989), pp. 271–81.

11. A. Martindale, *Heroes, Ancestors, Relatives and the Birth of the Portrait* (The Hague, 1988); Binski, *Westminster Abbey*, pp. 199–204.

12. D. Gordon (ed.), *Making and Meaning: The Wilton Diptych* (National Gallery, London, 1993), pp. 22–4, fig. 7.

13. Gordon, *Wilton Diptych*, p. 21; H. Van Os *et al.*, *The Art of Devotion in the Late Middle Ages in Europe 1300–1500* (London and Amsterdam, 1994).

14. Martindale, *Heroes*; F. Seibt (ed.), *Kaiser Karl IV. Staatsmann und Mäzen* (Munich, 1978), figs 10–18; C. R. Sherman, *The Portraits of Charles V of France (1338–1380)* (New York, 1969).

15. J. Pope-Hennesey, *The Portrait in the Renaissance* (London, 1966); P. Simons, 'Women in frames: the gaze, the eye, the profile in Renaissance portraiture', *History Workshop*, 25 (1988), 4–30.

16. Binski, *Westminster Abbey*, p. 204.

17. E. Panofsky, *Early Netherlandish Painting* (Cambridge, Mass., 1953), pp. 51–74; T. Veblen, *The Theory of the Leisure Class* (New York, 1899); J. J. G. Alexander, '*Labeur* and *paresse*: ideological images of medieval peasant labour', *Art Bulletin*, 72 (1990), 436–52.

18. I refer here to A. Appadurai, *The Social Life of Things: Commodities in Cultural Perspective* (Cambridge, 1986), pp. 3–63, 25, 31; S. M. Newton, *Fashion in the Age of the Black Prince: A Study of the Years 1340–1365* (Woodbridge, 1980), pp. 131–2.

19. R. Branner, *St Louis and the Court Style in Gothic Architecture* (London, 1965).

20. Binski, *Westminster Abbey*, pp. 93–107; Branner, *Court Style*, pp. 123–8.

21. M. T. Clanchy, 'Did Henry III have a policy?', *History*, 53 (1968), 203–16; D. A. Carpenter, 'King, magnates and society; the personal rule of Henry III, 1234–1258', *Speculum*, 69 (1985), 39–70.
22. Duby, *Private Life*, pp. 85–93.
23. R. Krautheimer, *Rome, Portrait of a City, 312–1308* (Princeton, 1980), pp. 203–28.
24. For Charles IV, see Seibt, *Kaiser Karl IV*, pp. 356–62, col. pls I–V.
25. Appadurai, *Social Life*, p. 38.
26. Hedeman, *Royal Image*; P. Binski, 'Reflections on *La Estoire de Seint Aedward le Rei*: hagiography and kingship in thirteenth-century England', *Journal of Medieval History*, 16 (1990), 333–50.
27. C. Sherman, 'The Queen in Charles V's "Coronation Book"; Jeanne de Bourbon and the "Ordo ad reginam benedicendam"', *Viator*, 8 (1977), 255–91; Binski, *Westminster Abbey*, pp. 126–30.
28. A. Vauchez, *La Sainteté en Occident aux Derniers Siècles du Moyen Age* (Rome, 1981), p. 194.
29. M. Kauffmann, 'The image of St Louis', in *Kings and Kingship in Medieval Europe*, ed. A. J. Duggan (London, 1993), pp. 265–86.
30. Binski, 'Reflections', 344–9.
31. C. Lévi-Strauss, *The Savage Mind* (London, 1966), pp. 257–62.
32. J. H. Burns (ed.), *The Cambridge History of Medieval Political Thought c.350–c.1450* (Cambridge, 1988), pp. 482–5.
33. Binski, *Painted Chamber*, pp. 71–103.
34. J. Vale, *Edward III and Chivalry: Chivalric Society and its Context 1270–1350* (Woodbridge, 1982), pp. 42–56.
35. Colvin, *King's Works*, i, 370–1.
36. Binski, *Westminster Abbey*, pp. 139–40.
37. M. Clanchy, *From Memory to Written Record: England 1066–1307* (London, 1979), pp. 26–7, 123–4.
38. Appadurai, *Social Life*, p. 26.

6 HERALDRY AND HIERARCHY: ESQUIRES AND GENTLEMEN (*pages 94–108*)

1. T. Hearne, *A Collection of Curious Discourses* (Oxford, 1720), p. 257.
2. A. Wagner, *A Catalogue of English Medieval Rolls of Arms* (Oxford, 1950), pp. 27–8 (Falkirk Roll), pp. 34–5 (Galloway Roll), p. 36 (Stirling Roll), pp. 39–40, 56–7 (1st and 2nd Dunstable Rolls).
3. T. Rymer, *Foedera* (Record Commission, 1816–30), I, pt i, 65; and see J. Barker, *The Tournament in England, 1100–1400* (Woodbridge, 1986), pp. 53–6.
4. *Statutes of the Realm* (Record Commission, 1810–28), i, 230–1 and *Rotuli Parliamentorum* (London, 1783), i, 85; and see Barker, *Tournament*, pp. 56–60, 191–2.
5. A. Wagner, *Heralds and Heraldry in the Middle Ages* (Oxford, 1956), pp. 9–10.
6. C. Carpenter, *Locality and Polity* (Cambridge, 1992), p. 90; J. Selden, *Titles of Honour* (2nd edn, London, 1631), pp. 874–5.

7. *Statutes of the Realm*, i, 380–2 (37 Ed. III, cc.8–15).

8. Ibid., ii, 399–401 (3 Ed. IV, c.5).

9. *Rotuli Parliamentorum*, iii, 57–8.

10. *Statutes of the Realm*, ii, 171 (1 Henry V, c.5).

11. See G. Sitwell, 'The English Gentleman', *The Ancestor*, 1 (April, 1902), 58–103, esp. 73–7.

12. G. Chaucer, *The Canterbury Tales*, Prologue, lines 38–40.

13. See Sitwell, 'English Gentleman', 68–73.

14. *Statutes of the Realm*, ii, 342 (23 Henry VI, c.14).

15. J. Fortescue, *De Laudibus Legum Angliae*, ed. S. B. Chrimes (Cambridge, 1949), pp. 68–9.

16. Wagner, *Catalogue of English Medieval Rolls*, pp. 42–50 (text printed in full in T. Palgrave, *Parliamentary Writs* (Record Commission, 1827), i, 410–20).

17. N. Denholm Young, 'Feudal society in the thirteenth century: the knights', in his *Collected Papers* (Cardiff, 1969), pp. 86–7.

18. C. Given Wilson, *The English Nobility in the Late Middle Ages* (London, 1987), p. 70; G. E. Mingay, *The Gentry* (London, 1976), p. 4.

19. See P. Coss, 'The formation of the English gentry', *Past and Present*, 147 (1995), 38–64, esp. 52–4; and his 'Knights, esquires and the origin of social gradation', *Transactions of the Royal Historical Soc.*, 6th ser. 5 (1995), 155–78.

20. Wagner, *Catalogue of English Medieval Rolls*, pp. 63–5 (Calveley's Book), pp. 68–9 (County Roll), p. 73 (Norfolk and Suffolk Roll).

21. N. H. Nicolas, *The Scrope and Grosvenor Controversy* (London, 1832), i, III.

22. These figures are based on A. Ayton, 'Knights, esquires and military service: the evidence of the armorial cases before the Court of Chivalry', in *The Medieval Military Revolution*, ed. A. Ayton and G. L. Price (London, 1995), p. 83.

23. See further, Coss, 'Knights, esquires', 156–60.

24. T. Rymer, *Foedera* (London, 1704–35), vii, 630.

25. Normally two shillings a day for a knight, one shilling for an esquire or man at arms.

26. See e.g. Nicolas, *Scrope and Grosvenor*, i, 51, 64, 70, 109, 126.

27. See further, P. Coss, *The Knight in Medieval England* (Stroud, 1993), pp. 60–71.

28. *Statutes of the Realm*, ii, 171 (1 Henry V, c.5).

29. Ibid., i, 380 (37 Ed. III, c.10).

30. Ayton, 'Knights, esquires and military service', 86. He finds 11 men in this category on the Morley Roll (Public Record Office (hereafter PRO), C47/6/1), out of a total of 160 witnesses (including 58 churchmen).

31. *Calendar of Patent Rolls 1381–5* (hereafter *CPR*), p. 462 (cited by Given Wilson, *English Nobility*, p. 70).

32. *Rotuli Parliamentorum*, iii, 58.

33. PRO, E101/55/13 (cited by C. T. Allmand, *Henry V* (London, 1992), p. 209).

34. S. Bentley, *Excerpta Historica* (London, 1831), p. 42. Bentley wrongly attributes these ordinances to John Talbot, earl of Shrewsbury; compare British Library, MS Cotton Julius F IV, fo. 322, where they are correctly attributed.

35. *Proceedings and Ordinances of the Privy Council*, ed. H. Nicolas (Record Commission, 1834–7), v, 74, cited by D. Morgan, 'The individual style of the English Gentleman', in *Gentry and Lesser Nobility in Medieval Europe*, ed. M. Jones (Gloucester, 1986), p. 22.

36. Ibid.

37. British Library, MS Harl. 2251, fo. 135.

38. Wagner, *Heralds and Heraldry*, app. C, pp. 136–7.

39. Ibid., pp. 77–8, 125–6.

40. British Library, MS Stowe 1047, fos. 247^B–248.

41. Rymer, *Foedera*, ix, 457–8.

42. *CPR 1416–21*, p. 341 (cited in Allmand, *Henry V*, p. 206).

43. Johannes de Bado Aureo, whose *Tractatus de Armis* was compiled for Richard II's Queen Anne, discusses grants made by Kings of Arms: see text in E. Jones, *Medieval Heraldry* (Cardiff, 1943), p. 130.

44. PRO, E28/97/1–35 (the writs and returns thereto; the Cambridgeshire writ is no. 4^A). I must thank Professor Allmand for drawing my attention to these documents.

45. PRO, E28/97/5^A (Cheshire), 8 (Devon), 21^A (Norfolk), 28 (Somerset), 4^A (Cambridge), 24^A (Oxford), 33^A (Wilts.), 25 (Rutland).

46. PRO, E28/97/10^C gives 16 names (the number of lances requested); 10^D gives six more, as some of the first 16 were unable or unwilling to serve. In the Essex list of those sworn to the peace in 1434 (*CPR 1429–36*, pp. 400–2) the surnames that reappear among the esquires are Tyrell or Terrell (John and Thomas 1419; Robert and Thomas 1434), Teye (Robert 1419; John 1434), John (Lewis 1419 and 1434), Doreward (John 1419 and 1434), Loveney (William 1419 and 1434), Langham (George 1419 and 1434), Spyce (Roger 1419 and 1434), Godmanston (1419 and 1434), Helyon (John 1419 and 1434). The two names that in 1434 have no title or dignity, by implication ranked as gentlemen, are those of Roger Deyncourt (1419 and 1434) and Richard Prior (1419 and 1434).

47. Hereford was asked to supply 16 lances: PRO, E28/97/12^A. There are two lists of names, one with 26 names (12^B) and one, presumably the final list, with 16 (12^C): there is a substantial overlap of names between the two. *CPR 1429–36*, pp. 376–8, lists those sworn to peace in 1434. The esquires' names or surnames occurring in both 1419 and 1434 are: William Crofte, Walter Hakelyt, Thomas Bromwych, John Abrehale, Thomas Delahaye, Richard de la Mare, John Mornington and Thomas Parker. John Mortymer, Henry Comyn and John Puy or ap Py also appear on both lists, but seem to be rated as mere gentlemen in 1434. Other Morningtons and Hakelyts, presumably kinsmen of the esquires of that name, appear on the 1434 list.

48. PRO, E28/97/32^B gives the 1419 Warwickshire list, here compared with Carpenter, *Locality and Polity*, apps 1 and 2, pp. 645–78. The 13 names are Ralph Bracebrygge (knight, 1419), Edward Odyngsele (knight, 1419), John Burdet (of a knightly family: Carpenter, pp. 671, 674), Thomas Stafford of Beginton (of a knightly family: Carpenter, pp. 80n, 666, 672), Richard Clodesdale (esquire: Carpenter, pp. 652, 672), William Peyto (esquire by 1410, knight by 1436: Carpenter, pp. 663, 672), Richard

Archer (esquire: Carpenter, pp. 646, 674), George Longville (esquire: Carpenter, pp. 659, 675), John Astley (probably of Wolvey Astley, members of which family appear both as esquires and as gentlemen: Carpenter, pp. 671, 676), John Cotes (esquire in 1436, but elsewhere of less status: Carpenter, pp. 81, 673, 676), Thomas Hugford (esquire in 1436, but of obscure origins: Carpenter, pp. 46, 658, 675), John Malory (not ranked as esquire 1410, but esquire in 1436: Carpenter, pp. 660, 673, 675), William Shukburgh (ranked as esquire 1410, but not ranked in that degree in 1436: Carpenter, pp. 46, 666, 676).

49. Wagner, *Heralds and Heraldry*, app. C, pp. 136–8, and for discussion see pp. 59–64.
50. Ibid., p. 61.
51. Rymer, *Foedera*, ix, 457–8.
52. Wagner, *Heralds and Heraldry*, pp. 9–10 (1530 commission), p. 137 (Clarence's ordinance).
53. See ibid., pp. 107–9.
54. R. L. Storey, 'Gentlemen bureaucrats', in C. H. Clough (ed.), *Profession, Vocation and Culture in Later Medieval England* (Liverpool, 1982), pp. 90–109.
55. Fortescue, *De Laudibus*, pp. 118–19.
56. N. Davis (ed.), *Paston Letters and Papers of the Fifteenth Century* (Oxford, 1972–4), pt ii, 551–2 (no. 897).
57. J. Selden, *Titles of Honour* (London, 1631), pp. 836–7.
58. Davis (ed.), *Paston Letters*, pt i, p. xiii and pt ii, pp. 551–2.
59. Bodleian, MS Eng. Misc. D227 (John Blount's translation of Upton, *De Studio Militari*), fo. 53r. I owe this reference to my research student, Mr Craig Walker.

7 THE RISINGS OF THE COMMONS IN ENGLAND, 1381–1549
(*pages 109–25*)

1. M. Bush, *The Pilgrimage of Grace: A Study of the Rebel Armies of October 1536* (Manchester, 1996), pp. 128, 236–7. The documentation for the 1536 uprising is largely to be found in *Letters and Papers, Foreign and Domestic of the Reign of Henry VIII*, ed. J. Gairdner (London, 1888–90), xi and xii (hereafter *LP*).
2. The other meanings of commons/commoners – that is, the freemen of the town, the elected members of parliament and manorial tenants with commoning rights – do not apply in this context.
3. *The Peasants' Revolt of 1381*, ed. R. B. Dobson (London, 1983), p. 141.
4. Ibid., p. 275.
5. I. M. W. Harvey, *Jack Cade's Rebellion of 1450* (Oxford, 1991), app. A.
6. *The Paston Letters*, ed. J. Gairdner (London, 1904), vi, 130–1. For recent examinations of this revolt, see M. A. Hicks, 'The Yorkshire rebellion of 1489 reconsidered', *Northern History*, 22 (1986), 39–62; and M. J. Bennett, 'Henry VII and the northern uprising of 1489', *English Historical Review*, 105 (1990), 34–55.

7. I. Arthurson, 'The rising of 1497: a revolt of the peasantry?', in *People, Politics and Community in the Late Middle Ages*, ed. J. Rosenthal and C. Richmond (Gloucester, 1987), pp. 1–18.

8. *Great Chronicle of London*, ed. A. H. Thomas and I. D. Thornley (London, 1938), pp. 275–8.

9. For Lincolnshire, see A. Ward, *The Lincolnshire Rising 1536* (Nottingham, 1986). For the 1549 revolts, see J. Cornwall, *Revolt of the Peasantry, 1549* (London, 1977); and A. Greenwood, 'A Study of the Rebel Petitions of 1549' (unpublished Ph.D. thesis, Manchester, 1990).

10. F. Rose-Troup, *The Western Rebellion of 1549* (London, 1913), app. K, pp. 492–4.

11. Included in Raphael Holinshed, *Chronicles of England, Scotland and Ireland* (London, 1807), iii, 944.

12. Printed in A. Fletcher, *Tudor Rebellions* (London, 1983), doc. 17.

13. See below.

14. See *LP* xii(1), 163 (2). For example, from the Pilgrimage of Grace when the commons of Beverley wrote, 'We shall be true to you (the Lincolnshire rebels) and other the commons of the realm': Public Record Office (hereafter PRO) SP1/107 (*LP* xi, 645); and from the uprising of 1450 when the men of Kent declared in a petition that they would seek remedy with the help of the king and 'all the commons of England' (Harvey, *Jack Cade's Rebellion*, pp. 188–9).

15. *The Tree of Commonwealth*, ed. D. M. Brodie (Cambridge, 1948), pp. 42–8.

16. G. R. Owst, *Literature and Pulpit in Medieval England* (Cambridge, 1933), pp. 72–5.

17. *The Vision of William concerning Piers the Plowman*, ed. W. W. Skeat (Oxford, 1886), i, 2–3, 12.

18. Ibid., p. 12.

19. Ibid., pp. 194–7.

20. *Reassessing the Tudor Age*, ed. J. Guy and A. Fox (Oxford, 1986), pp. 124–5.

21. *Humanist Scholarship and Public Order*, ed. D. S. Berkowitz (London, 1984), p. 119.

22. J. C. Holt, *Robin Hood* (London, 1989); H. C. White, *Social Criticism in Popular Religious Literature of the Sixteenth Century* (London, 1944), ch. 1. The literary tradition continued to develop throughout the fifteenth and sixteenth centuries: see Holt, *Robin Hood*, ch. 7; and White, *Social Criticism*, pp. 24–40.

23. Dobson, *The Peasants' Revolt of 1381*, p. 381.

24. Ibid., p. 382.

25. Ibid., pp. 383–4.

26. *The Paston Letters*, vi, 131.

27. Dobson, *The Peasants' Revolt of 1381*, p. 381.

28. *Piers Plowman*, pp. 178–80, 182, 192.

29. Ibid., p. 562.

30. See M. L. Bush, 'Captain Poverty and the Pilgrimage of Grace', *Historical Research*, 65 (1992), 17–36.

31. M. Bateson, 'The Pilgrimage of Grace', *English Historical Review*, 5 (1890), 344.
32. Bush, *Pilgrimage of Grace*, pp. 408–9.
33. Ibid., pp. 103–8.
34. Bush, 'Captain Poverty', 21–7.
35. See above, n. 21.
36. *State Papers, Henry VIII* (London, 1830), i, 506–10; PRO E36/121, fos 25b–26.
37. PRO SP1/117, fo. 50 (*LP* xii(1), 687); *LP* xii(1), 193; PRO SP1/118, fo. 213, 213b (*LP* xii(1), 965).
38. For the term 'pilgrimage of grace for the commonwealth', see Bush, *Pilgrimage of Grace*, p. 11. For first meaning of commonwealth, see *LP* xii(1), 393. For second, see *LP* xi, 1244; *LP* xii(1), 44.
39. For a levelled society, see PRO SP1/118, fo. 213. For wealth of commons, see PRO SP1/107, fo. 116 (*LP* xi, 622). Also see Bush, *Pilgrimage of Grace*, p. 396.
40. For oath and first petition, see PRO SP1/109 (*LP* xi, 902(2)). For second petition, see Fletcher, *Tudor Rebellions*, doc. 9 (articles 2, 4, 5, 7, 8, 18, 19). For Aske's two proclamations, see *LP* xi, 622; *State Papers, Henry VIII*, i, 466–7 (*LP* xi, 705(2)).
41. *State Papers, Henry VIII*, i, 485 (*LP* xi, 826).
42. PRO SP1/107 (*LP* xi, 645).
43. Bush, *Pilgrimage of Grace*, pp. 105–9, 213–14.
44. *LP* xii(1), 163.
45. As an indication that the commons were firm believers in articles 2 and 7 of the 24 articles (Fletcher, *Tudor Rebellions*, doc. 9), see, for example, the commons petitions PRO SP1/114, art. 4 (*LP* xii(1), 138); *LP* xii(1), 163.
46. See Bush, *Pilgrimage of Grace*, pp. 104–5.
47. See the first petition submitted by the pilgrims to the government: PRO SP1/109 (*LP* xi, 902 (2)). The 'shearman' jibe is made in Pickering's song, which was based on rhymes supplied him by the yeoman, John Hallom. See PRO SP1/118 (*LP* xii(1), 1021(5)).
48. Printed in M. H. and R. Dodds, *The Pilgrimage of Grace, 1536–7 and the Exeter Conspiracy, 1538* (Cambridge, 1915), i, 290.
49. PRO E36/122, fo. 65–65b (*LP* xi, 1128).
50. Bush, *Pilgrimage of Grace*, p. 84.
51. Bush, 'Tax reform and rebellion in early Tudor England', *History*, 76 (1991), 399–400.

8 TIDY STRUCTURES AND MESSY PRACTICE: IDEOLOGIES OF ORDER AND THE PRACTICALITIES OF OFFICE-HOLDING IN RAGUSA (*pages 126–46*)

1. According to the *Cronachetta* kept by the Venetian Martino Sanuto. See R. Finlay, *Politics in Renaissance Venice* (London, 1980), p. 59.
2. Manuscript sources consulted for this study are from the Historijski arhiv u Dubrovniku (Historical Archives in Dubrovnik, hereafter HAD). I am

very grateful to the Director and staff of the archives for their welcome and assistance.

3. There is one qualification: some patricians had illegitimate children. These, and their descendants, formed commoner sections of noble houses. They were not eligible for offices, however.

4. HAD, Acta Consilii Maioris 9, fos 102–103.

5. HAD, Manuali practici de Cancelliere, 8 (Ceremeniale, 2 vols).

6. HAD, Manuali practici de Cancelliere, 1 (Specchio, hereafter referred to as such).

7. L. Stone, *The Past and the Present Revisited* (London and New York, 1987), esp. ch. 2 'Prosopography'.

8. The methods are discussed more fully in D. Rheubottom, 'Hierarchy of office in fifteenth-century Ragusa', *Bulletin of the John Rylands University Library of Manchester*, 72 (1990), 155–67. The values given on pp. 162–3 of that article differ somewhat from those which appear in Table 8.1 here. While the same methods were used in both instances, the new values are based upon a larger and corrected sample.

9. The term is borrowed from E. A. Wrigley 'The prospects for population history', *Journal of Interdisciplinary History*, 12 (1981), 214.

10. E. Sundt, *On Marriage in Norway* (Cambridge, 1980).

11. R. Lee, 'Models of preindustrial dynamics with applications to England', in C. Tilly (ed.), *Historical Studies of Changing Fertility* (Princeton, 1978), p. 195.

12. HAD, Specchio, fo. 389v.

9 'THREE ORDERS OF INHABITANTS': SOCIAL HIERARCHIES IN THE REPUBLIC OF VENICE
(pages 147–68)

1. R. Mousnier, *Social Hierarchies, 1450 to the Present*, trans. P. Evans, ed. M. Clarke (London, 1973), p. 23.

2. These remarks owe much not only to Mousnier's *Social Hierarchies*, but also to E. E. Bergel, *Social Stratification* (New York, 1962), pp. 68–97, 145–6, 160–1; G. Duby, *The Three Orders: Feudal Society Imagined*, trans. A. Goldhammer (Chicago and London, 1980); Y. M. Bercé, *Revolt and Revolution in Early Modern Europe. An Essay on the History of Political Violence*, trans. J. Bergin (Manchester, 1987); and *Social Orders and Social Classes in Europe since 1500: Studies in Social Stratification*, ed. M. L. Bush (London and New York, 1992).

3. *John Howes' MS, 1582*, ed. W. Lemprière (London, 1904), pp. 45–7.

4. Mousnier, *Social Hierarchies*, pp. 67–73, 81–2.

5. Cf. Duby, *Three Orders*, pp. 51, 345.

6. Ibid., pp. 111–17.

7. M. Luther, 'Address to the Christian nobility of the German nation', in *Luther's Works*, ed. J. Pelikan and H. T. Lehmann (55 vols, Philadelphia, 1955–86), xliv, 127.

8. E. Muir, *Civic Ritual in Renaissance Venice* (Princeton, 1981), pp. 77, 88–9, 251–88; R. Finlay, *Politics in Renaissance Venice* (London, 1980), pp. 121,

123; G. Cozzi and M. Knapton, with G. Scarabello, *La Repubblica di Venezia nell' Età Moderna* (2 vols, Turin, 1986–92) (hereafter CK), ii, 175.

9. R. Mackenney, *Tradesmen and Traders, The World of the Guilds in Venice and Europe, c.1250–c.1650* (London and Sydney, 1987), pp. 233–4.

10. *Venice: A Documentary History, 1450–1630*, ed. D. Chambers and B. Pullan, with J. Fletcher (Oxford, 1992) (hereafter VDH), pp. 254–5.

11. Ibid., pp. 81–4, 102–3.

12. For an introduction to this subject, see J. C. Davis, *The Decline of the Venetian Nobility as a Ruling Class* (Baltimore, 1962).

13. E. Muir, *Mad Blood Stirring. Vendetta and Factions in Friuli during the Renaissance* (Baltimore and London, 1993), p. 35.

14. Ibid., p. 244; CK, ii, 487.

15. G. Contarini, *The Commonwealth and Government of the Venetians*, trans. L. Lewkenor (London, 1599). On Contarini, see especially E. G. Gleason, *Gasparo Contarini: Venice, Rome and Reform* (Berkeley, Los Angeles and Oxford, 1993). For accounts of the myth of Venice, see Muir, *Civic Ritual*, pp. 13–61; and D. E. Queller, *The Venetian Patriciate: Reality versus Myth* (Urbana and Chicago, 1986), pp. 3–28.

16. Contarini, *Commonwealth*, pp. 15, 94–5.

17. Davis, *Decline*, pp. 133–8.

18. Contarini, *Commonwealth*, p. 16.

19. M. Sanudo the Younger, *De Origine, Situ et Magistratibus Urbis Venetae, ovvero La Città di Venetia (1493–1530)*, ed. A. Caracciolo Aricò (Milan, 1980), p. 22.

20. D. Giannotti, *Libro de la Republica de Vinitiani* (Rome, 1542), fo. 16r–v.

21. Quoted in A. Zannini, *Burocrazia e Burocrati a Venezia in Età Moderna: i Cittadini Originari (sec. xvi–xviii)* (Venice, 1993), p. 284. For other examples, ibid., pp. 12, 272; and U. Tucci, 'The psychology of the Venetian merchant in the sixteenth century', in *Renaissance Venice*, ed. J. R. Hale (London, 1973), p. 360. On the subject of two- and three-fold divisions, B. Pullan, *Rich and Poor in Renaissance Venice. The Social Institutions of a Catholic State, to 1620* (Oxford, 1971), pp. 99–100; and Zannini, *Burocrazia*, pp. 51–8.

22. Contarini, *Commonwealth*, pp. 138–9, 141–2.

23. Cf. Zannini, *Burocrazia*, p. 53.

24. A. Contento, 'Il censimento della popolazione sotto la Repubblica Veneta', *Nuovo Archivio Veneto*, 19 (1900), 1–42, 179–240, and 20 (1900), 1–96, 171–235; J. Beloch, 'La popolazione di Venezia nei secoli xvi e xvii', *Nuovo Archivio Veneto*, new series, 3 (1902), 1–49; D. Beltrami, *Storia della Popolazione di Venezia dalla Fine del Secolo xvi alla Caduta della Repubblica* (Padua, 1954); P. Burke, 'Classifying the people: the census as collective representation', in his *The Historical Anthropology of Early Modern Italy: Essays on Perception and Communication* (Cambridge, 1987), pp. 27–39.

25. Pullan, *Rich and Poor*, pp. 252–4; VDH, pp. 303–6.

26. Cf. D. Romano, *Patricians and Popolani. The Social Foundations of the Venetian Renaissance State* (Baltimore and London, 1987), p. 91.

27. Pullan, *Rich and Poor*, p. 43.

28. B. Cecchetti, *La Republica di Venezia e la Corte di Roma nei Rapporti della Religione* (2 vols, Venice, 1874), i, 130–1, 153–8; Pullan, *Rich and Poor*, pp.

134–5; M. J. C. Lowry, 'The church and Venetian political change in the later cinquecento' (Warwick University Ph.D. thesis, 1971), pp. 239–50, 258–65; VDH, p. 146.

29. VDH, p. 104.

30. Ibid., p. 226.

31. CK, ii, 13–14.

32. Ibid., 22–3; A. Niero, *I Patriarchi di Venezia da Lorenzo Giustiniani ai Nostri Giorni* (Venice, 1961), pp. 72–87.

33. For an ample recent account, see W. J. Bouwsma, *Venice and the Defense of Republican Liberty* (Berkeley and Los Angeles, 1968), pp. 339–482.

34. G. Cracco, '"Relinquere laicis que laicorum sunt." Un intervento di Eugenio IV contro i preti notai di Venezia', *Bollettino dell' Istituto di Storia della Società e dello Stato Veneziano*, 3 (1961), 179–89.

35. Cecchetti, *Republica*, i, 133; CK, i, 242–3, 247–8.

36. P. Prodi, 'The structure and organization of the Church in Renaissance Venice: suggestions for research', in *Renaissance Venice*, ed. Hale, p. 414.

37. VDH, pp. 203–4, 208, 224. On some Venetian nunneries, see V. J. Primhak, 'Women in religious communities: the Benedictine convents in Venice, 1400–1550' (University of London Ph.D. thesis, 1991).

38. Cf. G. Cozzi, *Il Doge Nicolò Contarini: Ricerche sul Patriziato Veneziano agli Inizi del Seicento* (Venice and Rome, 1958), p. 37; CK, i, 233–4, 239–42, and ii, 13–14, 19–21, 79, 160–1, 162–3.

39. See B. Pullan, 'The occupations and investments of the Venetian nobility in the middle and late sixteenth century', in *Renaissance Venice*, ed. Hale, pp. 397–400; O. Logan, *The Venetian Upper Clergy in the Sixteenth and Early Seventeenth Centuries. A Study in Religious Culture* (Lewiston, Queenston and Lampeter, 1996), pp. 64–84.

40. VDH, pp. 117, 244, 305–6, 321.

41. P. Pirri, *L'Interdetto di Venezia e i Gesuiti. Silloge di Documenti con Introduzione* (Rome, 1959).

42. G. Ruggiero, 'Modernization and the mythic state in early Renaissance Venice: the Serrata revisited,' *Viator: Medieval and Renaissance Studies*, 10 (1979), 249–50.

43. For statistics, Davis, *Decline*, p. 137.

44. On the closure, see, for example, F. C. Lane, *Venice: A Maritime Republic* (Baltimore and London, 1973), pp. 112–17. But cf. S. Chojnacki, 'In search of the Venetian patriciate: families and factions in the fourteenth century', in Hale, *Renaissance Venice*, pp. 47–90.

45. For the mainland, A. Ventura, *Nobiltà e Popolo nella Società Veneta del '400 e '500* (Bari, 1964); for the maritime dominions, CK, ii, 374–5, 377, 380–82, 384.

46. M. L. King, *Venetian Humanism in an Age of Patrician Dominance* (Princeton, 1986), pp. 92–7.

47. VDH, pp. 244–6; V. Hunecke, 'Matrimonio e demografia del patriziato veneziano (secc. xvii–xviii)', *Studi Veneziani*, new series, 21 (1991), 301–6.

48. Zannini, *Burocrazia*, pp. 66–7; cf. A. F. Cowan, *The Urban Patriciate: Lübeck and Venice 1580–1700* (Cologne and Vienna, 1986), p. 71.

49. Pullan, *Rich and Poor*, pp. 106–7.

50. King, *Venetian Humanism*, pp. 118–31.
51. Contarini, *Commonwealth*, pp. 16–18.
52. Davis, *Decline*, pp. 18–19; Chojnacki, 'In search', pp. 53–4, 82; Romano, *Patricians*, pp. 155–6.
53. For an ample account of the new nobility, Cowan, *Urban Patriciate*, pp. 64–89. See also J. Georgelin, *Venise au siècle des lumières* (Paris and The Hague, 1978), pp. 688–90; CK, ii, 173.
54. CK, ii, 176–7; A. Viaro, 'La pena della galera: la condizione dei condannati a bordo delle galere veneziane', in *Stato, Società e Giustizia nella Repubblica Veneta (sec. xv–xviii)*, ed. G. Cozzi (Rome, 1980), pp. 398–9; VDH, p. 18 (but compare p. 97).
55. For the term, see J. C. Hocquet, *Le sel et la fortune de Venise* (2 vols, Lille, 1978–9), ii, 358.
56. Tucci, 'Psychology', 346–8; King, *Venetian Humanism*, pp. 134–6.
57. G. Botero, *The Reason of State*, ed. and trans. from the Venetian edition of 1598 and published with *The Greatness of Cities* by P. J. and D. P. Waley (London, 1956), pp. 20–1.
58. CK, ii, 269.
59. Cowan, *Urban Patriciate*, p. 199; cf. Pullan, 'Occupations', pp. 380–7.
60. Compare the estimates in Tucci, 'Psychology,' 372, and Cowan, *Urban Patriciate*, p. 73.
61. For an example, B. Arbel, 'A royal family in republican Venice: the Cypriot legacy of the Corner della Regina', *Studi Veneziani*, new series, 15, 131–52; VDH, pp. 251–4.
62. Finlay, *Politics*, pp. 77–9, 80–1, 171; Hunecke, 'Matrimonio', pp. 289–91; VDH, pp. 257–60. On the Quarantie, Contarini, *Commonwealth*, pp. 94–5.
63. Hunecke, 'Matrimonio', pp. 271, 280.
64. Lane, *Venice*, p. 264; Finlay, *Politics*, pp. 200–2; VDH, pp. 78–9.
65. Georgelin, *Venise*, pp. 634–47; Hunecke, 'Matrimonio', pp. 290–1.
66. G. Trebbi, 'La cancelleria veneta nei secoli xvi e xvii', *Annali della Fondazione Luigi Einaudi*, 14 (1980), 69.
67. R. Zago, *I Nicolotti. Storia di una Comunità di Pescatori a Venezia nell' Età Moderna* (Abano Terme, 1982), doc. vii, pp. 232–3; Zannini, *Burocrazia*, pp. 32–3.
68. Pullan, *Rich and Poor*, pp. 100–3; Tucci, 'Psychology', pp. 363–4; CK, i, 7, 117, 133–41, 201; VDH, pp. 276–9; Zannini, *Burocrazia*, pp. 26–32.
69. CK, i, 147.
70. Cozzi, *Nicolò Contarini*, pp. 139–46; CK, ii, 93–4.
71. Contento, 'Censimento', xx, 55–6; Burke, 'Classifying', 33.
72. CK, i, 133–5.
73. King, *Venetian Humanism*, pp. 76–7.
74. Trebbi, 'Cancelleria', 68–70; Zannini, *Burocrazia*, pp. 39–42.
75. Trebbi, 'Cancelleria'; M. Neff, 'A citizen in the service of the patrician state: the career of Zaccaria de' Freschi', *Studi Veneziani*, new series, 5 (1981), 33–61; M. Neff, *Chancellery Secretaries in Venetian Politics and Society 1480–1533* (Ann Arbor, 1985); VDH, pp. 272–4; Zannini, *Burocrazia*, pp. 120–32.

76. Trebbi, 'Cancelleria', pp. 104–5, 117–24; G. Trebbi, 'Il segretario veneziano', *Archivio Storico Italiano*, 144 (1986), 54–8, 67–73; Zannini, *Burocrazia*, pp. 64–5.

77. Contarini, *Commonwealth*, p. 139.

78. Neff, *Chancellery Secretaries*, pp. 3, 13; Trebbi, 'Segretario', 47.

79. Trebbi, 'Cancelleria', pp. 80–3; Zannini, *Burocrazia*, pp. 15, 183–96, 209–10, 231–40; R. C. Davis, *Shipbuilders of the Venetian Arsenal. Workers and Workplace in the Preindustrial City* (Baltimore and London, 1991), pp. 48, 60–2, 69.

80. Trebbi, 'Cancelleria', p. 78; Neff, *Chancellery Secretaries*, pp. 190–2; VDH, p. 259; Zannini, *Burocrazia*, pp. 268, 281, 283.

81. Trebbi, 'Cancelleria', pp. 70–2; Neff, *Chancellery Secretaries*, pp. 14, 21–2, 34; Trebbi, 'Segretario', p. 42; Zannini, *Burocrazia*, pp. 14, 45–6, 64–5, 67, 70, 88.

82. Cowan, *Urban Patriciate*, p. 67.

83. Zannini, *Burocrazia*, pp. 262–3.

84. Ibid., and Finlay, *Politics*, pp. 58–9; Neff, *Chancellery Secretaries*, pp. 89–90, 300; VDH, pp. 259–60, 268–72.

85. King, *Venetian Humanism*, pp. 61–2; Romano, *Patricians*, pp. 10, 36, 50–1, 55, 144–7; Finlay, *Politics*, pp. 45, 57; Trebbi, 'Cancelleria', p. 75; Zannini, *Burocrazia*, p. 83; VDH, pp. 264–5.

86. Zannini, *Burocrazia*, pp. 66, 98–100.

87. VDH, p. 270; cf. Contarini, *Commonwealth*, p. 144.

88. Neff, *Chancellery Secretaries*, pp. 67–9, 79–80; M. Casini, 'Realtà e simboli del Cancellier Grande veneziano in età moderna (secc. xvi–xvii)', *Studi Veneziani*, new series, 22 (1991), 195–251; VDH, pp. 274–6.

89. Trebbi, 'Segretario', pp. 72–3.

90. For recent statements, Mackenney, *Tradesmen*, pp. 4–7; and B. Pullan, 'Religious brotherhoods in Venice', item ix in his *Poverty and Charity: Venice, Italy, Europe 1400–1700* (Aldershot, 1994), pp. 2–4.

91. Mackenney, *Tradesmen*, p. 56.

92. Romano, *Patricians*, pp. 68–9; Mackenney, *Tradesmen*, pp. 82–3.

93. Lane, *Venice*, pp. 156, 161, 312–13.

94. Mackenney, *Tradesmen*, pp. 222–3.

95. R. A. Goldthwaite, *The Building of Renaissance Florence: An Economic and Social History* (Baltimore, 1980), pp. 242–5.

96. For a list of them, see Sanudo, *De Origine*, pp. 174–5; also VDH, pp. 286–7.

97. Zago, *Nicolotti*, pp. 25–9.

98. Pullan, *Rich and Poor*, pp. 145–56; Mackenney, *Tradesmen*, pp. 218–32. For the printers' guild, H. F. Brown, *The Venetian Printing Press* (London, 1891), pp. 83–91, 213, 243–8.

99. Zannini, *Burocrazia*, pp. 75–6.

100. Mackenney, *Tradesmen*, pp. 223, 227.

101. Romano, *Patricians*, pp. 67–75.

102. Pullan, 'Religious brotherhoods', 4, 9–10; VDH, pp. 287–9.

103. Archivio di Stato, Venice, Senato, Terra, filza 214, under date 11 June 1615.

104. Mackenney, *Tradesmen*, pp. 94–5, 103–4, 110–11.
105. For examples of protest, VDH, pp. 108–13, 289–91.
106. Zago, *Nicolotti*, pp. 12–16, 19–21.
107. Romano, *Patricians*, pp. 78–80; Davis, *Shipbuilders*, pp. 7, 83–9.
108. Davis, *Shipbuilders*, pp. 29–36, 44–5.
109. Ibid., pp. 135–52, 156–66; R. C. Davis, *The War of the Fists. Popular Culture and Public Violence in Late Renaissance Venice* (New York and Oxford, 1994). See also Zago, *Nicolotti*, p. 93.
110. M. Weber, 'Class, status and party', in *From Max Weber*, ed. H. H. Gerth and C. Wright Mills (London, 1948), pp. 85–6.

BIBLIOGRAPHICAL GUIDES

1 APPROACHES TO PRE-INDUSTRIAL SOCIAL STRUCTURE

A general survey of models of social stratification is provided by S. Ossowski, 'Old notions and new problems: interpretations of social structure in modern society', in A. Béteille (ed.), *Social Inequality* (Harmondsworth, 1969). For Marx and Engels's social theory, see S. H. Rigby, *Marxism and History: A Critical Introduction* (Manchester, 1987) and *Engels and the Formation of Marxism: History, Dialectics and Revolution* (Manchester, 1992); and for Marxism as adopted by historians, S. H. Rigby, 'Marxist historiography', in M. Bentley (ed.), *Companion to Historiography* (London, 1997). Classic statements of the functionalist approach are to be found in R. Bendix and S. M. Lipset (eds), *Class, Status and Power* (London, 1954), while this method is applied to pre-industrial societies in: J. Blum, *The End of the Old Order in Rural Europe* (Princeton, 1978); P. Crone, *Pre-Industrial Societies* (Oxford, 1989); G. Fourquin, *The Anatomy of Popular Rebellion in the Middle Ages* (Amsterdam, 1978); and R. Mousnier, *Social Hierarchies: 1450 to the Present* (London, 1973).

For closure theory, see: R. Murphy, 'The structure of closure: a critique and development of the theories of Weber, Collins and Parkin', *British Journal of Sociology*, 35 (1984); R. Murphy, *Social Closure* (Oxford, 1988); G. Neuwirth, 'A Weberian outline of a theory of community: its application to the "Dark Ghetto"', *British Journal of Sociology*, 20 (1969); F. Parkin, 'Strategies of social closure in class formation', in F. Parkin (ed.), *The Social Analysis of Class Structure* (London, 1974); and F. Parkin, 'Social stratification', in T. Bottomore and R. Nisbet (eds), *A History of Sociological Analysis* (London, 1979). Runciman's social theory can be found in: W. G. Runciman, 'The three dimensions of social inequality', in Béteille (ed.), *Social Inequality*; Runciman, 'Towards a theory of social stratification', in Parkin (ed.), *Social Analysis*; and Runciman, *A Treatise on Social Theory*, ii (Cambridge, 1989). S. H. Rigby, *English Society in the Later Middle Ages: Class, Status and Gender* (Basingstoke, 1995), provides a critical assessment of closure theory as applied to medieval society.

2 EUROPEAN AND MIDDLE EASTERN VIEWS OF HIERARCHY AND ORDER IN THE MIDDLE AGES: A COMPARISON

The best general overviews of Islamic thought in an historical context are M. Hodgson, *The Venture of Islam: Conscience and History in a World Civilization*, 3 vols

196

(Chicago, 1974), esp. i, 315– , ii, 62– , 152– (but his attempt at a comparison with Western 'corporativism' (ii, 329–) is not successful); and I. Lapidus, *A History of Islamic Societies* (Cambridge, 1988), esp. pp. 162–91, 253–64. For general histories of Islamic political thought, see E. I. J. Rosenthal, *Political Thought in Medieval Islam* (Cambridge, 1958), and A. Lambton, *State and Government in Medieval Islam* (Oxford, 1981); but Rosenthal exaggerates the role of Greek philosophy, and Lambton, though very informative, is not easy reading.

Hierarchy and order were not the subject of systematic discourse in pre-modern Islam, and there has been relatively little systematic study of these topics by modern scholars. The best general introductions are G. E. von Grunebaum, 'The body politic: the social order', in von Grunebaum, *Medieval Islam: A Study in Cultural Orientation* (Chicago, 2nd edn, 1953), pp. 170–220; and R. Levy, *The Social Structure of Islam* (Cambridge, 1957), chapter 1 ('The grades of society'). The articles in *Encyclopaedia Islamica* on *khassa wa'umma* (élite and masses) and *re'ayya* (common people) are extremely helpful. R. Mottahedeh offers a systematic account of status relationships in early Islam: *Loyalty and Leadership in an Early Islamic Society* (Princeton, New Jersey, 1980), chapter 3 ('Loyalties of category'). Agrarian relations are studied in A. Lambton, *Landlord and Peasant in Persia: A Study of Land Tenure and Land Revenue Administration* (Oxford, 1953); brilliant insight is given into commerical, artisan and labour relations in S. D. Goitein, *Studies in Islamic History and Institutions* (Leiden, 1966), chapters 11–13. For the status of various occupations, see R. Brunshvig, 'Métiers vils en Islam', *Studia Islamica*, 16 (1962), 41–60. P. Guichard, *Structures Sociales 'Orientales' et 'Occidentales' dans l'Espagne Musulmane* (Paris, 1977), is most illuminating, especially on family relationships. The absence of familiar European categories and the dominant role of the household is tellingly set forth by M. Chamberlain, *Knowledge and Social Practice in Medieval Damascus 1190–1350* (Cambridge, 1994).

3   DANTE: ORDER, JUSTICE AND THE SOCIETY OF ORDERS

The edition of the *The Divine Comedy* from which quotations in this chapter are drawn (trans. C. Singleton, 6 vols, Princeton, 1970–5) incorporates Petrocchi's critical text, a sound translation, and the fullest commentary available in English, with a wealth of explanatory material, literary, historical, and doctrinal. The other major sources for Dante's political views are also well served by clear and reliable modern translations: *The Banquet* (trans. C. Ryan, Saratoga, 1989), book iv of which concentrates on the question of nobility; and *Monarchia* (ed. and trans. P. Shaw, Cambridge, 1995), a fine edition incorporating a new critical text, translation, and notes. As a general history of Italy in the thirteenth and fourteenth centuries, J. Larner's *Italy in the Age of Dante and Petrarch 1216–1380* (London, 1980) remains the standard account; just as the much older F. Schevill, *History of Florence from the Founding of the City through the Renaissance* (New York, 1961; first published 1936), continues to be the fullest study in English of the political fortunes of Dante's native city.

The most important recent contributions in English to an understanding of Dante in his general historical context are the work of C. T. Davis and G.

Holmes. G. Holmes, *Florence, Rome. and the Origins of the Renaissance* (Oxford, 1986) relates Dante's achievements to the political, economic, and cultural conditions and developments in the period through which the poet lived. C. T. Davis, *Dante's Italy and Other Essays* (Philadelphia, 1984) gathers conveniently into one volume a number of significant studies on Dante's theology of history and political thought and the influences that helped to shape them – essays such as 'Dante's vision of History' (pp. 23–41) and 'Poverty and escatology in the *Commedia*' (pp. 42–70).

Of work available in English on Dante's political thought, C. T. Davis, *Dante and the Idea of Rome* (Oxford, 1957), retains its importance, as do the fundamental studies by E. Gilson, *Dante the Philosopher* (London, 1952), and A. P. d'Entrèves, *Dante as a Political Thinker* (Oxford, 1952). Mention must be made too of E. H. Kantorowicz's magisterial study, *The King's Two Bodies: A Study in Mediaeval Political Theology* (Princeton, 1957), the concluding chapter of which is devoted to Dante's political thought. For an introduction to this area of Dante's thinking, see A. Black, *Political Thought in Europe 1250–1450* (Cambridge, 1992), pp. 56–8 and 96–100 of which consider the poet's views on Church and State, Empire and Nation; J. F. Took, *Dante Lyric Poet and Philosopher: An Introduction to the Minor Works* (Oxford, 1990), cap. 4 of which deals largely with the *Monarchia*; and J. M. Ferrante, *The Political Vision of the Divine Comedy* (Princeton, 1984). The essay by K. Foster, 'Religion and philosophy in Dante', in *The Mind of Dante*, ed. U. Limentani (Oxford, 1965), pp. 47–78, deals in the author's characteristically precise and illuminating fashion with the notion, crucial to Dante's political thought, of the two ends of human existence. P. Armour, *Dante's Griffin and the History of the World* (Oxford, 1989), ostensibly an essay on the religious–historical pageant with which *Purgatorio* concludes, is this and much more besides, and includes extremely well-informed discussion of Dante's notions concerning History, Empire, and the relationship between Church and State.

4   FROISSARDIAN PERSPECTIVES ON LATE-FOURTEENTH-CENTURY SOCIETY

The only comprehensive study of Froissart's *Oeuvre* remains that by F. S. Shears: *Froissart, Chronicler and Poet* (London, 1930). Well-written and wide-ranging, it needs to be complemented by more recent scholarship. A useful starting-point for exploration of modern approaches to the chronicler is K. Fowler's sympathetic and well-informed essay, 'Froissart, chronicler of chivalry', *History Today*, 36 (1986), 50–4. See also C. T. Allmand's perceptive study, 'Historians reconsidered: Froissart', *History Today*, 16 (1966), 841–8. For an important compendium of articles examining different facets of Froissart as historian, including an article on patrons and patronage, see J. J. N. Palmer (ed.), *Froissart: Historian* (Woodbridge, Suffolk, and Totowa, NJ, 1981). A fundamental aspect of the chronicler's aristocratic ideology is dealt with in K. McRobbie, 'The concept of advancement in the fourteenth century in the *Chroniques* of Jean Froissart', *Canadian Journal of History*, 6 (1971), 1–19.

For a comprehensive treatment of literary, textual and socio-political issues raised by the Chronicles, see P. F. Ainsworth, *Jean Froissart and the Fabric of*

History: Truth, Myth, and Fiction in the 'Chroniques' (Oxford, 1990), which contains a full bibliography. For an examination of symbolism in book iii, see P. F. Ainsworth, 'Knife, key, bear and book: poisoned metonymies and the problem of *translatio* in Froissart's later *Chroniques*', *Medium Aevum*, 59 (1990), 91–113. Modern French and English sources are listed in P. F. Ainsworth, 'Froissart', in J.-P. Beaumarchais, D. Couty and A. Rey (eds), *Dictionnaire Bordas des littératures de langue française* (Paris, 4 vols, 2nd edn, 1987), i, 851–4. Most of the texts studied in the article published here feature in an edition of the Chronicles due to be published in 1998: *Les Chroniques de Jean Froissart (extraits)*, i, ed. G. T. Diller (livre I) et P. F. Ainsworth (livre II) (Paris, 1998). For the reader familiar with French, an excellent presentation of the principal ideological and political questions raised by the Chronicles, plus a provisional inventory of the extant manuscripts of Froissart's historical works, is to be found in G. T. Diller, *Attitudes chevaleresques et réalités politiques chez Froissart. Microlectures du premier livre des 'Chroniques'* (Geneva, 1984). Finally, a selection of miniatures from the British Library manuscipts of the Chronicles is reproduced in G. G. Coulton, *The Chronicler of European Chivalry* (London, 1930).

5 HIERARCHIES AND ORDERS IN ENGLISH ROYAL IMAGES OF POWER

Two standard reference works for England are provided by H. M. Colvin (ed.), *The History of the King's Works: The Middle Ages* (London, 2 vols, 1963), with exemplary documentation; and J. J. G. Alexander and P. Binski (eds), *Age of Chivalry, Art in Plantagenet England 1200–1400* (Royal Academy of Arts, London, 1987), with critical and historical essays, accompanying the 1987 exhibition of English Gothic art. For royal representation, see P. Binski, *Westminster Abbey and the Plantagenets: Kingship and the Representation of Power 1200–1400* (New Haven and London, 1995); and for the decoration of the Palace of Westminster under the Plantagenets, see P. Binski, *The Painted Chamber at Westminster* (London, 1986). R. Branner, *St Louis and the Court Style in Gothic Architecture* (London, 1965), is a seminal work on the development of French court patronage in the thirteenth century, and see M. Camille, *The Gothic Idol: Ideology and Image-Making in Medieval Art* (Cambridge, 1989). An illuminating study of the social and ideological context of chivalry is found in J. Vale, *Edward III and Chivalry: Chivalric Society and its Context 1270–1350* (Woodbridge, 1982); and for the Wilton Diptych see D. Gordon (ed.), *Making and Meaning: The Wilton Diptych* (National Gallery, London, 1993).

6 HERALDRY AND HIERARCHY: ESQUIRES AND GENTLEMEN

The best modern treatment of early English heraldry is A. Wagner, *Heralds and Heraldry in the Middle Ages* (Oxford, 1956). The questions that have been the principal focus of this chapter were opened up, in modern historiography, by Sir George Sitwell in a remarkable essay, 'The English Gentleman', *The Ancestor*,

1 (April 1902), 58–103. For many years the principal major scholar to take up his leads was N. Denholm-Young, in his *History and Heraldry, 1254–1310* (Oxford, 1965) and *The Country Gentry in the Fourteenth Century* (Oxford, 1969); also in his notable essay 'Feudal society in the thirteenth century: the knights', *Collected Papers* (Cardiff, 1969), pp. 83–94. More recently, the subject has attracted much more attention, especially in the writings of P. Coss, D. Crouch and A. Ayton. Coss's most important contributions are 'The formation of the English gentry', *Past and Present*, 147 (1995), 38–64, and 'Knights, esquires and the origins of social gradation', *TRHS*, 6th ser. 5 (1995), 155–78; also important are chapters 4–6 of his *The Knight in Medieval England* (Stroud, 1993). David Crouch treats illuminatingly the early history both of heraldry and of squires in England in *The Image of the Aristocracy in Britain, 1000–1300* (London, 1992). A. Ayton's paper on 'Knights, esquires and military service: the evidence of armorial cases before the Court of Chivalry', in *The Medieval Military Revolution*, ed. A. Ayton and G. L. Price (London, 1995), is particularly interesting on esquires' military service: also very illuminating is chapter 6 of his *Knights and Warhorses* (Woodbridge, 1994). A very perceptive article on the gentleman is D. Morgan, 'The individual style of the English gentleman', in *Gentry and Lesser Nobility in Medieval Europe*, ed. M. Jones (Gloucester, 1986), pp. 15–38. Regional studies of the English gentry in the late Middle Ages are now legion. Two that have seminal and general things to say on the topics discussed in this chapter are C. Carpenter's magisterial *Locality and Polity: A Study of Warwickshire Landed Society, 1401–1499* (Cambridge, 1992), esp. pt. i; and N. Saul, *Knights and Esquires: The Gloucestershire Gentry in the Fourteenth Century* (Oxford, 1981).

7 THE RISINGS OF THE COMMONS IN ENGLAND, 1381–1549

Useful for the medieval revolts are: R. B. Dobson (ed.), *The Peasants' Revolt of 1381* (London, 2nd edn, 1983); R. Hilton, *Bond Men Made Free* (London, 1973), pt. ii; the essays in *The English Rising of 1381*, ed. R. H. Hilton and T. H. Aston (London, 1984); and I. M. W. Harvey, *Jack Cade's Rebellion of 1450* (Oxford, 1991). For the Tudor revolts, see the following: M. Bush, 'Tax reform and rebellion in early Tudor England', *History*, 76 (1991), 379–400; R. B. Manning, *Village Revolts: Social Protest and Popular Disturbances in England, 1509–1640* (Oxford, 1988); M. Hicks, 'The Yorkshire rebellion of 1489 reconsidered', *Northern History*, 22 (1986), 39–61; I. Arthurson, 'The rising of 1497: a revolt of the peasantry?', in *People, Politics and Community in the Late Middle Ages*, ed. J. Rosenthal and C. Richmond (Gloucester, 1987), pp. 1–18; A. Ward, *The Lincolnshire Rising, 1536* (Nottingham, 1986); S. J. Gunn, 'Peers, commons and gentry in the Lincolnshire revolt of 1536', *Past and Present*, 123 (1989), 52–79; M. Bush, *The Pilgrimage of Grace: A Study of the Rebel Armies of October 1536* (Manchester, 1996); D. Bownes and M. Bush, *The Defeat of the Pilgrimage of Grace: A Study of the Postpardon Revolts of December 1536 to March 1537 and their Effect* (forthcoming); A. Greenwood, 'A Study of the Rebel Petitions of 1549' (Manchester Ph.D., 1990); J. Cornwall, *Revolt of the Peasantry, 1549* (London, 1977); B. L. Beer, *Rebellion and Riot: Popular Disorder in England during the Reign of Edward VI* (Kent State, 1982); and D. MacCulloch, *Suffolk and the Tudors* (Oxford, 1986), ch. x.

For social theory, see: G. R. Owst, *Literature and the Pulpit in Medieval England* (Cambridge, 1933); F. Caspari, *Humanism and the Social Order in Tudor England* (Chicago, 1954); W. R. D. Jones, *The Tudor Commonwealth, 1539–59* (London, 1970); and T. F. Mayer, *Thomas Starkey and the Commonweal* (Cambridge, 1989). Useful for Piers Plowman is H. C. White, *Social Criticism in Popular Religious Literature of the Sixteenth Century* (London, 1944); and for Robin Hood, J. C. Holt, *Robin Hood* (London, enlarged edn, 1989).

8   TIDY STRUCTURES AND MESSY PRACTICE: IDEOLOGIES OF ORDER AND THE PRACTICALITIES OF OFFICE-HOLDING IN RAGUSA

While there is a large literature on Ragusa (Dubrovnik), most of the sources are in Serbo-Croatian. The best general history of this period in English is B. Krekic, *Dubrovnik in the 14th and 15th Centuries* (Norman Oklahoma, 1972). S. Stuard, *A State of Deference: Ragusa/Dubrovnik in the Medieval Centuries* (Philadelphia, 1992) concentrates on an earlier period, but provides a stimulating, if controversial, interpretation of Ragusan society and culture. F. Carter, *Dubrovnik (Ragusa), a Classic City-State* (London and New York, 1972) contains useful material on trade and Ragusa's geographical setting. The historical chapters, however, borrow heavily from L. Villari's *The Republic of Ragusa* (London, 1904) and are dated. A work which sets Ragusa in its regional and historical context is J. Fine Jr., *The Late Medieval Balkans* (Ann Arbor, 1987). A more complete discussion of the hierarchy of offices in Ragusa is to be found in D. Rheubottom, 'Hierarchy of office in fifteenth-century Ragusa', *Bulletin of the John Rylands University Library of Manchester*, 72 (1990), 155–67. Using a computer simulation of Ragusan marriage, his '"Sisters First": betrothal order and age at marriage in fifteenth-century Ragusa', *Journal of Family History*, 13 (1988), 359–76, discusses marriage and political alliances challenging conventional interpretations of the Mediterranean marriage pattern. His 'Genealogical skewing and political support: patrician politics in fifteenth-century Ragusa (Dubrovnik)', *Continuity and Change*, 9 (1994), 369–90, examines the implications which age at marriage has for the configuration of kinship relations and sources of political support.

9   'THREE ORDERS OF INHABITANTS': SOCIAL HIERARCHIES IN THE REPUBLIC OF VENICE

The most manageable general histories of Venice, which contain much information about social orders and groupings, are F. C. Lane, *Venice: A Maritime Republic* (Baltimore and London, 1973); and G. Cozzi and M. Knapton, with G. Scarabello, *La Repubblica di Venezia nell' Età Moderna* (2 vols, Turin, 1986–92). Lane was a distinguished economic historian famed for his interests in money, shipping and overseas trade. His volume concentrates heavily on the city of Venice itself, whereas the work of Gaetano Cozzi and his collaborators, part of the multi-volume UTET (Unione Tipografico Editrice Torinese) history of Italy, provides a comprehensive account, not just of the dominant city, but also of its dominions in northern Italy and the eastern Mediterranean between about 1381 and 1797. D. Romano, *Patricians and Popolani. The Social Foundations of the Venetian Renaissance State* (Baltimore and London, 1987), presents a general portrait of social groupings, defining their characteristics and exploring the relationships between them, across the years from 1297 to 1423. J. R. Hale has edited an important collection of sixteen essays by various authors, some of them dealing with social history, under the title *Renaissance Venice* (London, 1973). D. Chambers and B. Pullan, with J. Fletcher, have edited a collection of documents in translation, drawn by them and a team of collaborators from the Venetian archives and other manuscript and printed sources, in *Venice: A Documentary History, 1450–1630* (Oxford, 1992). Part vi, pp. 239–94, is devoted to 'Social Orders'. On particular orders, N. S. Davidson provides a serviceable introduction to 'The clergy of Venice in the sixteenth century', *Bulletin of the Society for Renaissance Studies*, 2 (2) (1984), 19–31, and J. C. Davis to the patriciate in *The Decline of the Venetian Nobility as a Ruling Class* (Baltimore, 1962). Ranging from the early sixteenth to the late eighteenth century, Davis's book lays particular stress on the problems caused by shrinkage in the number of nobles.

In *Politics in Renaissance Venice* (London, 1980) R. Finlay provides a lively analysis of the political activities of Venetian noblemen, mainly in the late fifteenth and early sixteenth centuries. D. E. Queller, *The Venetian Patriciate: Reality versus Myth* (Urbana and Chicago, 1986) describes iconoclastically, with numerous examples, the failure of the Venetian nobility to live up to its impossibly lofty ideals of selfless service to the state. Two comparative studies bring the Venetian nobility into a wider perspective. P. Burke, in *Venice and Amsterdam: A Study of Seventeenth-Century Elites* (London, 1974), attempts to identify the characteristics of an inner ring of rulers within the Venetian nobility, while A. F. Cowan, in *The Urban Patriciate: Lübeck and Venice 1580–1700* (Cologne and Vienna, 1986), is especially informative about the new nobility who entered the Great Council in and after 1646. On the citizenry, in so far as they were administrators and civil servants, there is Mary Neff's published Ph.D. thesis, *Chancellery Secretaries in Venetian Politics and Society 1480–1533* (Ann Arbor, 1985), and the ambitious and comprehensive work of A. Zannini, *Burocrazia e Burocrati a Venezia in Età Moderna: i Cittadini Originari (sec. xvi–xviii)* (Venice, 1993). On craftsmen and shopkeepers, see R. Mackenney, *Tradesmen and Traders. The World of the Guilds in Venice and Europe, c.1250 – c.1650* (London and Sydney, 1987), which makes illuminating comparisons with other European cities. R. C. Davis, *Shipbuilders of the Venetian Arsenal. Workers and Workplace in the Preindustrial City* (Baltimore and London, 1991) is an exciting account of a large, cohesive body of privileged workers engaged in an enterprise managed by the state, mainly in the seventeenth century.

INDEX

Note: this selective index pays particular attention to medieval and early modern authors and to the categories and themes especially associated with social orders.

203